THE LOU HALSELL RODENBERGER PRIZE IN HISTORY, CULTURE, AND LITERATURE

ALSO IN THIS SERIES:

Dressing Modern Maternity: The Frankfurt Sisters of Dallas and the Page Boy Label
by Kay Goldman

The Lady Makes Boots: Enid Justin & the Nocona Boot Company
by Carol A. Lipscomb

A Promise Fulfilled: The Kitty Anderson Diary and Civil War Texas, 1861
edited by Nancy Draves

Their Lives, Their Wills: Women in the Borderlands, 1750–1846
by Amy M. Porter

daughter of a song

a memoir

SARAH CURTIS

TEXAS TECH UNIVERSITY PRESS

Copyright © 2025 by Sarah Curtis

All rights reserved. No portion of this book may be reproduced in any form or by any means, including electronic storage and retrieval systems, except by explicit prior written permission of the publisher. Brief passages excerpted for review and critical purposes are excepted.

To protect the privacy of certain individuals, names and identifying details have been changed.

This book is typeset in Adobe Caslon Pro. The paper used in this book meets the minimum requirements of ANSI/NISO Z39.48-1992 (R1997). ♾

Designed by Hannah Gaskamp
Cover design by Hannah Gaskamp
Cover photo from author's collection

Library of Congress Cataloging-in-Publication Data

Names: Curtis Graziano, Sarah author Title: Daughter of a Song: A Memoir / Sarah Curtis Graziano. Description: Lubbock: Texas Tech University Press, 2025. | Series: Lou Halsell Rodenberger prize | Includes index. | Summary: "A biographical memoir of motherhood, music, and the mythic figure of rock 'n' roller Sonny Curtis"—Provided by publisher.
Identifiers: LCCN 2025016923 (print) | LCCN 2025016924 (ebook) |
ISBN 978-1-68283-274-5 paperback | ISBN 978-1-68283-275-2 ebook
Subjects: LCSH: Curtis, Sonny | Curtis Graziano, Sarah | Singers—United States—Biography | Rock musicians—United States—Biography | Fathers and daughters—United States—Biography | LCGFT: Biographies
Classification: LCC ML420.C989 C87 2025 (print) | LCC ML420.C989 (ebook) |
DDC 782.42166092 [B]—dc23/eng/20250410
LC record available at https://lccn.loc.gov/2025016923
LC ebook record available at https://lccn.loc.gov/2025016924

Texas Tech University Press
Box 41037
Lubbock, Texas 79409-1037 USA
800.832.4042
ttup@ttu.edu
www.ttupress.org

For my parents, in love and harmony

Come and sit by my side if you love me
Do not hasten to bid me adieu
But remember the Red River Valley
And the cowboy who loved you so true

—"RED RIVER VALLEY," CAMPFIRE FOLK SONG,
AUTHOR UNKNOWN

We reach here the very principle of myth: it transforms history into nature.

—ROLAND BARTHES, *Mythologies*

CONTENTS

ILLUSTRATIONS		XI
PART 1: The Gun and the Gods		
Leitmotif		5
CHAPTER 1:	Twelve by Fourteen	7
CHAPTER 2:	Daughter of a Gun	23
CHAPTER 3:	Lifting Buddy Holly	45
CHAPTER 4:	"I Fought the Law": A Love Song	73
CHAPTER 5:	Civilized	83
CHAPTER 6:	Countrypolitan	95
CHAPTER 7:	Burning Out	109
PART 2: Back to the Land		
CHAPTER 8:	The Glass House	121
CHAPTER 9:	The Last Waylon Party	139
CHAPTER 10:	Sonny Comes Home	155
CHAPTER 11:	Frog Song	171
CHAPTER 12:	Miseducation	183
CHAPTER 13:	Dead Awakening	197
PART 3: Earth Mother		
CHAPTER 14:	A Noble Goal	207
CHAPTER 15:	Sky Mother	221
CHAPTER 16:	The Shadow of a Song	229
CHAPTER 17:	The Winter Dance Party	241
CHAPTER 18:	The Meanders of the Creek	249
CHAPTER 19:	The Ghosts of Lubbock	259
ACKNOWLEDGMENTS		277
INDEX		279

ILLUSTRATIONS

42	Author's great-grandfather Will Curtis on Texas farm
69	Pete Curtis watching over Sonny onstage, circa 1945
70	Buddy and Sonny swapping guitars onstage, mid-'50s
70	Don Guess, Thelma King, Sonny, Buddy, Clara Cobble, and Sonny's brother Dean, spring 1956
93	Phil and Don Everly, Joe B. Mauldin, J. I. Allison, and Sonny, *Alma Cogan Show*, London, April 1960
107	Author's mother in L.A., 1969
116	Everly Brothers tour of England, 1964
116	Sonny at the hospital after author's birth
138	Sonny and author on Easter Sunday, 1978
152	Sonny before a Waylon tour rig, circa 1980
152	Seventies party: J. I., Joe B., Don Everly, Joanie, author and her mother, Karen Everly
169	Author as a child with her father
273	Author's grandfather's tractor

daughter of a song

PART 1

The Sun and the Gods

LEITMOTIF

During our second winter in Tennessee, while a rare blizzard thrashed the siding of our tumbledown farmhouse, my parents recorded three eight-track tapes of me singing. I was two years old. I can't remember recording the tapes, but I can envision the scene: me in footed pajamas toddling around my mother, sitting cross-legged on the floor holding a tape recorder. Behind her, my long-haired father sits on the orange tweed sofa, tuning his guitar. It's clear the Nashville music scene has already gotten its hooks in me; when I sing "Away in a Manger," I drawl the last word like Loretta Lynn, with two syllables: "Asleep in the ha-yeeeeee." My mom coos with delight after each song, but my dad is a tougher critic. Throughout the tapes, he coaches me constantly: *back up from the mic, count it off, stand up straight* (a strange directive for an audio performance) and, at several points, *sing on key!* Once or twice he stops strumming and lectures me about being flat, a word he never defines. He just assumes I speak his language.

"Let it go," my mom pleads at one point.

"Okay," he grumbles, his voice on edge.

I can't explain his overbearing presence here, other than to say he's always been a perfectionist when it comes to music, and music came more naturally to him than fatherhood. But as I recently listened to the recordings for the first time in decades, I heard something else. Even at age two, I gave my father as good as I got. When he lectures me, I snap, "Hush up, Sonny." When he takes a guitar break I yell, "You play now!" and he complies.

As I listen to these tapes, I realize I'm hearing my family's leitmotif, one that carries through to this day. I am the rhythm: the heartbeat at the center of the phrase, the unifying pulse. My mother's laughter provides the harmony: the ease of tension, the ear's release. My father is the melody: the force that creates that tension but also creates the resolution. The part of the song you remember most.

CHAPTER 1

Twelve by Fourteen

Moon, moon, silvery moon
Light up the heavens tonight
　　　　—"MOON, MOON, SILVERY MOON," 1951

If my father were a song, he would have been untitled. Conceived from dirt, he was born in a dugout, thousands of miles beneath a sliver of a new moon. The hole was hollowed six feet into the earth like a grave with a tin roof on top, yet populated with the living. The fifth child, his birth made seven of them down there.

Dugouts were common in the American Southwest during the westward migration of the early twentieth century. One of the most ancient forms of human housing, they were cheap and well insulated, nestled safely below the frost line. But living in them was hard. They flooded, for one thing, and teemed with insects, especially in more humid climates like that of Oklahoma. Some families poured scalding water over the dirt walls to kill the hatchlings, or coated the walls with canvas tarps. My father's oldest brother Pete, my only living relative who remembers the dugout, says he can't recall the bugs. On the arid plains of West Texas, they had deadlier adversaries: rattlesnakes.

When my grandma Violet's labor pains kicked in that Saturday night in May 1937, my grandad Arthur drove to Brownfield and fetched Dr. Jacobson. He delivered my father on the mattress where the family slept, laid flat on the dirt floor. My father arrived in the early hours of Mother's Day, born with his mother's full moon of a face, her almond-shaped eyes, and her little round peak on the tip of his nose, like he was balancing an India rubber ball. It was not an easy birth. He had trouble breathing at first, and the doctor worried he might be a "blue baby," a baby born with a heart condition that prevents oxygen from traveling through the blood, but he recovered quickly. Maybe his tiny lungs filled with dirt. With no running water, did they even try to sanitize the bedclothes? Or was the mattress bare? Did his four older siblings huddle around to watch, kneeling in the tamped-down soil? My modern mind envisions the birth like a crime scene.

When Dr. Jacobson asked my grandparents what name he should write on the birth certificate, they looked at each other blankly. *We was so busy, we hadn't thought of one!* That was the story Violet always told, her ample chest quaking under her faded muumuu. Dr. Jacobson said that was fine, just as long as they picked out a name within a few weeks and registered it at the courthouse.

I was so poor, I was born in a dirt hole, my father used to tell me. That kind of image leaves a stain on a child's mind, hard to scrub out. When my father seemed distant and I didn't know why, I suspected it had something to do with that dirt hole, like a black hole of meaning, the source of all his silence.

I have wanted to write the story of my father, a songwriter and musician who eventually acquired a name, Sonny Curtis, since I was a journalism student in my twenties. Like a Texan Forrest Gump, he's lived through the tail end of the Dust Bowl, the birth of rock 'n' roll, the California hippie scene, and the country music outlaw movement of the eighties. He's written songs that helped define their musical eras, like "I Fought the Law" and "Love Is All Around," the theme song to *The Mary Tyler Moore Show*, and he's toured with some of the most famous music stars of his day, from Buddy Holly to the Everly Brothers to Waylon Jennings. Through it all, he's witnessed the tragic fallout of fame, so many friends and colleagues cut down by accident or addiction. For a young woman with writerly aspirations, my father's life seemed like a treasure chest. I, his only child, held the key.

But treasure has a weight. My father's story was so big, I couldn't see myself in it, nor my mother, the people standing offstage who fade into the background once the house lights go down. Besides, I was busy—busy working, or busy raising three young daughters, or busy renovating a nineteenth-century Michigan farmhouse. There was always a good reason not to write about my father.

Then the same week my youngest daughter turned six, I received the kind of call I'd long dreaded. My mom phoned to tell me my dad had been diagnosed with stage III esophageal cancer. My first emotion was fear and my second was guilt—guilt for living three states away from my parents and guiltier for not keeping in closer contact with my dad. Except for the occasional email and those brief moments when I called my mom and he picked up, we rarely spoke. Daydreamers and introverts, neither of us are very good on the phone. I loved him deeply but I'd avoided those calls, blinded by the most mortal of illusions: endless time.

After I hung up I called my husband, who was traveling for work and didn't pick up. I stood frozen in my bedroom holding the phone, wondering who else to call. Noises from downstairs drifted up— my three daughters just home from school, arguing and unpacking their homework and clamoring for snacks. However combative their connection, I envied it. I ached for a sibling of my own like a phantom limb.

Life marched on, as it has a habit of doing. That weekend, my husband and I threw a birthday party for our daughter at an apple orchard. It was early October, the Michigan air turning crisp, the green giving way to gold. While waves of copper sunflowers surrendered their seeds to the northwest wind, I handed out cake and cups of cider to messy-haired, careless first graders and felt flattened by metaphor. Death attached itself to everything in my life like a shadow, especially the lovely things. My camera roll from that time reveals photo after photo of a Japanese maple outside my bedroom window whose red leaves fluttered down each evening under our porchlight. I fixated on capturing those dreamlike leaves, the beauty of dying. It was a melancholy season.

A year before my father's diagnosis, I'd asked him to write me some memories of his life so I could start assembling my research. To my surprise, he did. He mailed me fifty single-spaced typed pages about his childhood and adolescence growing up in West Texas. While I was grateful for his effort, the memoir wasn't the sweeping Robert Caro saga I'd hoped for. He wrote about close calls with rattlesnakes and tumbleweed fires, goofy mishaps from elementary school, and corny dating experiences that did not age gracefully. In each story, my father portrayed himself as a hapless rube bumbling through life, a theme reflected even in the silly font: bold Comic Sans. It was a trait I knew well, a deeply planted seed of West Texas humility that made me cringe.

Like many West Texas farmers of their day, my father's parents lived by the laws of the almanac, planting their crops and castrating their bulls and weaning their babies according to the phases of the moon and stars. My dad was born under a new moon, a planting moon, and that was especially true during that spring, the tail end of the Dust Bowl, when the family was hanging on by a milkweed. According to laws of the almanac, the days immediately following a new moon are the most important ones for planting crops that grow above the soil, when the earth is fertile and wet. And so as soon as she could stand, Violet swaddled my father in muslin and pitched a tent for him under the meager shade of a mesquite while she hoed beside him. It was a hot, dry month. As my father grew, he developed more of an olive complexion than his brothers and sisters, which Violet attributed to the time he spent under that mesquite, soaking up the West Texas sun. They believed in earth and sky, stardust and folklore.

There was no downtime for Violet, no time to stand around that spring letting the weeds grow under her feet. She now had three children to nurse, for five-year-old Dean and two-year-old Alene were still at the breast, her milk the cheapest nourishment she could provide. Those were the years before they'd saved enough money to buy the tractor, so all the field work was done with mules and hand tools—the kind of work that could drain your spirit as well as your body. Dishes to wash, children to nurse, chickens to pluck, and, if she was lucky, a few more rows of cotton in the ground. From dawn until dusk, she jumped around like grease on a hot skillet.

And still there was that blank space on the birth certificate. Legality aside, a kid needs a name for practical reasons, so my grandfather started calling my father Sonny boy, though that didn't seem like the kind of name you should put on a formal record. By the time the cotton was planted, the name had stuck. They never made it to the courthouse.

It's a strange story, one I can't get my head around. "You have to understand, my folks were country. Simple," my father once explained, a folksy take that does little for me. As a mother who has named three children of my own (you might even say obsessively named them, drawing inspiration from Dickens, dreams, astronomy, and high school French), I can't imagine carrying a child for nine months—a wanted child, from what I understand—without giving any thought to the baby's name. No amount of poverty or labor or simplicity explains away the fact that my father was denied the most basic human possession, as if he were born outside of language itself, like a mark meant to be erased. Maybe this is what he was formed to seek: the lyrics to compose himself alive.

Dugouts were intended to be temporary housing. As farmers assembled the materials to build more traditional homes above the earth, they did so. By the time my father was a year old, my grandfather had gathered enough lumber to build a plywood shack one hundred yards from the dugout. At twelve by fourteen feet, the shack was technically smaller than the dugout, which my uncle Pete remembers being twelve by twenty feet. But despite its spatial limitations, the shack signified an upgrade: the family literally ascending from the dirt alongside their cotton crops. As my father joked in his memoir, "Our social and economic status was definitely on an upward trajectory." In the shack, Violet gave birth to her last child, my dad's younger sister Jean. And now they were eight.

Life improved in the shack. Violet no longer spent her hours shaking dirt out of blankets and clothes and kitchen wares, a Sisyphean task if there ever was one. How does any semblance of cleanliness exist in a room made of dirt? My father was too young to remember that dusty life in the dugout, but he does remember the shack. His first memory took place there around 1939. He was a toddler, gazing out the window at an apocalyptic sandstorm from the safety of his mother's hip. The sky was black with towering clouds of topsoil that smudged out the few signs of life—chicken coop, plow, melon patch, gone. A macabre child's snow globe of a landscape.

That sandstorm, those impossible numbers. *Eight people, twelve by fourteen feet.* They're details I might want to forget, but my father sought to remember them—so much so, he built an equipment shed with a tool storage room exactly that size behind the Tennessee farmhouse where he and my mother raised me. That farm was located in a small town called Dickson, forty minutes from Nashville's Music Row. When I was a child, I sometimes meandered through our back lawn to the shed, where I ducked into the room. Inside I breathed the scents of motor oil and cattle feed and tried to make sense of it all. *Eight people, twelve by fourteen feet. How could it be?* I knew the house my parents and I lived in spanned over 2,000 square feet, and still we bumped into each other leaving bathrooms. Though of course they didn't have a bathroom in the shack—all their water was pumped by a windmill.

My parents sold the farm over twenty years ago and bought a house closer to Nashville on five acres of land, where they live still.

Behind this new house, my father built another toolshed—smaller and more cheerful than the last one because he had sold the farm equipment—with yet another twelve-foot-by-fourteen-foot room to remind him of his childhood shack. He painted it cherry red. When I saw it for the first time, I thought, *So much depends on a red toolshed.*

The February following my father's diagnosis, I showed the shed to my two youngest daughters, six and eight at the time, who were on midwinter break from their elementary school. We'd left my oldest daughter and husband in Michigan the day before to fly to my parents' house in Tennessee, where we traded Midwestern snow for dark skies and rain. The mood inside my parents' house was equally dreary. My dad lay on the couch staring hollow-eyed out the window at his bluebird house, the chemo pump at his hip simultaneously drowning him and keeping him afloat. My mom hadn't slept in days, and in her eyes I saw the glazed-over terror of unknowing.

My parents' home had always been filled with background music, practice pieces my father strummed over and over on his guitar, like Chopin's "Prelude to Les Sylphides," Hoagy Carmichael's "Stardust," and the Beatles' "Blackbird": songs imprinted on my psyche from an early age like the soundtrack of my life. Now, the concert was over. Dad's Martin guitar gathered dust in the unused dining room. He'd once tried to teach me to play this guitar when I was young, pressing the pads of my fingers along the fretboard until I whimpered, "That hurts!"

He snapped, "Well, yeah, it hurts in the beginning! You gotta train your fingers, grow some calluses!" Our one and only lesson.

Now my parents' home felt haunted by his melodies, and melody-makers. Several of my dad's closest musician friends had recently died, including Phil Everly of the Everly Brothers, Joe B. Mauldin of the Crickets, and singer Bobby Vee. These were men he'd toured with for more than fifty years, men he shared a road language with, men he met for soup and salad at O'Charley's. The Sonny Curtis fan page I'd started for him as a fun lark on Facebook a decade earlier had turned into a grief machine, one maudlin tribute after another. An era was passing, and my dad seemed next in line.

CHAPTER 1

The first morning of our trip, I came downstairs to find him listless on the couch, finishing a crossword puzzle and periodically nodding off. The father I grew up with was round-bellied and full-faced. Now he appeared sallow and gaunt, as if cancer had stripped him of all but the essentials. All morning my mom bustled around him, retrieving his empty coffee mug and straightening his newspaper pile, as if she were mowing around a tree stump. I blended him a peanut butter smoothie to boost his weight, but he barely managed to drink half. My daughters sprawled on the couch beside him, watching a cartoon they were too old for, and my chest tightened as I surveyed the scene: mother working, father distant, child(ren) bored. I felt as if I'd floated a time machine back to my own childhood.

"Time to put on our rain boots and have an adventure!" I chirped, switching off the TV. My girls trailed after me into the drizzle, whining like cats. It didn't take long for my youngest to realize the word "adventure" had been, at its least fraudulent, a gross exaggeration. "What are we supposed to *do* out here?" she asked, the rain making ringlets of her red curls. I gathered a palmful of acorn hats and toadstools, little signs of fairies, for they were both still young enough to want to believe. When this hunt grew old, I did the only thing I could think of to entertain them. I led them through the thicket of slender birches to my father's shed, where I flipped up the wooden latch to the tool room.

"Eight people lived in a room this size. Can you girls believe that?" My daughters shook their heads, able to believe in a winged sprite who trades cash for teeth but as unable to believe in those numbers as I had been as a child, as I still was. "Where did they sleep? Where did they eat?" my logistically minded eight-year-old wanted to know.

The patter of rain on tin made me realize my father had built the room not only to evoke his childhood shack; he'd also outfitted it with a corrugated tin roof, just like the one in the dugout. The room was empty except for a shelf of forgotten tools, a Shop-Vac, and three unopened bags of fertilizer. It was clear my father rarely came out here, that the room was pretty useless from a practical perspective. In other words, nothing much depended on this red toolshed.

The outside world exhausted of its meager adventure, my daughters and I trudged back to the house, where we found my father still slumped on the living room sofa. As we kicked off our boots, I told him how I'd explained the meaning of the tool room's dimensions to his granddaughters.

At that moment a shimmer of my perfect world flashed before me. It was a world where my father would set down his puzzle and pull my youngest onto his lap, patting the cushion beside him for her sister. "Girls, have you ever heard of the Dust Bowl?" he'd begin, and they would shake their heads in wonder. My father would sigh heartily and give them a brief meteorological summary before telling them about his family, about long days spent in the fields pulling bolls by hand, how he and his siblings would drag each other around on the canvas picking sacks if their parents weren't looking. He'd tell them about his mother and her daily chores, so different back then. How she'd wring a chicken's neck to make supper, or how each Thursday she'd pay a nickel at the laundromat and let him turn the hand crank to get the soap out. He'd talk about his little Texas hometown, and how it was so dry, he and his best friend once started a brush fire lighting a tumbleweed with a match. He'd delight them with grisly tales of the town's annual hog-killing party, which, despite its bloody main stage, was a soap-making, kick-the-can-playing "hooki-la," as the old-timers used to say. Of course, there were hard times too; he couldn't deny it. His parents had been desperately poor, but they always managed to grow enough food to eat, and they were resourceful. Once when he had an ear infection as a small child, his mother wrapped a warm towel around a fried egg and laid it upon his ear—oh, how it soothed. Yes, he'd admit, twelve by fourteen feet was small, but everyone was poor back then! His family was rich in other ways like music and fun, which is why he'd built the shed to remind him of those days, both the good and the bad. In the shimmer of my perfect world, my father would grant his poverty context and just the right amount of levity, spin it into a narrative my girls could gain a finger hold on.

But as I live in the actual world and not a Wilford Brimley oatmeal commercial, my father said none of these things. Instead he glanced up from his puzzle in irritation. "No, you're thinking of the old toolshed, the one at the farm," he snapped, jabbing a thumb toward the backyard. "This one's not the same size."

My girls trailed off, our mission now fruitless in their eyes. "I—no, I don't think so, Dad," I said, reminding him he'd taken me out there once or twice to show me the dimensions.

"Nope," he repeated. "You're thinking of the farm."

It was a disagreement easily resolved. I rummaged through a kitchen drawer where I found a tape measure, then stepped back into my rain boots. "I'll just go measure it and see," I said. My father shrugged as if to say, *Suit yourself.*

My feet stomped through the sodden leaves with new purpose as I thought about those numbers, and how I wished my father would give me an inch. He was making me doubt more than the dimensions of the shed. Was my memory of him showing it to me wrong? No matter—it was *my* memory, fractured by time, but still mine. He couldn't just erase it.

Ten minutes later, I slid the living room door back open. "It's twelve by fifteen feet!" I announced, kicking off my boots. As far as I was concerned I'd won the argument, but he just shrugged again and gave a bemused "Huh," as if the room had assumed the measurements of its own accord. "That's pretty close," I added, rubbing it in. He ignored me completely.

A year before I would have picked an argument. The two of us used to argue heatedly, usually over politics after a few glasses of wine. We were both born under the sign of Taurus, and we could be bullish. But now I was just glad he was alive, regardless of how much he disliked the Obama administration. "Dad," I said, sinking into the armchair beside him. "Maybe you can draw me a picture of the shack someday? So I can really see it?"

"Well sure, I can do that," he said, looking up from his puzzle. "I remember it pretty well." And with that, our quibble was over. Cancer had gentled us.

Our last evening together, we sat watching *Jeopardy!* with the sound turned down while my dad nursed a Guinness, his one daily indulgence. Out the patio window, the sun finally burned through the storm clouds and hung red and swollen in the sky. My daughters were playing upstairs and my mom, chopping vegetables at the kitchen counter, was prattling in a forced chipper tone about how well my dad was doing, how he only had a few more months of chemo to go, and how *Nobody was dying around here, dammit.* That was a refrain she echoed a lot during those months: "Nobody's dying around here!" she'd yell like a drill sergeant, apropos of nothing. I'd be emptying the dishwasher or making a sandwich, my mind wandering while my dad dozed nearby. Then suddenly my mom would march into the room with a basket of laundry and loudly remind us that contrary to appearances, nobody was dying around here. Not on her watch.

"Well, you definitely can't die until I've written about you, Dad!" I cried. "What else am I going to do with my life?" My dad attempted a wan chuckle and patted me on the knee, though I was only half-joking. After staying home to raise my three daughters for nearly a decade, I'd begun writing again, mostly pithy articles for parenting websites. The closest I ever came to going viral was an essay titled "Being an Only Child Was Great. It's Being an Only Adult That Sucks." The piece was widely hated by parents of only children, some of whom, like my own mother, had suffered infertility. After that, I strenuously avoided conflict (and readership) with articles like "Five Best Read-Aloud Books for Siblings," or "Five Reasons You Should Garden with Your Kids." I never met a parenting issue I couldn't turn into a five-point listicle.

So that's where I was on that gray winter night, facing my dad's uncertain future as well as my own. My decision seemed stark and clear: I could continue writing fluff about raising kids or I could

CHAPTER I

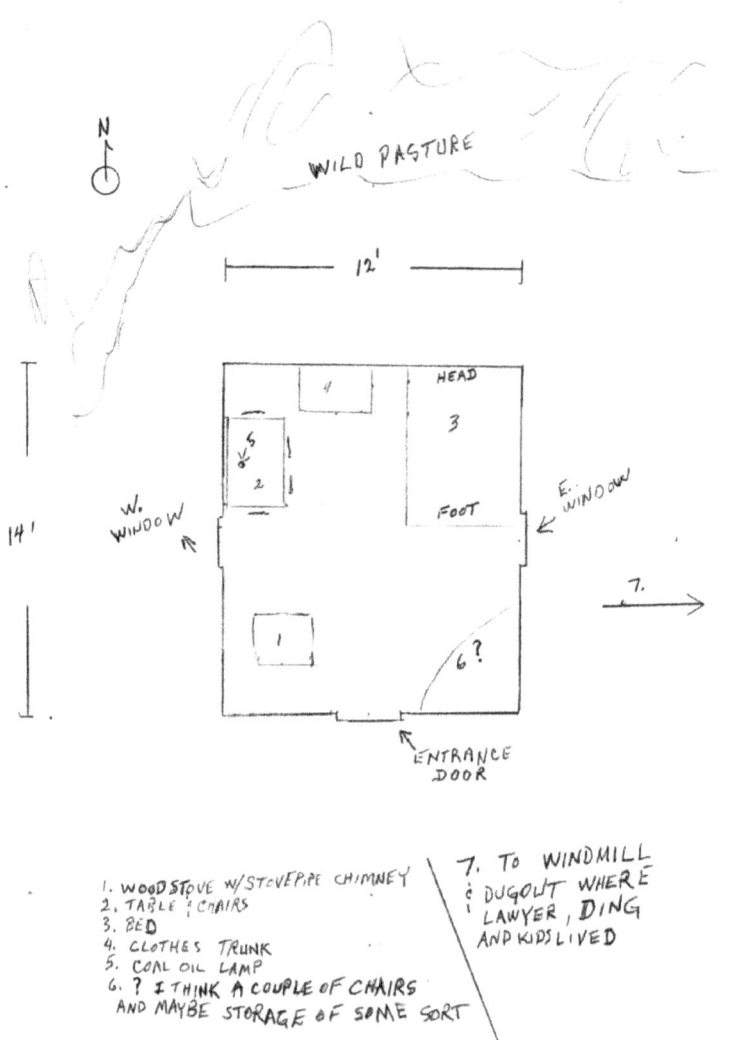

write the best story I knew, the story of Sonny Curtis. Hovering over the project was an aura of magical thinking. Maybe if I spun a good enough yarn, I could keep him alive.

Before I returned to Michigan, I reminded him once more about the drawing of the shack, then forgot all about it until I opened my mail two weeks later to find a surprise.

Before I comment on the drawing, note my father's meticulous capital lettering and perfectly protracted right angles. And of course he would never dream of drawing a diagram without including a compass. Children growing up in West Texas have few trees or land markers to guide them between their shadow and the horizon. By necessity, they learn their directions before they learn their letters. My dad tells the story of his second-grade teacher hanging a map on the wrong wall, with the northern arrow pointing east. Who thinks about actual directions before hanging a map? My second-grade father. *That map confused me all year*, he told me once. *Every time I'd look at it, I'd see Pittsburgh goin' south!*

After he mailed me the drawing, he emailed a few clarifications. The bed in the top right corner was actually two mattresses stacked on top of each other. His parents slept on the top mattress with baby Jean, and at bedtime they'd pull the bottom mattress out for the five other kids. The two oldest girls slept head to foot while my father and his two brothers slept foot to head. The clothes trunk also served as seating, a sort of makeshift couch.

Lawyer and Ding, referred to at the bottom right, were a Black couple who helped my grandparents farm the land, along with their children: Noonie and Chug, both boys, and Ruth, the youngest, my father's age. Years later when I read about the horrific way Black farmhands were treated during the Dust Bowl in James Agee's *Let Us Now Praise Famous Men*, I immediately thought of Lawyer and Ding. My grandparents held some racist views, but my father says that he and his siblings spent so much time with the couple's children growing up, they felt like "one big family." After Ruth, Ding gave birth to a stillborn baby, and the two families mourned together, holding a funeral in the field. The baby's gravestone remains there to this day.

I examine the drawing as if I expect it to solve a mystery I'm still articulating to myself. And though it does answer some questions about life in the shack, it poses others. What happened when a baby cried through the night? And speaking of babies, how was Jean conceived amidst this chaos? Why did Violet and Arthur have so many kids, anyway? My understanding is that they were loving parents, if lax. They enforced no bedtimes, which seems self-defeating in such a small space. They did, however, take great pains when it came to fairness, treating all their children the same no matter the circumstance, and doling out praise rarely, if ever.

Mainly I'm confounded by the challenge of water—drinking, diapering, dishwashing, and especially bathing. Baths proved a challenge for the family for years, even after they moved into a small house in the nearby town of Meadow. That house did have running water, though no indoor plumbing. When the brood started school, kids on the bus made fun of them for smelling bad. My grandparents were too busy working the fields to remedy the situation, but my father's oldest brother Pete refused to let his family become a town joke. Each morning at the break of dawn, he dragged his younger siblings out of bed to rinse them off, one by one, under the cold garden hose. My mother told me that story years ago; my father would never speak of it. Even writing the words on the page now brings tears to my eyes, as if I am revealing a shameful family secret, as if I too bear the scars of my father's poverty.

That story—and the silence surrounding it—illustrates the Curtis family's deep desire to escape the painful stigma of white trash cotton farmers. A 1940 novel called *The White Scourge* by a Texan named Edward Everett Davis shows how dehumanizing this stigma was. In it, Davis attacked Texas cotton culture for attracting "lowly blacks, peonized Mexicans, and moronic whites." But he saved most of his ire for the whites, for the perceived threat they posed to the white race, describing them as "America's worthless human silt" and people with "just enough intelligence to beget children, hew wood, draw water, and pick cotton."

Still, there must have been some beauty in that old shack, or my father wouldn't have built two tool rooms to its proportions. In the memoir he wrote me, he waxes sentimental about #5, the coal oil lamp.

One of my fondest memories is lying on the floor at night between Pete and Dean, listening to the lonesome howl of the coyotes. It was a virtual canine choir. And when I blew out that coal oil lamp, the only light came from the heavens. Our nearest neighbors were Grandpa and Grandma Curtis who lived half a mile to the north of us. There were no electric lights anywhere. It was glorious.

Eight people, twelve by fourteen feet. In the end, I'll never fathom the meaning of those mythical numbers. I'm also not sure why my father built two tool rooms with those dimensions but claims to have built only one. Perhaps those numbers used to show him how far he'd traveled in life, a starting point for all the measurements that followed: the hit songs, the millions of air plays, the halls of fame. But so much has been subtracted: four siblings, two parents, and a way of life. Maybe now that my father's an old man, those numbers just remind him of what was lost inside that tiny room, a room so small to hold a world.

"Our lovers, our husbands, our wives, our fathers, our gods—they are all beyond us," Tim O'Brien wrote in his novel *In the Lake of the Woods*. "And we wish to penetrate by hypothesis, by daydream, by scientific investigation those leaden walls that encase the human spirit, that define it and guard it and hold it forever inaccessible." My father's spirit walls are more like fortifications against attack. I have tried to chip away at them, to find—as much as we can ever locate another's soul—the man within the myth. But that man will always remain a bit of a mystery to me.

And yet the myth of him, with its sweeping history, wild changes of fortune, and artistic salvation, has lived inside me all my life. Now that I am a middle-aged mother making my own art while raising daughters of my own, it's time to see if I can live inside of it.

CHAPTER 2

Daughter of a Gun

Robbin' people with a zip gun
I fought the law, and the law won
—"I FOUGHT THE LAW," 1959

In 2012, the Hatch Show Print shop, a historic letterpress company in downtown Nashville, designed a poster commemorating my father. His manager called him after he'd seen the print. "They put guns on your poster, Sonny," he said. "Is that okay with you?" When my father later told me about this conversation, we both laughed, sharing the same unspoken thought. *What a silly question.*

The guns were a nod to my dad's most famous song, "I Fought the Law," which he wrote when he was twenty-two. Hundreds of artists have covered it, from The Bobby Fuller Four to The Clash to Bruce Springsteen to Johnny Cash to me, once, in my twenties. At Lonnie's Western Room karaoke bar in Nashville, I confused the tempo with my father's blues version—the only version I'd ever heard him play at home—and rightly bombed. Otherwise, few women have touched it. It's a masculine song, and men are drawn to it. It's a violent song, and each man who covers it stamps it with his own brand of violence. Texan Bobby Fuller didn't rob people with the original "zip gun" (a crude firearm used among 1950s teenage gangs) but a more Westernized "six gun." In concerts, The Clash changed the line "I miss my baby and I feel so bad" to "I killed my baby and I feel so bad."

It's no accident my father wrote a song mythologizing guns. Guns play a crucial role in his family's mythology, as stories hinge on whether or not the protagonist had a sidearm. If I begin unspooling the yarn at the spot where the gun mythology was formed in my father's family, I can see the places where it looped and knotted, spinning on and on, until it reached me.

I didn't inherit much from my Texan grandparents, but I did inherit these stories. They have been written to me by my father and corroborated by my father's oldest brother Pete and Pete's daughter, Karen. They are my spoken heirlooms, subjective truths hammered out in living rooms after Sunday suppers, one brother's feelings and observations fused with the thing his sister overheard—memory as alchemy, or sculptures chiseled over time to form the contours of my family's reality.

Every mythology, including this one, has a genesis. This genesis story does not contain a flood or a birth, but rather a death, a murder. Later there would be redemption, a righting of wrongs, a place where the myth took root in the dry West Texas dirt, alongside endless rows of cotton. Through the ages, its branches spread, sprouting habits and convictions that still exist in my family today. And on one branch, if I listen closely enough, I can even hear a song about a gun.

MAY 1913

The house was unusually quiet when my great-grandfather Will Curtis awoke that Sunday morning, alone. The familiar morning clamor—Pearl banging a pan onto the stove to fry the hoecakes, the children's small, hungry voices—was missing, the house silent except for the cry of a lonesome chickadee, the breeze susurrating the Indian grass. Throughout his life, Will would replay that day in his mind so frequently that the neural pathways became as trodden as the Arkansas backroad he called home in those days.

The kids were gone and his second wife Pearl was visiting family nearby. Will had the place to himself—not that the Ol' Bob Place, as it was known throughout the town, was his to begin with. He was only a tenant farmer, tall and rangy with a body like a wild dog at the end of winter. The farm was located on a scruffy patch of land in the backcountry of Paron, Arkansas, smack in the middle of the state among the rolling hills west of Little Rock, just before the land grows thick with hardwoods ridging the flinty peaks and valleys of the ancient Ouachita Mountains to the east. There is beauty there, though the Ol' Bob Place was just a one-mule homestead with a rickety shack, nothing much to speak of. Still, it could be Will's soon enough, if the drought eased up and that spring's crops cooperated. Finally, he could be a landowner.

The evening before, Will's ex-wife Ida had sent word that she wanted their three children to spend the night at her house a half-mile up the road. One night wouldn't hurt, Will had figured. It was May, peak planting month for cotton, and he could get a lot more done without the kids underfoot. Maybe it was even good for them to see their mother every once in a while, crazy though she was. He'd agreed to let them go for one night, and had sent seven-year-old Freeman, five-year-old Arthur, and three-year-old Etta over the hill to their mother's.

Harrowing the land with his mule and plow for hours on end that Sunday, Will must have let his mind wander to Ida's house. She and her husband Henry—a common-law husband, according to my father—were rumored to be housing transient hillbillies. It wasn't the kind of atmosphere Will wanted his kids around, though should it keep them from seeing their mama? He had no guideposts on this road; he was just trying to do right by his kids, better than any parent had ever done by him.

Who was my biological great-grandmother Ida? My cousin Karen suspects she might have been a saloon girl. My father says she was "not all there." I don't know how much of Ida's character has been molded through the years to fit the narrative. I also don't know the exact custody arrangement she and Will had worked out after their divorce. Karen thinks Will took the boys while Ida kept Etta, a more common arrangement in those days. Whatever their initial agreement, what does seem clear is that at some point, Will began to believe all three kids were better off with him, and Ida disagreed—but only when it came to Etta.

The day wore on until suppertime, and the kids were due home. Will was outside working a stubborn patch of ground, watching for them to come over the hill. Before long, sure enough, two small figures emerged. Just two? "Whoa," he signaled the mule, steadying its chain in order to get a better look. He made out the pant legs of the boys— no sign of Etta. She'd probably stopped to pick daffodils or collect a sparkly rock. She was often straggling behind like that, distracted by God knows what, never minding instructions. Just like her mama.

"Where's Etta?" he called out when the boys reached earshot.

"Mama wants to keep her another night," Freeman answered. Arthur shuffled his feet around, unable to meet Will's disapproving eye. A sensitive boy, he felt his father's moods before they landed.

"The hell she will," mumbled Will. He chained up the mule and walked into the house. *Damn that Ida, what's she up to now?* he wondered. She never made anything easy for him. He should have known better than to take her at her word, he thought, fishing through a desk drawer for a slip of paper. On it, he wrote down a clear order: *Send Etta home.*

"Freeman, run back up the hill and give this to your mama," Will said, handing over the note. Maybe he hoped the written word would carry more weight than his little boy could deliver, an official decree of sorts. Or did he have a darker premonition? Did he send Freeman because something told him that going himself would only bring trouble? Freeman did as he was told while Arthur stayed back at the house with Will.

Before long Freeman returned, this time bearing a new note, one written in Ida's shaky scrawl. *You want Etta, you come and get her*, it read. *Damn Ida.*

As Will set out to retrieve the little girl, his younger brother Dick happened to pass by on his way to Sunday evening church service.

Dick was twenty-four and not yet married. At some point, he'd discovered Christ, a faith that would elude Will until later in his life. In those days, Will worshipped more immediate gods, ones foretold in his precious, dog-eared farmer's almanac: early frosts, new moons, and spring rains.

Will told Dick where he was headed and asked his brother if he'd like to join him on the walk. Dick paused. Something about the situation made him wary. "You expectin' any trouble?" he asked Will.

"Naw," answered Will. By my father's account, he had decided to leave his gun at home. Dick, on the other hand, sensed a danger that Will did not. Perhaps Will was just worn down, tired of dealing with his ex-wife's folly. Perhaps he thought he was used to Ida's brand of trouble by now. He was wrong.

Dusk was falling as the brothers approached Ida's house. Dick stopped under a tree about thirty yards away, perhaps still uneasy about accompanying Will to resolve such a private family matter. The moment Will touched his right hand to Ida's picket gate, the first shot rang out. The bullet struck Will in his wrist before lodging in his chest. Doubled over, he frantically scanned the house for a sign of the shooter, and there it was—a rifle jutting from a front window. Before Dick could run to his brother's aid, Will saw a second gunman lean around the back corner of the house. He yelled for Dick to run, but it was too late. The gunman fired a bullet straight to Dick's head.

The gunmen were coming for the brothers now. Will dashed fifty yards to a nearby creek bed, where he scrambled under a downed tree, shrouded in the newly fallen darkness. He huddled there all night, his thumb plugging the bullet hole in his chest. Around midnight, he watched the long silhouettes of the gunmen pass by with their rifles as they called his name. "Come on out, Will. Here, kitty kitty," they beckoned, their lantern light sweeping the brambles. Along the embankment above him, his brother lay dead.

Freeman and Arthur spent that night at the Ol' Bob Place, alone. At some point, word of the ambush reached Ida's uncle Simon Garrett, who had remained friends with Will after the couple divorced. Garrett gathered a team and a wagon and drove to Ida's house, where they set out on a search. This time when Will heard his name called, he answered.

The search team lifted him up the hill to where Ida's house now stood empty, she and the gunmen having deserted it in the dead of night, Etta in tow, after they were unable to hunt down Will. The team carefully laid him on Ida's bed and summoned Pearl, who arrived with a country doctor. The doctor removed the bullet from deep within Will's chest, then asked Pearl for her silk scarf. As the story goes, he threaded it in through Will's chest and out his back, weaving it back and forth to clean the wound. Will lay on his ex-wife's bed in a laudanum fog for several days, his life still a question hanging in the air, until he was well enough to be moved back to the Ol' Bob Place.

The day after the murder, the *Muskogee* (Oklahoma) *Times-Democrat* ran an article all but pronouncing Will dead. Under the headline "Child Leads to a Killing," it read, "Henry Coburn, a young farmer, shot and killed Dick Curtis and probably fatally wounded his brother, Will Curtis, in Saline County. . . . Trouble over a young child of Will Curtis and Mrs. Coburn, from whom he was divorced two years ago, caused the shooting. Coburn surrendered today, claiming self-defense."

The doctor told the family that Will was lucky to be alive because the bullet had barely missed his heart and because the cold creek water had clotted his blood and prevented him from bleeding out. That was the only good news. Will stayed in bed recovering for months, and by the time he was able to work again, he'd lost crucial wages that cost him the Ol' Bob Place. Among his injuries was a permanently closed right fist that he would thrust in the air to wave hello to people, much to his future grandchildren's curiosity.

Four months after the shooting, Henry Coburn was indicted on two counts: assault with intent to kill Will and the voluntary manslaughter of Dick. Whatever happened to the second gunman—the one Will saw lean around the back corner of the house and actually shoot Dick—remains a mystery.

The trial began nearly a year later, on the morning of Thursday, March 5, 1914. Henry and Ida showed up for court looking like refugees, in a covered wagon bulging with furniture, clothes, and kitchen wares, seemingly all their earthly possessions. They had something else with them too: Etta. The little girl had been staying with her mother and her uncle's accused murderer ever since the shooting.

It took less than three hours for the jury to deliver its decision. For Dick's murder, Coburn was found not guilty of voluntary manslaughter. As for the second charge against him, assault with intent to kill Will, the court reporter's slanted longhand declared it "nol-prossed," a misspelled attempt at the Latin term *nolle prosse*. In other words, the state dropped the case.

The court adjourned for lunch. Ida walked outside and climbed into the waiting buggy, her makeshift home on wheels. Henry picked up Etta and handed the little girl to her mother. Ida held the child in her lap as the couple drove away from the courthouse to start a new life in East Texas.

In his memoir, my father wrote about the Arkansas justice system back then:

> At the end of the 19th and beginning of the 20th centuries, civil society, at least in [Will's] hardscrabble world, wasn't all that civil. Sometimes the law could be non-existent and what little law there was seemed way over on the other side of the mountain. As I was told by my dad, disagreements and grievances were settled on the spot, without judge or jury, in whatever way that was deemed necessary. I suppose there was some sort of flimsy, frontier justice, but it wouldn't pass for much today. Also, I imagine a lot of things didn't get settled at all. They just festered, and people learned to live past them.

Will tried to do just that for a few years after the trial. He moved off the Ol' Bob Place and onto a different one-mule homestead. He took any tenant farming job he could find to support his family, which was growing. Pearl, who had been pregnant at the time of the murder, gave birth to a baby boy they named Alvin. Two years later, they welcomed another son, Argust. But the tragedy cast an indelible shadow on the family. It festered. In early 1918, almost four years after the trial, Will looked at the unlucky cards left in his hand and decided to fold. He and Pearl packed the boys into a covered wagon and got the hell out of Arkansas.

Like the story of so many white American settlers, theirs was a story of leaving. For generations, Will's ancestors had been packing light and traveling westward with the sun. Coaxed by soaring agricultural prices brought on by World War I and the prospect of an open range, Will aimed his wagon as far west as it could go before it tipped into the sea: the promised land of California. Five generations later, I can see the faint ripples and waves of this migratory pattern, us Curtises born with a wandering heart, an itch to pack up and cut out.

The pilgrimage was a grueling, five-year journey of stops and starts. A year in, the family crossed over to Texas and began making their way through the fabled Red River Valley, surviving on sharecropping jobs along the river. Will chartered a boxcar to Quanah, named after the last great Comanche chief Quanah Parker, though those fearsome warriors were fifty years gone from the region by then, dislocated and betrayed by the US government, or cut down by the white man's pox. In Quanah, everyone pulled cotton again. Pearl gave birth to another baby boy who died at six months from pneumonia. The couple drove his body twenty miles east through a lonely stretch of pasture, where they buried him in a cemetery near the railroad town of Chillicothe. After four years of grinding labor in Quanah, the family had nothing to show for it. They packed up and left again, the dream of California growing ever more distant.

Will had heard about the town of Lubbock, where there was rumored to be cheap, uncultivated farmland for sale. Deciding to take a chance, he and Pearl bought the older boys train tickets and sent them ahead while the couple packed up the family's few possessions. When Will arrived in Lubbock, he saw nothing but grass for miles on end: raw earth, perfect land for planting cotton. He took yet another sharecropping job until the following year, when the owner of the sprawling L7 Ranch west of Lubbock sectioned off 640 untouched acres, located in a small town aptly named Meadow. The L7 owner, an old gold miner from Illinois, was asking two thousand dollars for the property. Will managed to come up with half for the down payment. The year was 1925—the war was over, agricultural business was booming, and Will, finally, was a landowner.

SUMMER 1925

Once in Texas, Will never again left the house unarmed. He carried two guns wherever he went: a sidearm on his body, and a rifle in his car. It's unclear how much of that choice was cultural (gun carrying was more prevalent in Texas, partly because so were snakes) and how much was situational (he'd vowed never to repeat the Arkansas tragedy). What is known is that Will got into street brawls in Texas, a lot of them. The open secret in the Curtis family was that many of these fights were over women. Will was a womanizer, at least when he was younger before religion got its claws in him, and these indiscretions were a lifelong source of shame for his children and grandchildren.

One altercation took place the summer Will bought the farm. The family's status had been upgraded from tenant farmers to landowners, though now they were mired in cultivating the ground to plant cotton. It was West Texan ground, riddled with mesquites. Will and his boys hadn't gotten much further than rooting them out, a punishing task that had to be done with shovels, axes, and grubbing hoes. Arthur and Freeman were the main grubbers, fated to spend decades bent under the paltry shade of those barbed canopies, digging away at the deeply interlacing roots.

After he cleared the mesquites, Will would turn over the sod. In this endeavor, he wasn't alone. Farmers throughout the Western frontier lured by federal land grants—migrants and sharecroppers

CHAPTER 2

and tenant farmers, all turned landowners now like Will—were doing the same, ripping out the thick Texas bluestem and the rest of the native grasses. Between the years 1925 and 1930, farmers plowed an area twice the size of Yellowstone National Park, 5.2 million acres. They would soon learn the error of their ways: how, without the grass, the topsoil couldn't hold. But they were desperate to survive in this unfamiliar terrain, and the land was all they had. They couldn't foresee the drought to come; in fact, a dangerously misleading superstition had once held that "rain will follow the plow," as if humans were gods with the power to change the climate. Earth and sky, stardust and folklore. But they would learn. The Dust Bowl was just around the corner, the decade where the ground became the sky.

All that would come later, though. On this morning, Will and Arthur had driven to the trading post in town when Pearl looked up from her washing to see a wagonload of cowboys from the L7 ranch drive up, the previous owners of Will's farm. Several of the men stepped out of the buggy and began yanking the six-foot cedar fence posts out of the ground. For the farmers who settled this land, fences were laws, protecting the land they had surveyed and fought over, paid for with blood and sacrifice. Wood was scarce in West Texas, so the cedar posts were in high demand. When Will bought the farm, he assumed the fence came with it. The L7 ranchers disagreed.

"Alvin!" Pearl hollered for her twelve-year-old son. "Hurry down to Brownfield and get your daddy and brother!" The road ran eleven miles to Brownfield, but the little boy knew a shortcut and ran as the crow flies, six miles across the sun-scorched pastures. He found his father and half-brother at the trading post and told them the news. The family jumped in Will's Model T and sped back to the farm, where they found the men still tearing out the posts.

"Stay in the car with the gun, son," Will instructed my grandfather Arthur, by then seventeen, before he jumped out of the car and ordered the ranchers to stop removing the posts, as well as to return the ones they'd loaded up in their wagon.

"He was a scrappy old guy," my father tells it. "Not afraid of anyone."

One of the ranchers, armed with a two-by-four fence stay, charged at Will. He swung it high and landed it hard against Will's side, knocking him backwards. Arthur watched from the front seat as the rancher steadied his footing and planted his legs wide, rearing for another blow. Behind him, one of the men climbed into the driver's seat and shook the reins, charging the horses in Will's direction.

Arthur looked down at the .22 rifle lying on the floorboard at his feet. There was no moment to think, no choice to be made.

He got out of the car and aimed it at his father's assailant. "Stop it or I'll shoot you!" he yelled. To Arthur's surprise, the rancher dropped the post. In that moment, Arthur knew the men were unarmed. Emboldened, he took a step forward, adjusting his aim. "Now y'all do exactly as my daddy told you," he said, summoning a lower register in his voice. "Give him back the posts you took."

The ranchers begrudgingly unloaded their wagon as Arthur stood guard under the gaze of his father. The L-7 cowboys never returned.

"Would you have shot him, Daddy?" my father used to ask my grandfather.

"Well, I reckon I would have," he'd shrug.

It was hard to imagine my grandfather hurting anything other than a rattlesnake. Quiet and unassuming, he walked with shoulders permanently bowed from decades of crouching in the fields, his eyes steady on the ground two feet ahead of him, as if scanning the milkweeds in a row of cotton. At times, his mannerisms evoked a punished dog, but when he spoke, there was an unexpected levity about him. He ended most of his stories with a jokey turn of phrase and a tremulous chuckle. When I grew older and learned more about his childhood, I wondered where he got his mirth.

I've wondered other things as well. Why didn't Will have a gun on him the day he went to retrieve Etta? It seems uncharacteristically naive of him to have gone unarmed, given his later reputation for street fighting. But that is the narrative I was told—Will was the victim, not the perpetrator—so that is what I wrote. An earlier version of this chapter was published and later anthologized. I figured that was the end of the story.

Then a few years ago I bought a subscription to an online newspaper database. After "Sonny Curtis" failed to turn up any salacious details, I searched for Dick's murder. I still had some lingering doubts about the version of the story I was given by my father and uncle, both of whom had also received the story secondhand, and both of whom had their own allegiances to Will. That's when an article popped up I hadn't seen before from the *Arkansas Democrat*, dated May 12, 1913.

> YOUNG FARMERS ENGAGED IN A FATAL AFFRAY
>
> A tragedy occurred in Jefferson Township, 25 miles southwest of this city, late Sunday afternoon, resulting in the death of Dick Curtis and the probable fatal wounding of his brother, Will Curtis, by Henry Coburn. All are prominent young farmers of the community, Coburn and Dick Curtis being about 25 years old and Will Curtis about 27.
>
> The trouble arose over the three-year-old daughter of Mrs. Coburn and Will Curtis, who were divorced about two and a half years ago. The custody of the child was awarded to Mrs. Curtis, who afterward married Henry Coburn.
>
> Curtis had called several times during the absence of Coburn and against his wishes, to see the child, and three weeks ago took the child away with him, and kept her until last Saturday, when he permitted her to return to her mother, sending word that she must come back Sunday.
>
> Sunday afternoon Will Curtis, accompanied by his brother Dick and Simon Garrett, called at the Coburn home to get the child. Mrs. Coburn answered the call and told them that she would not permit the child to go with them. The little one began crying when her father opened the gate and started toward her. Hearing this, Coburn, who was in the house, seized his Winchester, and going to the door, opened fire. Six or seven shots were fired, killing Dick Curtis and severely wounding Will Curtis.

Coburn came to town and surrendered to the sheriff, claiming self-defense, as he said Will Curtis was reaching toward his hip pocket when he fired upon him. He said that he did not intend to kill Dick Curtis, who was his friend.

In Will's defense (or maybe this is my own Curtis allegiance talking), the *Arkansas Democrat* does not reveal one single source until the end, and because that source is Henry Coburn, it's reasonable to assume that this is Coburn's version of events. Despite the discrepancies between his story and the narrative I was given, certain details do match up. My cousin Karen was correct—the original custody arrangement awarded Etta to Ida and the boys to Will (presumably Ida only wanted Etta, not the boys). Will *did* decide to go back on that arrangement for some reason. And he *was* shot while entering the gate. But according to the article, he brought Simon Garrett with him as well as Dick (and there's no mention whatsoever of the mysterious second gunman at the house). The fact that Simon was Ida's uncle and keen to help Will rather than his own niece indicates that he too thought Etta was better off living with Will. I can't imagine that Simon would want to bring guns into this family dispute, but there it is, my suspicions seemingly confirmed: Will was reaching for his hip pocket when Henry fired. When I read this line, I remembered something my father told me years ago about a signature move Will made during street fights. If he suspected his opponent was armed, he would put his hand on his pocket and say, "Don't do it. I got the drop on you." My dad said Will sometimes did this as a trick even when he wasn't armed. Yet the article states that Coburn only *heard* the argument between Will and Ida before grabbing his Winchester. By his own admission, there was little time for Will to reach for anything before Coburn fired wildly into the dusk.

The article raises questions I'll never resolve. But it did lend a new dimension to the story—a human, sorrowful one. I find a few details terribly sad, like when Etta, the "little one," cried as Will threatened to separate her from her mother. And though I still believe Henry

Coburn is the villain here (as well as a bad shot), the last sentence gets me: "He did not intend to kill Dick Curtis, who was his friend."

Coburn opened fire on three possibly unarmed men, killing one who was his friend. That is a heinous act of murder. And yet his actions made sense within his ethical universe—he protected the females of his household with a gun. He operated within the moral code of his time and place. I know this to be true. How? Because a jury acquitted him.

As for Will, his experience in Arkansas became a myth in my family. Each time it was passed down, its rough edges and inconsistencies were sanded and honed until it took on the sheen of a parable. The lesson it teaches—*A gun will protect you*—was the one Will learned that night, too late, as he lay fetal in the cold black creek. How he must have longed for a gun, a god, anything that could have saved him and his brother. When he emerged the next day from those frigid waters, he was baptized into a new mythology.

In French essayist and philosopher Roland Barthes' 1957 book *Mythologies*, he asserts that myths occur when society's institutions, cultural or political, create and foster cultural beliefs that are in turn adopted by the masses. Barthes writes of his "feeling of impatience at the sight of the 'naturalness' with which newspapers, art and common sense constantly dress up a reality which, even though it is the one we live in, is undoubtedly determined by history." It is easy to draw a straight line between my Texan family's penchant for guns to any number of events, be they personal, political, or artistic (my dad's infatuation with old Western movies, for example). I may not always agree with it, but I can relate to this primal need for self-protection expressed so cleanly in the form of a weapon.

When I was a child, mass shootings were extremely rare, and with the exception of the 1966 University of Texas Tower shooting well before my time, school shootings were practically nonexistent. I understood growing up that we owned guns for the same reason my friends' parents did, because like the locks on our doors or our faithful guard dog Sandy, they protected the household. We weren't exactly "responsible gun owners" by today's definition, for my father kept guns within easy access, always loaded. As his own father used to say, what good was a gun if it wasn't loaded? He gave me strict warnings never to touch his guns without him around, and fortunately because I was a dreamy child more interested in books and dolls than weapons, I followed his orders. Sometimes I'd open the top drawer of his bedside table, where a snub-nosed pistol lay alongside stray guitar picks, a stick of Absorbine Jr., and slips of paper with lyrics he'd scribbled in the night. When I reached to grab something and saw the gun, I quickly shut the drawer like slamming the lid on Pandora's box.

That box was reopened in July 2018. My second cousin Lisa, Will's youngest grandchild, was murdered by her husband Kurt at their house on the family farm. I didn't know Lisa well, but I'd met her at a few family gatherings over the years. Wiry and blonde, she struck me as one of those tireless matriarchs who buttresses the family in ways big and small.

Like too many people in this country, Kurt owned an arsenal of guns despite a history of substance abuse and mental illness. One night when Kurt and Lisa's grandchildren were staying over, Kurt began acting erratically. Lisa called her daughter to pick up the children so they wouldn't witness his rage. Before her daughter left with the kids, she asked Lisa to come too, get out of the house for a night and let Kurt cool off. But Lisa refused, saying that leaving would just make him angrier. Later that evening, an argument between the couple escalated and Kurt grabbed his gun. While Lisa ran for her life to her pickup truck, Kurt shot her in the back. She tried calling her son and 911 as she drove off down their country road, but she was losing too much blood. She skidded into a ditch and died behind the wheel.

Typing Lisa's name online pulls up a website honoring Texas victims of domestic and intimate partner violence. The list covers one year, 2018, and 211 deaths alphabetized by county. Sparse details are provided for each victim, and I read a few pages before they all start running together. Nearly every victim is a woman and a mother (Lisa had three adult children, two with Kurt and one from a previous marriage), many of them pregnant at the time of their murders. Nearly every woman was shot in her home by her husband or boyfriend or ex, often as she was attempting to end the relationship. Often the gunman then turned the gun on himself; Kurt did not. He went to jail where he remains today. "He should have just shot himself," was something I heard a few members of my Texan family say after the murder. Another thing I heard them say: "How in the world could this *happen?*"

I reach out to my cousin Karen, Pete's youngest daughter, on Facebook to help answer that question. Every writer tackling her family history should have a relative like Karen. A tenacious saleswoman in her fifties, Karen is both brash and warm, with waves of silver-streaked dark hair and a fondness for colorful clothing and funky eyeglasses. She's been through a lot of hardship in her life, yet she retains a deep sense of both faith and humor. Because she's lived mostly in or around Lubbock, she's entrenched in the Curtis family in a way I am not. I joke with her that she's my intrepid boots on the ground, willing to answer whatever question I throw her way, no matter how big or small (I once asked her to photograph an elm tree).

Still, I hesitate before writing to Karen about Lisa's murder. Her politics are radically different from mine. For one thing, as I know because I follow her on Facebook, she's a vocal gun advocate. I worry she'll think I'm painting our family as violent hillbillies or, worse, exploiting Lisa's death for my own agenda. But Karen does as she always does, gives me the benefit of the doubt and an honest answer.

She writes back that she remembers Lisa as "sweet but nervous," unhappy in her long-lasting marriage but unwilling to offer many specifics as to why. Though Kurt was a recluse, Karen manages to send me one fairly recent photo of the couple. In it, Lisa and Kurt are standing in a modest living room wearing jeans and flannel jackets. Kurt appears stocky and smug, with a ten-gallon cowboy hat and a bottle of Budweiser in hand (Karen says he had a drinking problem).

Lisa leans into his side, both her arms wrapped around his right arm in a gesture both protective and loyal. Her closed-mouth smile is tight. Her eyes are hollow and expressionless.

I ask Karen if she saw any warning signs with the couple and she delivers a big one: Lisa once made an offhand comment to Karen that she thought Kurt might kill her. Rattled, Karen asked if she really believed that and Lisa laughed it off. "No," she said rolling her eyes, "but I hate him." *Maybe it was just a joke*, Karen thought. After all, the couple had been married over twenty years. Lisa was fifty-eight at the time of her murder, long past the age of youthful vulnerability.

According to the National Coalition Against Domestic Violence (NCADV), gun-related intimate partner femicides in Texas have steadily crept up in recent years, from an average of seventy-seven women annually between 2010 and 2014 to ninety-six women annually between 2015 and 2019. Unsurprisingly, this number rose during the pandemic—204 women's killings in 2021. It's no coincidence that Texas's femicides have risen as its gun laws have loosened. The NCADV estimates that an abuser's access to a firearm increases the risk of intimate partner femicide by *400* percent.

Kurt should not have owned a gun given his state of mind, but since he had no prior arrests that I'm aware of, perhaps no one could have prevented him from doing so. He lived on a wild farm teeming with rattlesnakes. I'd probably own a shotgun if I lived there too. I believe many, if not most, gun owners in this country are responsible citizens who own guns for the same reason my relatives do—because they live on a farm, or believe the only thing that can stop a bad guy with a gun is a good guy with a gun, and maybe they can even point to evidence of that theory somewhere back in their family history like I can, especially in Texas, a land forged and flamed in blood, a land where the terms "good guy" and "bad guy" are highly subjective. That's how myths work: they take history and mistake it for nature.

As tragic as Dick Curtis's murder was, it followed a frontier logic, its meaning easy to decipher: two husbands, each protecting his own family. Lisa's murder defiles that moral framework. Karen says my

CHAPTER 2

uncle Pete couldn't bear to speak of the crime because it upset him so. Of course it did. It bastardized everything he was raised to believe about men being the providers and protectors of the family. And the way Kurt shot Lisa in the back while she was running away infuriated him. The most cowardly way to win a gunfight. "Most people wouldn't do that to an animal," Karen remembers him saying.

Approximately fifty American women are killed each month by guns, according to a 2018 report from the Violence Policy Center. As Rachel Louise Snyder points out in her excellent book *No Visible Bruises: What We Don't Know About Domestic Violence Can Kill Us*, this figure is almost certainly lower than the reality (some of the reporting is voluntary) and does not factor in the deaths of innocent bystanders such as children or coworkers. Nor does it include law enforcement officers caught in crossfire. If we live by the myth that a gun will protect you, then we also have to acknowledge the growing number of human casualties of its ideology.

A man killed Lisa—a man crazed by violence and possibly drink, a man raised in a violent state located at the boot heel of a nation birthed by violence. But I believe a myth killed her too.

Snakes lurked everywhere on the rural Tennessee cattle farm where my parents raised me, hidden under the tall timothy grass. Two pastures from our house, the Piney River gently glided over glossy brown rocks that I longed to skip, but my father deemed the path "too snakey" and I was only allowed to go after he cut the grass for hay. *Where did the Piney River start? Where did it end?* I used to wonder as a child, its origin and journey as mysterious as the songs my dad seemingly pulled from the air to buttress our life. The grass surrounding the river teemed with copperheads, the river itself with venomous water moccasins. I learned from an early age to walk through our pastures head down, ever alert for the snakes with diamonds on their backs. Perhaps that was one of my earliest life lessons: to look for the dangers in the grass, to doubt life's placid surface.

But I never doubted my father's love for me. Despite his frequent absences in my early years, or his tendency to hole up in his consciousness, I knew he loved me deeply, nervously. I was his only child, small for my age, in need of protection. Guns weren't a symbol of power in our house; they were a symbol of my father's love—a love tinged with righteous fear.

Our farm was a treasury of peril, my father its archivist. For almost every danger, we had a gun. For the copperheads, rattlesnakes, and puff adders, we owned a slender .410-bore shotgun with the words "Snake Charmer" scrolled in cursive across the barrel. A single-barrel shotgun, it only fired once before it needed reloading, so it required careful aim—just right, to quote my father, "for snakes and suicides."

After I left for college, my parents sold the farm and moved to a pristine white clapboard house overlooking a less threatening road, one closer to town. The cowboys and copperheads are gone but the mythology remains. My father suffers from lifelong insomnia, and when I visit him, I wake to find the television invariably tuned to the late-night Western channel. Though he no longer lives in a Western, he still sleeps with two rifles under his bed and that same snub-nosed black pistol in his bedside table. I find that most of my father's guns come complete with a story, and this pistol is my favorite. It once belonged to a friend of my father's from his Hollywood days, a character actor fittingly best known for his role in the television show *Gunsmoke*. The man's wife had left him and their two small children to hole up with her lover in a high desert bungalow. One night, the actor showed up at my father's house, drunkenly raving that he planned to drive up there and kill them both. My father managed to wheedle the gun away from his friend before the actor drove off in a fit of rage. Soon afterwards we moved to Tennessee, and though my father never saw his friend again, he keeps the pistol in his bedside table, equal parts protection and souvenir from his youth.

CHAPTER 2

Will Curtis on Texas farm. (From author's collection.)

My father doesn't display his guns; it's not his style to show them off. He hides them, sometimes accidentally from himself. As with any protective amulet, a crucifix or rabbit's foot, the awareness of its presence matters more than the object itself. For my father, that knowledge is vital, and enough.

Sometimes after we have dinner together, the wine blurs our boundaries and warms our blood, and my father will lean into me. "I know you don't believe in them . . ." he'll trail off before narrowing his eyes and slowing his speech for effect, "but you should really think about owning a gun." And so he instills the mythology that was long ago instilled in him. It isn't rote instruction. It's his truth—the truth of his experiences, and the experiences of those who came before him. My truth is different. I suppose I followed in the footsteps of my Wisconsin-born mother, a stranger to his Texan lore. Now that I too am a mother, one raising children in a country plagued by constant mass shootings, my terrain is fraught with terrors hidden like the copperheads in the timothy grass, only on paths I can't avoid, or arm myself against.

For now, the guns I own are made of paper: two printed revolvers, framing my father's name on that Nashville commemorative poster. It hangs above my dining table where my husband and I nightly feed our family, spinning more peaceful mythologies for our daughters than the ones I inherited.

Sometimes my eyes rest upon those six-guns, and I think of Will, and begin to understand. I can see why the gun represented redemption for him after the terrible loss of his brother. I see too how that mythology seeped through my bloodline, from Will to Sonny to Lisa to me. If I listen closely, I can hear a straight-eight guitar intro and a gunshot drumbeat, like the pounding heartbeat of a frightened teenage boy, forever frozen in time. He is looking through the windshield as the rancher raises the fence post, as his father cowers, unarmed. He is the law and the lick, the son and the father, the birth of a song. It's time for him to make his debut.

CHAPTER 3

Lifting Buddy Holly

I just came down to see The Buddy Holly Story
*I guess it don't matter none, but they told it wrong
So I'm gonna try and tell you what really happened
But it's gonna be tough to tell a story that long in a song . . .*
—"THE REAL BUDDY HOLLY STORY," 1978

In the living room of my childhood farmhouse in Tennessee, a bronze statue of Buddy Holly perched high on a floor-to-ceiling bookshelf, holding a guitar I would later learn was called a Stratocaster. He stood about a foot tall, overseeing the room where my parents and I spent most of our time, his bespectacled gaze upon us as we went about the business of our daily lives.

I must have learned about Buddy when I was very young, still cataloguing the people and objects in my world—for all I know, I learned the opening chords to "Maybe Baby" in my mother's womb. Yet I don't remember asking my dad about him when I was growing up. I definitely don't remember him reminiscing about their teenage friendship. I don't remember a moment of Buddy Holly discovery ever taking place in my early life, though I knew Buddy's ghost required certain things of us. It required us to have two phone numbers, one listed and one not. Friends and family called the unlisted line, but the listed number fed directly to an answering machine filled with

CHAPTER 3

messages from Buddy Holly fans or, as my father called them—sometimes affectionately, sometimes not—*pervs*. Coined by the Crickets' drummer J. I. Allison, the term was a frequent part of their road lexicon, just as country music fans were *melons*. Not all country music fans, of course, but a specific brand, the tourists who swarmed downtown Nashville, especially during the summer exhibition that used to be called Fan Fair but is now the CMA Music Festival. *Avoid driving to Nashville this week unless you want to get melon juice on your car*, my father might say behind the newspaper, and I could picture them in my mind, the men in shiny cowboy boots and the women in Daisy Dukes, sun-blinded and drunkenly weaving outside Tootsie's Orchid Lounge: melon headquarters. Pervs were obsessive music fans, or "musos" as they're called in the industry, but melons cared more about stardom. They traveled in herds. They stood in hours-long lines for a fleeting moment with a country star. In the Venn diagram of fandom, melons and pervs rarely overlapped, though I suppose one could be a perv in the sheets and a melon in the streets. The term melon was always a pejorative, but my dad had a soft spot for pervs. The impression I got from him was that they were more intelligent than melons, and also more persistent. And where melons were gender neutral, pervs were usually men, many with British accents. England, my father said, was full of pervs.

Buddy's ghost also required my dad to field calls from music journalists and radio DJs around the world. I can still see him sitting in the living room under Buddy's cold gaze, wearing jogging pants and a concert T-shirt, his stocking feet propped on the glass coffee table and his bifocals atop his balding head. Gazing out the window at his pasture, he'd rest the phone against his shoulder and give different answers to the same question. Though I couldn't hear it, I knew what it was.

Who was Buddy Holly?

"He was just a good ole boy, you know?"

"Yes, a very talented guitarist, but also a great songwriter. Sometimes people forget that."

"That's right, I left the band in 1956, before the Crickets formed."

"Well, yes and no. I admit we had a rivalry, but it was mainly teenage ego stuff. Seems a little silly now."

Buddy Holly felt important in our family, even honored, but in a workmanlike way: a question to answer, an event to attend, a responsibility to shoulder. A weight.

Perhaps because I lacked a sense of discovery about Buddy growing up, I tried to recreate one later in life, as I learned that not everybody lives in the shadow of a dead rock 'n' roll star. The Buddy era was one piece of my father's puzzle I couldn't make fit. What *had* happened between them all those years ago? Was my dad bitter? He didn't seem bitter, but I might be if I were him. I began calling him more during his cancer battle and quizzing him when he felt up to it. Sometimes my questions made him tired, other times they seemed to perk him up. Sometimes it was just an excuse to call.

Over time I acquired so much useless Buddy Holly trivia, I couldn't keep it straight in my brain. I bought rolls of butcher paper and colored Sharpies and devised a timeline of that era that soon spanned an entire wall—so many songs and dates! My father is a near savant when it comes to remembering dates. But every time I wrote a draft of this chapter, something was missing. My dad had given me the same answers he'd given all those reporters before me, answers that could be gleaned from countless Buddy Holly biographies (I know, because I read most of them). I once had a professor who liked to say that writing is either alive or dead on the page. Every time I tried to write about Buddy Holly and my dad, my writing gasped its final breath and crossed the rainbow bridge.

I knew my dad's situation with Buddy backwards and forwards. But what was the story? Was it a story of rivalry and regret? A story of the complexities of fate and fame? A story of cultural appropriation? A story of tragedy and redemption? I knew how to begin the story, but where did it end?

CHAPTER 3

"Can't you tell me *anything* about Buddy you never told anyone before?" I once asked my dad in frustration. As his only child, I thought I deserved more than the boilerplate answers. Hadn't I orbited Buddy's ghost like a distant satellite? Didn't I have a small claim on his legacy too?

My dad was quiet for a moment before coming up with an answer. To pass the time driving home from late-night gigs, Buddy and their bandmate Bob took turns spooking each other with ghost stories while my dad listened from the backseat. "Those stories used to scare the fire out of me," he said. He didn't think he'd told anyone that before.

Breaking news, I thought. *Buddy Holly was a typical teenager who liked to be scared.*

Later, it stupidly dawned on me.

Maybe this is a ghost story.

♪

They met on a blustery spring day in 1953, though they likely crossed paths before, knocked elbows at some high school jamboree, which is to say their meeting was inevitable. They were both hungry teenage guitarists orbiting the same West Texas country scene, angling for opening spots on *Louisiana Hayride* shows. But their official meeting unfolded like a formally arranged date. When sixteen-year-old Buddy tuned into a local television variety show one night, he saw my dad performing a Grand Ole Opry tune called "Uh-Huh, Honey." Fifteen and angel-faced, my dad had just won the statewide Future Farmers of America talent contest, earning him media attention. A gangly brunet like Buddy, his hands were adept at fingerpicking and his voice was strong and eager, an unadorned honky-tonk twang.

My father learned to play guitar from his aunt Lorena when he was four, so young he could only play on the top four strings because his fingers couldn't stretch all the way across the neck. In a photo I once saw of Lorena, she was tall and pretty with a wide smile and hair the color of a wheat field at dusk. She was married to my grandfather's older brother Freeman, the one who'd delivered the note to Ida on that fatal Arkansas day so long ago. Lorena grew up on the panhandle, where her parents, the Mayfields, ranched cattle. She'd learned the guitar from her mother, who played in a fingerpicking style thought to have originated in the late 1800s by Black blues guitarists imitating ragtime piano. Her father played the fiddle, and the couple taught their eight children to play instruments as soon as they could hold them. They were a talented family, but not exactly unique. Music was integral to Texas culture, one of the only acceptable paths people had to transcend the punishing forces of dust, drought, and Depression.

Three of Lorena's six brothers, Herb, Smokey, and Edd, went on to form a band called the Mayfield Brothers (sometimes, in the style of popular band names of the day, they called themselves the Green River Boys). In 1953, Edd Mayfield caught the attention of the father of bluegrass himself, Bill Monroe, who hired him as one of his Bluegrass Boys.

So the lineage is this: Bill Monroe took aspects of folk, ragtime, gospel, and country and crystallized them into a new genre called bluegrass, which rubbed off on the Mayfields. The family introduced the genre to my father's family, especially the sons. In turn, my father and his two brothers started their own trio, the Curtis Brothers. Playing guitar and singing lead was Pete, the oldest at eighteen, tall and broad-shouldered with a crew cut and chiseled jaw. Fifteen-year-old Dean, winsome with light brown curls and dimples, played the fiddle. My nine-year-old father wore a cowboy hat too big for his head and khakis that hung off his narrow hips. He also played the fiddle, and his brothers let him sing one song per show. For a while, it was Ernest Tubb's cutesy "Throw Your Love My Way." From the photos I've seen, my father was cutesy too, a bluegrass version of Michael Jackson, or Donny Osmond—the baby of the band, coasting on his charm.

He performed on his own for the first time in third grade when his mother signed him up to play in a school assembly. He was so nervous, he cried himself to sleep the night before the show. *Just look at me the whole time and you'll be fine*, Violet told him. *Forget all them other folks.* The next day she dressed him in a matching blue button-down and pants, like a pint-sized Texaco attendant. When he stepped up to the mic, the men in the audience chuckled and the ladies sighed and clasped their chests. The kids didn't know what to think seeing their classmate Sonny, the scrawny boy who sat in the back reading *Li'l Abner*, now standing before them holding a guitar. He held his breath until he spotted his mother. Then his fingers began to dance across the strings, plucking out "Good Old Mountain Dew," a quick-tempo Prohibition tune made famous by The Stanley Brothers. Nobody was chuckling now. Someone hollered, and the room exploded with applause and whooping, the cacophony lifting my father high, high above the crowd, high above the roof, into a new stratosphere where the air was charged and he became something other than himself, something other than human almost, a part of the bigger picture, like a cloud or a breeze. Like a star.

Fast forward to 1953, when Buddy saw my father perform on TV. He recognized a kindred bluegrass lover, for Buddy too had grown up idolizing the Mayfield Brothers. He'd formed a duo with his best friend from Lubbock High School, a kid named Bob Montgomery, and they could use a third band member. In what would be a fated coincidence, my dad and Buddy had a friend in common named Olan, and Buddy asked Olan to introduce them.

One day soon after, my dad skipped his last two periods of school and drove thirty miles into Lubbock to meet Buddy. It was March, sandstorm season, and one was blowing that day, he recalls. A sandstorm blows through so many of his early memories, I wonder if West Texas exists in his mind behind a haze of ruffled earth. He headed to the Gin Café, a country diner Bob's parents owned on the outskirts of Lubbock (named after the cotton gin of course; Lubbock was dry as a brick). As he waited inside the diner, a yellow school bus pulled in front and a boy with a thick mop of dark, wavy hair bounded off. He introduced himself as Bob, then suggested they drive over to Buddy's house and get to picking.

I've asked my father what he and Buddy talked about that day, but he remembers their conversation as well as I remember the first words I spoke to any of my high school friends, which is to say, not much. What he does remember are his impressions, that Buddy seemed shy, and Bob more aggressive. This dynamic carried over to their duo, where Bob was the lead singer and Buddy his backup. Buddy had dyed his hair blond a few months prior, and its half-grown-out state reminded my father of a black-and-tan coonhound. My father guessed Bob was the star of the duo, the one who got the girls. With his glasses and funny hair, Buddy seemed awkward. Ordinary.

Later, my dad would find out that Buddy had a goofy side, that he could be a smart aleck prone to irreverent outbursts, and that he was far from ordinary. But in that moment, they were just music-obsessed teenage boys. They wasted little time on chitchat but picked up their guitars and spoke their first conversation in song (something by Hank Williams, my father thinks). When reporters ask him about the first time they met, he always gives some version of the following answer: *We said hello, shook hands, and started pickin'*. Sometimes he adds this sweet reflection: *I think Buddy and I were friends before we met*.

Maybe at its heart, this is a story about friendship.

♪

The two had much in common, both rascally younger sons, the beloved baby boys of their families. Their fond nicknames bear this out: Buddy and Sonny. Buddy also grew up in a family of avid musicians. As a boy, he too played the fiddle and guitar with his older brothers. But unlike my dad, Buddy grew up middle-class, his father a tailor and salesman in a Lubbock clothing store.

Soon after meeting Buddy and Bob, my father joined their band, picking gigs at county fairs, roller rinks, grocery store parking lots—anywhere that would book them ("We'd play at the opening of an envelope," he jokes). They played a mix of bluegrass, country, and Western swing; Flatt and Scruggs's "Salty Dog Blues" was one of their signature tunes. Buddy and my dad took turns playing rhythm and lead guitar. Sometimes Buddy would play the banjo and my dad the fiddle. Bob played the flat-top guitar, and they all took turns singing harmonies and lead. Their roles were nebulous but their desire was clear—they overflowed with ambition to be big Grand Ole Opry stars like their heroes, Red Foley and Ernest Tubb. When a local country music radio station owner named Dave Stone needed acts to fill out bills featuring Marty Robbins or Hank Snow, he'd often call them and they'd gladly pick for free just to breathe the same air as their heroes.

What fueled their hunger? I can't speak for Buddy, but for my dad, it stemmed from more than a love of music. "Well, I might as well say it. I liked the attention," he once told me. That school assembly long ago had shown him the healing balm of applause.

Soon my dad's relationship with Buddy deepened into friendship. They cruised the Hi-D-Ho and double dated at the State Theater with Lubbock girls (Buddy and Bob both had a crush on the same girl, melodically named Echo McGuire). They loved seeing movies, both with and without their dates—especially shoot-'em-ups like 1956's classic Western, *The Searchers*. By this point, the band included Buddy's Lubbock High School friend, J. I. Allison. Two years younger than my dad and Buddy, J. I. was a skinny seventeen-year-old kid who looked younger than his age and played the drums with a sly smile and a noodle-armed exuberance. One scorching summer day after seeing *The Searchers* with Buddy and J. I., my dad drove back to Meadow while Buddy and J. I. ambled over to J. I.'s house to tool around on their instruments. At some point, Buddy said to J. I. that it sure would be nice if they could write a hit song.

"That'll be the day," J. I. answered, reciting a line from the film in his best gravelly John Wayne voice. And that's the song they wrote.

On weekend nights after gigs, the band headed to Lubbock's North Mexican town, where the bootleggers lived. A few houses had converted windows into makeshift drive-throughs, and a dollar apiece would get each of them a quart of Lone Star beer. They drank them in vacant fields under the upturned bowl of Texas stars, their laughter piercing the silence of the open prairie.

Texas may not have been part of the Deep South geographically, but it inherited much of its ideology. As Texas historian Neil Foley writes in his book, *The White Scourge: Mexicans, Blacks, and Poor Whites in Texas Cotton Culture*, most Anglo Texans were descended from transplanted Southerners like Will, many of whom "had fought hard to maintain the 'color line' in Texas and to extend its barriers to Mexicans." In other words, as the South's cotton culture advanced westward, so did its white supremacy. In keeping with this practice, Lubbock was deeply segregated, beholden to a 1928 ordinance forbidding Black people from owning property outside the southeast side (the law remained on the books for seventy-eight years, until the city council abolished it in 2006).

When Buddy and my father were teenagers in the 1950s, rhythm and blues was so verboten, white DJs refused to play Black artists on the air. But somehow Buddy and my father discovered a radio show called Stan's Record Rack, a Shreveport broadcast that played popular Black music of the day. The sound was different, with a heavy downbeat like a raw throb. It grabbed on and took hold.

In a 1996 interview with biographer Spencer Leigh, my father recalled:

> Then along came Little Richard, Fats Domino, Ray Charles—he was a little more sophisticated, we couldn't figure out some of his chords—and, of course, Chuck Berry. At the outset, we couldn't listen to some of that music 'cause it was considered "race music." We'd have to go out in the car late at night and listen to this show out of Shreveport, Louisiana, which played the greatest music in the world. I used to spend the night with Holly. We'd go out at midnight and sit in his car, and fall asleep listening to the music.

CHAPTER 3

♪

If you Google my dad's name, there's a good chance you'll stumble upon the word *pioneer*. A search of "Sonny Curtis" + "pioneer" yields 34,000 results. Growing up, I watched enough *Little House on the Prairie* episodes after school to understand what that word meant. He was not Michael Landon driving a covered wagon westward into an uncertain horizon as Will had done, but I knew he had been first at something, something big and important.

Over the years, I figured out what any half-educated rock 'n' roll fan has long known. My dad and Buddy were pioneers in the same way the Ingalls family were pioneers: whites trailing a path already forged. In today's terms, it's a classic example of cultural appropriation. It's strange researching my father's career through his past interviews and seeing his answers through the lens of a trending topic. And while that lens makes sense, the story is more complicated. He grew up alongside the children of Black and Mexican sharecroppers and migrant laborers, all of them running barefoot together through the cotton fields. A Mexican café near his house played norteño music on weekends, and he loved to stand on his porch at night and listen to the jangle of accordions. His close experiences with Black and Mexican cultures molded him from an early age, just as they molded other white artists like Carl Perkins, who learned guitar from a Black field hand on his parents' cotton farm.

My dad and Buddy weren't the only white boys listening to rhythm and blues. On January 6, 1955, Elvis Presley played Lubbock for the first time at the Fair Park Coliseum. My seventeen-year-old father was on the bill that night, playing guitar for a country duo. The concert organizers stacked cotton bales against the stage to separate Elvis from the crowd, and my father remembers "the most beautiful girls in Lubbock" climbing over them, grasping at the singer's pant legs. "I remember being made aware of something happening, that there was more to music than *making* music," he once told me. "I don't know if the term 'groupie' even existed back then, but before that night, I'd thought of a fan as someone who liked someone else's music. I mean, I was a Hank Snow fan. But this was different, the effect Elvis had on people. Especially girls."

Elvis had co-opted more than the rhythm-and-blues sound, blatantly copying Black performers like Otis Blackwell and Big Mama Thornton. He'd also borrowed the language—billing himself as the Hillbilly "Cat," fifties slang for a Black man—and the clothes. My father vividly remembers his outfit that night: white suede bucks, red flannel pants, and an orange jacket: decidedly *not* Western wear.

When Buddy saw Elvis, he "flipped out," according to my father, and instantly converted from country to rock 'n' roll. My dad was more impressed by Elvis's guitar player Scotty Moore, whose playing echoed that of his childhood hero, Chet Atkins. He was fixated on imitating Atkins's style, which merged bass and guitar in a way that created an orchestra to the ear. A few months before that night, he'd hitchhiked to Lubbock to track down a local TV cameraman rumored to know the method. The man showed him how to play the rhythm with his thumb and the melody with his fingers. Afterwards, my dad practiced constantly until he nailed it. And here was Scotty Moore, doing the same trick.

Elvis planted a seed in Buddy's head that night. Since Elvis's three-piece band was comprised of lead guitar, rhythm guitar, and bass, his band would be too. Buddy would imitate Elvis, singing lead and playing rhythm. His high school friend Don Guess would play the slap bass in a percussive style like Elvis's bassist Bill Black. My father would play lead guitar like Scotty.

They dug in the next day after school, teaching themselves songs from Elvis's early catalog, like "Baby, Let's Play House." You couldn't get in to see Elvis? No problem. You could see my father, Buddy, and Don. Gigs began lining up from Dallas to Amarillo. Later, they would name themselves the Two Tones, based on matching Elvis-inspired suits they bought from a haberdasher in Oklahoma City: white pants, blue shirts, and orange jackets.

CHAPTER 3

The following summer, 1956, the *Lubbock Avalanche-Journal* ran an overwrought series on the dangers of rock 'n' roll, which the author Phyllis Battelle described as "a poor white trash version of rhythm and blues." Throughout the series, Battelle made no effort to hide her racism for rock 'n' roll's "primitive jungle beat," as she called it. She interviewed a Boston disc jockey, who said, "I suppose the natives must have been worked into a frenzy by tom toms. It works the same on kids." The editors ran a photo of the band playing a seedy club where kids were dancing the "dirty bop," a sort of choreographed dry hump. They blacked out the bandmates' eyes, so sinful was the scene.

One Friday afternoon when my father was eighteen, a guitarist for the famous blues pianist, Charles Brown, came into Adair Music, the shop where my dad worked after school, to buy strings. My dad introduced himself as a fan of Brown, and the guitarist invited him to see their brass orchestra perform that night at Lubbock's Cotton Club. Like all the joints, the club was segregated, hosting different nights for white and Black performers. My dad arrived alone that night, the only white person in the house. Perhaps to put him at ease, the guitarist pulled up a chair beside him onstage, where my dad sat for the entire show, electrified. When he returned to school, he couldn't wait to tell a muso friend about the concert. A boy overheard their conversation in the hall. "What do y'all see in that n----- music?" he sneered.

When my dad told me this story a few years ago, we were eating breakfast at a Lubbock diner, our eggs growing cold between us. "Weren't you embarrassed?" I asked. "Sitting onstage, not playing an instrument? The only white person there?"

No, no, no, he insisted with a dismissive wave of his hand. "Maybe I was too stupid to be embarrassed. But he made me feel like a guest. He just welcomed me with such . . . warmth." *Warmth,* I scribbled in my notebook, pretending not to see the tears welling up in his eyes. Now that he's an old man, he becomes emotional when he remembers mentors who were kind to him in his youth.

I admit it's a sweet conclusion, but the problem with the narrative is it doesn't work both ways. The word "segregated" itself is one-sided, for no young Black man would have been invited onstage at one of the Cotton Club's all-white performances. That's also, I think, why the memory affects my father so. He knows it wasn't the guitarist's job to invite a white teenage music store employee to the show, much less treat him as a VIP. The man could have paid for his strings and breezed out the door. But in an act of grace, he reached across the barrier.

When white acts came along like Elvis, the Beatles—and yes, my father and Buddy Holly—they offered this Black music up for white consumption and profit. They may have thought they were doing it out of respect; or more likely, they were just kids who didn't think much about it at all.

Maybe this is a story about racial reckoning.

♪

Memphis had Elvis and Carl Perkins, and Nashville wanted its own rhythm-and-blues star. In the summer of 1955, a Nashville talent scout approached Buddy following a Two Tones show and asked him to send over some demos. Buddy did, and the scout passed the acetates up the ladder until the band landed a deal with Decca, Nashville's most prominent publishing house. Famed producer Owen Bradley would oversee four sessions in Bradley's Barn, the Quonset hut studio behind his house where he'd launched country artists such as Patsy Cline, Conway Twitty, and Loretta Lynn into the stratosphere.

The deal was potentially huge, and Buddy knew it. He borrowed money from his older brother for clothing and equipment, the lion's share of which he spent at Adair Music on a new amp and soon-to-be-signature instrument, the curvy, futuristic Fender Stratocaster. In January 1956, the band piled into Buddy's parents' black-and-white Oldsmobile and set out for Nashville.

The band may have been Elvis clones, but they differed from the star in one significant way. Unlike Elvis, Buddy and my father were already writing many of their own songs. This was atypical for the time period, as Jeff Merron noted in a 2018 article in *Mental Floss*: "Before Holly came along, pop music performance and songwriting were, for the most part, separate businesses; composers crafted tunes in places like New York's Brill Building, and performers picked from among those songs to record and sing in concert."

At the second Decca session, the band recorded "Rock Around with Ollie Vee," a catchy bop my dad wrote. Ollie Vee was an actual woman he knew, the wife of a Black farmhand named Willie who worked for his father. I imagine my teenage father and Willie nodding politely at each other from their respective tractor perches as they pass at the turn row. From a distance, my father spots Ollie Vee hauling water from the windmill. Like I've seen him do so many times, he pats out the tempo on his knee, spinning music from life.

Over two decades after those Decca sessions, my dad and the Crickets would fly to Dallas to attend the 1978 premiere of the Hollywood film, *The Buddy Holly Story*. The band would watch in horror as the events and characters onscreen bore no resemblance to their memories (my dad was so incensed by the film, he went straight back to his hotel room and wrote his own version, "The Real Buddy Holly Story.") Gary Busey may have turned in an Oscar-winning performance as Buddy, but my dad couldn't recognize his old friend in the character, a rude teenager who wore ill-fitting pants and worse, the ultimate fifties fashion faux pas: *white socks with black shoes*. Buddy had impeccable manners—he always called his elders Ma'am or Sir—and he dressed sharp, in pressed shirts and leather moccasins. His dad was a tailor, after all.

But of all the scenes in the film, my father most hated the one depicting the Owen Bradley sessions. In the film, Bradley's character is named T. J., a cigar-chomping racist who strongarms the band into churning out a hillbilly version of "That'll Be the Day." When Buddy pushes back, T.J. tells him, "Why don't you get your n-----lovin' ass right back out there where you belong?" The session ends when Buddy punches the producer in the face.

It makes for a helluva scene, but little of it was true. Owen Bradley was no-nonsense but polite, my dad remembers, and as for the band, "We were nice boys from Texas and we were trying to put our best manners forward," as he told a Buddy Holly biographer in 1997. "We were on our toes and it was 'Yes sir, Mr. Bradley,' and 'Whatever you say, Mr. Bradley.'"

But for all the film's gross exaggerations, it warped an underlying truth. Owen Bradley was a country producer, and he failed to harness Buddy's rock 'n' roll energy. Weirdly, he didn't let him play his Stratocaster on the first session, assigning the Strat, the lead guitar, to my dad and standing Buddy in the corner with only a microphone. (On the song "Blue Days, Black Nights," my dad reportedly made history as the first person to play a Stratocaster on a rock 'n' roll recording.)

The album flopped. Decca barely marketed it, and the band had to turn over most of the $43 they were each paid to join the musicians union. Soon after the album's release, the boys found themselves back in Texas, hauling bricks for Buddy's older brother, Larry, who owned a tile company. Swigging bootleg beer after picking joints was fine when they were in high school, but they'd graduated now. My father was dead broke, and antsy about the future Buddy envisioned for them. On some level he clung to the old ways, the values he'd been raised with. He preferred country to rock 'n' roll, financial security to risk. He couldn't afford otherwise.

Shortly after the deal with Decca fizzled, recording engineer and musician Norman Petty offered my dad a job playing guitar with his band, the saccharine Norman Petty Trio. (Petty was a better engineer than musician and would later become the Crickets' producer.) Lured by the prospect of a steady gig, my dad reluctantly called Buddy to tell him he was quitting the band.

Buddy pushed back. "Don't go play that Mickey Mouse music with Norman Petty. You'll hate it!" he argued. "We're about to make it, man!"

"How long, Buddy?" my father remembers asking. "How long is it going to take us to make it?"

CHAPTER 3

Buddy barely gave it a thought. "About as long as it took Elvis," he said. To my dad, it was a naive, absurd answer.

Buddy could be cheeky like that, maybe a little entitled. Growing up, his parents gave him more than access to their Oldsmobile—they gave him an unlimited supply of encouragement. Ella, his mother, even helped him in the recording studio, writing "Maybe Baby," one of his first hits, herself.

My father's parents, on the other hand, were loving but detached when it came to his musical career—too busy, as his father Arthur used to say, "makin' a living to make any money." The family reaped a few bumper cotton crops in the forties, but drought struck in the fifties, lingering throughout my father's teenage years, his years with Buddy. Unlike Buddy's parents, his didn't attend his concerts, even when he was older and no longer picking seedy joints. "It wasn't their thing," he told me once with a flip of his hand. Maybe not. Maybe they were too busy in the fields. Yet from what I understand, they rarely told him they were proud of him, out of some West Texan attachment to humility, a fear of letting success go to his head.

Modern-day parents catch a lot of flak for raising our children without grit, lavishing them with meaningless medals and empty praise. My father had grit in spades, perseverance all day long, and it served him well in life. What he lacked was Buddy's effortless surety, his irrational belief that he, too, had a place reserved in the pantheon.

Maybe this is a story about faith.

Their breakup may have been as inevitable as their meeting. As Buddy's guitar playing improved, he began to break away from Elvis's model, wanting to play lead guitar, not rhythm. My dad had occasionally swapped lead with Buddy, an arrangement that worked fine in the early years when everything was "loosey-goosey," as he puts it. But from what I understand, this dynamic shifted around the time the band returned to Nashville for a second Decca session, and the producers began giving Buddy more chances to play his own lead guitar.

They didn't argue, my father tells me. They weren't mad at each other. It was more like an unspoken understanding: a band can't have two lead guitarists. Buddy's no-name rhythm player was not the star my dad was aiming for. He was Sonny Curtis, after all—a hotshot guitar prodigy, a statewide Future Farmers of America talent contest winner, a go-to opening act for the *Louisiana Hayride*, the pride of Meadow, Texas. As his friend Waylon Jennings wrote in his 1996 autobiography, "My hero then was Sonny Curtis. He was so far advanced to what I was as a guitar player that I seemed struggling compared to him.... Sonny could play in that fingerpicking style. I admired him so much I wanted to change my name to Sonny. I even tried to stand like him."

When country singer Slim Whitman offered my dad a well-paying job on his tour, it wasn't even a choice. My grandparents were too poor to support him now that he'd graduated high school, and Slim was a bona fide star, known for his smooth "countrypolitan" vocals. This time when he told Buddy he was quitting, Buddy was relieved to let him go.

After my dad left the band he and Buddy remained on decent terms, occasionally catching up at concerts, and once at a Nashville DJ convention. Yet there would be no more double dates or weekend matinees or late-night jam sessions. They would never play their guitars together again, a fact that strikes me as sad for two kids who once "shook hands and started pickin'." The breakup may have been amicable, but as my dad once put it to me in a rare moment of vulnerability, it led to "a finality of feeling."

The Slim Whitman tour lasted only six months. With no car and little money left over, my dad hitchhiked to Nashville in the summer of 1957 with the hopes of landing a record deal. He hung around the country music publishing house Cedarwood, run by a hard-drinking songwriter named Wayne Walker who lent him his couch to crash on. Each day Wayne sent my dad to The Jungle, a bar on 17th Avenue, to fetch him a bottle of whiskey, allowing him to keep the $1 change. From there, my dad would walk forty-five minutes across town to Krystal on Church Street, where he bought his one daily meal: a bowl of chili, a carton of milk, and a packet of crackers. He still remembers the total came to .26—a quarter plus a penny tax.

Perhaps in an effort to get my dad off his couch, Wayne arranged for him to meet with Wesley Rose, the head of Acuff-Rose Music. An oily, mustachioed powerhouse, Wesley was a capable businessman and an even more capable asshole, better known for crushing dreams than making them. My dad drove Wayne's car through a pounding rainstorm to the Acuff-Rose building downtown thinking, *This is it. The day I'm discovered.* Inside Wesley's office, he handed the executive an acetate with four songs on it. Wesley skipped through the first bars of each song before he clicked off the machine. "You better go back to Texas, boy," he said. "You don't have anything different enough to make it here."

Those words would imprint themselves on my father's psyche his entire life. They would remain there even after he learned the commonality of his story, how so many aspiring Nashville musicians had collected similar insults from Wesley Rose, other artists who, like him, somehow found the fortitude to soldier on. But how many didn't? How many left that office and turned the car back to Little Rock or Flagstaff or Tuscaloosa? How many dreams died at the muscular hands of Wesley Rose?

Meanwhile, Buddy's band renamed itself the Crickets and regrouped with J. I. on drums, Niki Sullivan on rhythm guitar, and Joe B. Mauldin on bass. In May 1957, mere months after my father left the band, they released "That'll Be the Day," catapulting them to fame.

Maybe this is a story about luck.

> Everybody had always thought Sonny was the one that would make it, and here Buddy had torn up the world.
> —Waylon Jennings, *Waylon: An Autobiography*

♪

I often think about an essay by the author Charles Baxter titled "Regarding Happiness," about happiness in narrative structure. In it, he recalls attending a summer festival on a lake when he was sixteen. The festival hosted a canoe race. After the race the winner, a popular, handsome young man, collected his blue medal then swung his arm around his gorgeous girlfriend, who gazed up at him with admiration and kissed him. Baxter watched with envy as the pair strolled off arm-in-arm in the direction of the lake.

Forty years later, Baxter writes that he still remembers every detail of that moment in a way the couple has probably long forgotten. Why? Because even in memory, the couple and their happiness are not the story. The story, he writes, is the "unhappy onlooker." He argues that this is the story in eighty percent of all narratives: Gatsby watching the partygoers, Iago watching Othello and Desdemona, even Satan watching Adam and Eve.

Buddy Holly biographies tell the story of the couple on the lake. Maybe this is the story of the unhappy onlooker.

> Q: How did you feel about missing out on the Crickets?
> A: I remember I was in a radio station one day looking at a *Billboard* magazine, and there was this big picture of my old friends, and I felt real good for them because they were my friends, but to tell the truth, I did have a sort of letdown feeling too. You know what I mean. The train has left the station and I'm not on it sort of feeling.
> —Sonny Curtis, interviewed by Jim Liddane for the International Songwriters Association

Over the next year, my dad's career cooled while the Crickets got "hot as a pistol," as he wrote in "The Real Buddy Holly Story." In the winter of 1957, he found himself living back in Texas and working on the family farm, Wesley Rose's words swiftly gaining ground. Each day he and his older brother, Dean, took turns on the tractor, picking up the ragged winter bolls littering the fields and hauling them to the gin, the gray hours stretching as long as the furrows.

One afternoon, the Crickets' producer Norman Petty called my dad to request a meeting at his studio two hours away in Clovis, New Mexico. My dad turned the tractor duties over to Dean and drove his newly bought car, a beat-up 1951 Oldsmobile, west into the flat horizon. He arrived at the studio and parked next to Buddy's shiny pink Cadillac. Norman ushered him in, explaining that the Crickets were upstairs meeting over whether to fire their rhythm player Niki Sullivan. He wasn't jibing with the rest of the band—they especially hated the way he imitated Chuck Berry's signature duck walk onstage—and they were considering replacing him with my dad. "Why don't you go see a movie or something for a few hours?" Norman suggested.

Instead, my dad took his D-28 Martin to a nearby park, where he sat strumming under the pallid winter sky, thinking it over. He hadn't loved being Buddy's rhythm player, but touring with stars beat farming cotton. I imagine he let himself feel hopeful, envisioning beautiful girls winking from the crowd, silver-domed room service trays, autographs and cocktails. The good road.

When he drove back to the studio, Buddy's Cadillac was gone. Only Niki and Norman remained. "Sorry, Sonny," said Norman. "Buddy decided he doesn't need another guitar player. They're going to be a trio from now on." As for Niki, not only was he out of a job, he was out of a ride. My dad gave him a lift back to Lubbock, which must have been one awkward journey.

"Weren't you disappointed?" I asked him over the phone.

"Not really," he said in a glib tone. "I just accepted it was how things would be."

Why didn't it hurt more? I wondered. Was he so numbed by failure at that point, he'd lost feeling in his fingertips? Or is he numb now, the sand blurring his memory with each recall, each interview, each regret? Now only the story remains for him, emptied of emotion: memory's modus operandi. It's the opposite for me. I have the emotion but not the memory, the wound but not the accident. Fame is an explosion that leaves a lot of shrapnel in its wake.

It's an inescapable fact of life that we're doomed to inherit some of the psychic traumas of our parents and caregivers. Had I inherited my dad's longing for fame like a secondhand wound? Was I writing a book about him to heal him, or myself?

Maybe this isn't my dad's story at all. Maybe I'm the unhappy onlooker.

♪

I know how to begin the story, but where does it end?

KLLL was a Lubbock radio station located on the top floor of the Great Plains Life Building, what used to be the tallest building in Lubbock. The station was a free-for-all among young musicians in the late fifties, a place where they could noodle around on their instruments, maybe even broadcast their music to the South Plains, to the land and people they loved best. Waylon worked as a disc jockey there before he became famous, and sometimes he'd let my dad pick on air or record jingles in the control room. In between picking and broadcasting there was no middleman, no mercenary studio head, no fear of rejection. There was only art and coffee flowing between them, the music their conduit, the language they'd always communicated in best. A coffee shop adjoined the station, and that's where my father saw Buddy alive for the last time.

It was late in the summer of 1958, right around the time the star married María Elena Santiago, the receptionist at the Crickets' New York publishing house, Peer-Southern Music. When Buddy had brought her to Lubbock to meet his family earlier that year, he was struck by the racism his Puerto Rican–born fiancée encountered—a waitress refused to serve her an ice cream cone until he awkwardly intervened. "It's just the way things are around here," he explained. He was learning the game, outgrowing Lubbock.

CHAPTER 3

My dad had known María Elena longer than Buddy had, for he too had signed a publishing deal with Peer-Southern. The deal covered his rent, if not much else, but the clouds were starting to clear (two songs he wrote for Southern during this period sum up his mindset: "Wrong Again" and "Laughing Stock"). In order to complete the publishing contract, he'd ordered his birth certificate to be sent from the Brownfield, Texas, courthouse to Peer-Southern's lawyers. And it was in their New York City law office that my father learned his legal name: Unnamed Baby Boy Curtis.

"Well, this won't do," the lawyer told him. "You'll have to go down there and name yourself, son." That summer my dad flew back to Texas, plunked down two dollars at the Brownfield courthouse, and named himself Sonny.

A few months later he was taking a coffee break with a DJ at KLLL when Buddy walked in and briefly joined them. They were "cordial," he tells me over the phone, "but a little distant."

"Because of fame or because you quit the band?"

"Fame. And because we were both so busy. Though, you know, his busy was more lucrative than mine." He attempts a chuckle.

I mention that I once read in a biography of Buddy that the star gave Waylon one of his songs to record because he said "he liked to see his friends make it."

"Do you think he wanted to see you make it, Dad?"

"Hmmm. I don't know what Buddy wanted for me," he says in a flippant tone that implies *and I don't care*.

"Well, did he ever say to you, 'Hey, Son, what are you up to?' And you'd tell him about your career, the songs you were working on?"

"Oh no, I never talked about that stuff to Buddy."

"But you rooted for him, right? You went to some of his shows and supported him. I'm just wondering if he also rooted for you, if he wanted you to make it?"

"I wouldn't necessarily say I *rooted* for Buddy."

Aha. So there it is, the old kernel of rivalry. "Why not?" I pounce. "Did fame go to his head?"

"I think fame goes to everyone's heads," he says, adding in a quieter tone, "Between you and me, I think fame went to the Crickets' heads . . . a little." I think about that winter day in Clovis, when none of his so-called friends stuck around to give him the bad news. How they made Norman do the dirty work.

Before I wrap up our call, I ask him what he and Buddy talked about that day at KLLL. But just as he can't remember the first words they spoke, he can't exactly recall the last. "We talked about 1950s muso stuff, you know?"

"No, I don't know, Dad. I don't know what 1950s musos talked about."

He sighs. The line falls silent except for a distant buzz, the static of ghosts. Just as I'm about to give up, he summons one. He thinks they discussed the arrangements on Ray Charles's latest hit. And he vaguely remembers Buddy asking him if he'd tried this incredible New York thing called cheesecake.

> Q: Where were you when you got the news about the plane crash?
> A: I had spent the night at J. I.'s folks' house. Mrs. Allison [J. I.'s mother] and I were at the kitchen table having coffee. Oleta Hall, a neighbor from across the street, came over and said she had just heard it on the radio. J. I. was still asleep, and I had the sad task of waking him up with the news.
> —Sonny Curtis, quoted in the *Lubbock Avalanche-Journal*, February 24, 2012

I wish I could leave them there, drinking coffee on the twentieth floor of the tallest building in Lubbock, two men now, no longer boys, figuring out how to harmonize ambition with friendship. But that ending is false.

On a bitterly cold February day in 1959, my father served as one of Buddy's pallbearers at Lubbock's Tabernacle Baptist Church. The funeral was "terribly sad," he told me, and for once, I didn't press. After the service, he gathered the acetates he and Buddy had made together in happier days, loosey-goosier days, and delivered them to Buddy's parents.

But the story doesn't end there either.

My father rejoined the Crickets (on lead guitar, naturally), and the band played on for over fifty years. They played high and they played low. They played Albert Hall and they played smoke-filled casinos. They played for Sir Paul McCartney and they played for trucker conventions. They survived fifty-plus-year marriages, cross-country moves, a handful of children and grandchildren, farm mortgages, livestock, drunken revelry, bitter arguments, inside jokes, European tours, fancy dinners, truck-stop breakfasts, good albums, not-so-good albums, middle age malaise, old age acceptance, health scares, hall of fame awards, and a long lifetime of friendship.

Buddy missed out on almost all those things.

Maybe this story has no meaning. Or maybe it has too much.

For years I've been trying to manipulate this chapter to fit a coherent narrative arc, to find, as the writer Vivian Gornick called it, "the story within the situation." But there isn't just one. It's a Russian nesting doll, a story that contains stories. It's a Rorschach test, one that means something different to the perv than it does to the oldies DJ than it does to my dad. But since I'm the author, I'll pick the one I like best.

I think it's a story of survival.

> Q: Who was Buddy Holly?
> A: I can't think of anything people wouldn't already know about Buddy.
> —Sonny Curtis, *Lubbock Avalanche-Journal,* March 14, 2009

Buddy talked in the middle of movies. He could be a smartass. His mother taught him to watch his diet by always leaving some food on his plate. He had a hard time sitting still. He lined up water glasses in restaurants and played them with a spoon. He collected souvenir

Pete Curtis watching over Sonny onstage, circa 1945. (From author's collection.)

spoons for his mother when he picked gigs out of town. His mother tapered his jeans for him. He believed in heaven and hell. He loved ghost stories.

Q: Who is Sonny Curtis?
A: A hothead Taurus, a hoarder of memories, a sharpshooter, an introvert, a sandstorm, a set list I know by heart, a pioneer, a shadow caster, a downbeat, a guitar pick on my coffee table, a beer can on my porch, a displaced Texan, a fallow field, a history buff, an

Buddy and Sonny swapping guitars onstage in the mid-fifties. (From author's collection.)

(L–R): Don Guess, Thelma King, Sonny, Buddy, Clara Cobble, and Sonny's brother Dean, spring of 1956. The band was in Nashville to record one of the Decca sessions at Bradley's Barn. (Photo courtesy of Thelma King.)

insomniac, a Reaganite, a gravel road, a Mason, a worrier, a folded hundred-dollar-bill pressed into my palm as he says goodbye, a loving grandfather, a theme song on TV, a tumbleweed, an overgrown dugout, a tricky chord progression, an "American singer and songwriter known for his collaborations with Buddy Holly . . ." (Wikipedia)

CHAPTER 4

"I Fought the Law": A Love Song

He never was blue, but he could sing the blues...
— "COWBOY SINGER," 1980

From: music@sonnycurtis.com
Sent: Monday, August 17, 2015 4:47 PM
Subject: Re: Two quick "I Fought the Law" questions

Hi Randal,

Thank you for your interest in "I Fought the Law." To answer your questions:

1) There was nothing other than my imagination that inspired me. I was alone in my living room one afternoon with a West Texas sandstorm going on outside, trying to write a song. I was just pickin' my guitar and letting my mind go, the way you do when you write a song. It only took about twenty minutes. It sort of scares me, but I don't think I ever wrote it down. I just carried it in my head 'til we needed it. But it's one of my best copyrights and I've always been grateful that the Rock and Roll gods came through for me and helped me make it happen.

2) I had no idea what a protest song was at the time and certainly didn't know what punk rock was. Genres like psychedelic, punk,

grunge, heavy metal, etc., didn't come along until years later.

I was really trying to write a country song, but when we recorded the album, *In Style with the Crickets*, I transcribed it to a rock 'n' roll song and there ye are. It has always amused me that people try to analyze it. I don't mean to sound flippant, but I've never taken it that seriously. To me, it's one of my songs that I'm real proud of. I'm just thankful that it stirs something in people and makes them like it, for whatever reason. I hope they, and you, continue to do so.

Thank you for your interest and support.

Very truly yours,
Sonny Curtis

It's a mystery even to my father how a brainstorm at age twenty-two would go on to define much of his life—and mine. It's certainly not my favorite song he ever wrote, nor is it his. Yet *Rolling Stone* magazine ranks it at #175 on the list of 500 Greatest Songs of All Time. It's as if the reaction to the song has eclipsed the song itself, which is more than the sum of its simplistic parts. A three-chord melody, lyrics a child could write: *I needed money, and I had none. I fought the law, and the law won.* Anarchy at its most elemental.

Perhaps the song's simplicity is its strength, the thing allowing it to serve so many agendas. It is what music publishers call an "evergreen" song, and indeed, it has resurfaced at least once a decade since The Bobby Fuller Four made it a hit in 1966. In the seventies, the Dead Kennedys released a punk parody of it as a social commentary after courts acquitted the man who assassinated San Francisco mayor George Moscone and the board supervisor, politician and gay rights activist Harvey Milk. In 1989, US troops blasted The Clash's version outside Panamanian dictator Manuel Noriega's compound until he gave himself up—one more person done in by rock 'n' roll. In 2004, the song was used as a marketing tool when Green Day covered it for a Pepsi/iTunes Super Bowl ad. Just the other day I opened my mailbox to find my father had sent me a larger birthday check than usual. When I called to thank him, he said, "Well, don't get too used to it, honey. 'I Fought the Law' had a good year in Australia."

To grow up surrounded by the physical manifestations of a parent's art is a complicated dynamic, especially when that art enters the public sphere. If my father had been a psychiatrist or a car dealer, I wouldn't be confronted with his work while strolling the cheese aisle at my local Meijer. My father's songs pierce my reality—and that's often what it feels like, a puncture, a breach—at strange and unexpected times: when I'm riding an elevator, or watching TV, or, as "I Fought the Law" did the other day, while wandering a vintage car show with my kids. While not unwelcome, these moments can feel lonesome. I would never announce to strangers in my vicinity, "My dad wrote this song!" Instead I inhabit a three-minute pocket of solitude, everyone around me oblivious to my father's words pulsing through my head, dredging up a lifetime of memories and associations that are mine and mine alone.

As a teenager I learned the song's currency, its cool factor, how when people (boys especially, it seemed) discovered my connection to it, they treated me a little nicer. I've used the song to my advantage a lot in life, even if only in my head. How many times have I hung on to it like my childhood security blanket when things were falling apart around me? *These people suck/That woman is rude/I'm no good at this job . . . but my dad wrote "I Fought the Law."* My own personal mythology, a legend if only in my mind.

It's hard not to wonder about the provenance of a song that has played such a significant role in my psyche. Fellini said, "The pearl is the oyster's autobiography." So at the risk of amusing my father, I, too, wonder what irritants combined to form his most famous pearl?

He wrote the song in the summer of 1959, five months after Buddy's death. He'd been bouncing around the country chasing gigs from coast to coast, but that summer he was crashing at a friend's house in Slaton, Texas, while playing lead guitar for the Crickets. With Buddy gone, their gigs were growing thin. When my dad was desperate for spending money, he occasionally hit up J. I., still flush with Cricket cash. He hated to do that, though J. I. never made him feel guilty or even asked for repayment. It was a generosity my father never forgot.

J. I. was still nineteen at the time, too young to process the grief and guilt of Buddy's death. Buddy had been his best friend in the world, a sympatico soul who understood him on both a musical and comedic level. They'd been friends since middle school and shared a dry, sarcastic sense of humor that my father occasionally found unkind. In 1956, after my father left the band but before the formation of the Crickets, a Lubbock skating rink hired Buddy and J. I. to play every Friday and Saturday night. Like the Beatles' stint in Hamburg, this period was transformative for the duo. They tightened their sound and formed their own identity far beyond that of Elvis clones. Buddy compensated for the lack of a rhythm player by playing lead in a rhythmic, straight-eight style, thrashing the downbeat. J. I.'s drum licks syncopated perfectly to Buddy's vocals and open-chord guitar strumming. They learned each other's moves in advance.

The friends had even gotten married the same month, July 1958—Buddy to María Elena, and J. I. to his Lubbock High School sweetheart Peggy Sue Garron, whose name they used for their hit song the year before. The two couples honeymooned together in Acapulco, but the trip was a disaster. Eighteen and fresh out of high school, Peggy Sue had nothing in common with the more urbane María Elena, and the women orbited each other in awkward silence. J. I. goofed off like he'd always done around Buddy, but María Elena found their jokes sophomoric.

The rift between the two women was indicative of a change occurring within the band. Buddy was enamored by New York—not only by its cheesecake, but by its more progressive culture and bohemian music scene. He and the Crickets made plans to move to New York City later in 1958, while building a recording studio in Lubbock. The move would involve breaking with their producer Norman, increasingly a controlling, Machiavellian figure who played fast and loose with song credits, falsely listing himself as a co-writer on many of the band's biggest hits like "That'll Be the Day."

Norman knew Buddy was lost to him, but he was able to convince J. I. and Joe B., still in their late teens, to stay in Lubbock, retaining the name the Crickets while Buddy forged a solo career in New York. The split broke Buddy's heart. María Elena would later say he cried over what he considered his friends' betrayal. In typical Norman fashion, the producer listed himself as the sole withdrawer from the Crickets' bank account, and after Buddy broke ties with him, he refused to pay the star, planning, as Joe B. would later recall him saying, "to starve him to death." In a sense, Norman did just that. When Buddy and María Elena moved to Greenwich Village, they needed money. Buddy hustled to support his new lifestyle, and that hustling included joining the Winter Dance Tour, the tour that took his life.

The details are well known, but they bear repeating. On February 2, 1959, Buddy played his final show at the Surf Ballroom in Clear Lake, Iowa. It was a routine stop on "the tour from hell," as he and his tour mates had nicknamed it. Their bus's heating system broke down and Buddy's drummer was hospitalized for frostbite. Several musicians caught the flu, including J. P. Richardson, known as The Big Bopper. A drafty bus, a frigid night, a mean stretch of highway, a flu virus spreading fast. Buddy decided to charter a plane to their next gig in Minneapolis. It wasn't a tough choice, I'm sure. What was fame for if you couldn't pull a few strings occasionally? Not only was he cold and tired, he had a suitcase full of dirty clothes. He wanted to reach their next destination a day early to catch up on sleep and laundry. Instead, just after midnight, the plane fell from the sky and careened into a desolate stretch of Iowa cornfield.

J. I. hated flying. Had he not been swayed by Norman, had he been on that tour, he would have talked Buddy out of chartering that tiny plane; he knew it. It was textbook magical thinking, all the ways he could travel back in time and save his friend, and it would haunt him for the rest of his life.

As for my father, the universe had granted his former wish—to be the lead guitarist of Buddy's band—but with Buddy dead, the victory felt fraught. Sitting on his friend's couch that day in July 1959, he let his mind wander as he looked out the window at the all-too familiar scenery: brown grass, flat road, dirty sky. *You better go back to Texas, boy.* The song came to him quickly, a twenty-minute brainstorm in a sandstorm. I've sometimes wondered if writing "I Fought the Law" was a subconscious attempt for him to impose order onto a chaotic world. First it was a Dust Bowl world, where the ground and sky could switch places. And later, it was a world where a teenage friend could shoot to international stardom, then fall from the sky. Maybe "I Fought the Law" came not from a place of anarchy but from a place of yearning, a desire for the stars to better align, for the laws of the universe to make sense.

My father was born into a world buckled under the weight of law. When he was five, his family cultivated enough cotton to move off the farm and into a small, yellow house in Meadow. It was around this time that he began attending the Church of Christ with his grandfather Will, who had (mostly) given up street fighting for Jesus. Before the move to Meadow, the family had been too mired in farming to worry about religion, their bible the almanac. And of course the cycles of farming provided their own doctrine, from harrow to harvest to harrow again, the jobs at the mercy of the season, the season at the mercy of the sky, the sky at the mercy of a law too powerful to comprehend. That's what church was for.

My dad has clear memories of the sweltering hot summer revival meetings, how the only relief came from the little handheld fans printed with pictures of Jesus and Mary that the church ladies passed out. In the memoir he gave me, he wrote:

> Brother Shannon and the other "country clergy" would shout and holler from the pulpit and remind you constantly that if you didn't get saved and walk the straight and narrow, you would burn in hell. Not just to the ground, once and for all. Hell no! Forever on out, eternity. As I grew older and was able to grasp the meaning of things, those dour teachings scared the hell out of me. I thought

often about what it would be like to just keep on burning with no end in sight.

I can't fully fathom this nightmare, having myself grown up in Protestant churches where hymns were warbled apathetically and Hell was an abstraction. But Hell was real in Meadow, Texas, and nobody escaped those fiery sermons unscathed.

The Church of Christ also forbade musical instruments from being played during service; only a cappella music was (and often still is) allowed. It was a hard law for my young father to understand. In his memoir, he reflects on a revival meeting he attended around age ten, led by a fire-and-brimstone pastor aptly named Brother Loveless. To lead the singing, the church brought in a song leader from a nearby congregation in a neighboring town. When the song leader approached the choir, he reached into his breast pocket and pulled out a tuning fork to set the key. After the song ended, Brother Loveless resumed the pulpit. *What you just witnessed was a man using an instrument of the devil!* he hollered. It wasn't a revival meeting without a hot blast of damnation, yet this one especially lodged in my father's brain. As he wrote in his memoir, "By the time he was finished, he had dragged that song leader right up to the gates of hell where he was ready to happily shove him through." The sermon split the church down the middle. The adults sent the kids outside after the service to discuss the situation. When the meeting adjourned, Brother Loveless was gone and the song leader stayed, but just barely.

In his memoir, *The Prince of Frogtown*, Rick Bragg writes about his own father's similar fire-and-brimstone religion around the 1940s that held their Appalachian cotton mill town in its grip. "They were still a new denomination then but had spread rapidly in the last fifty years around a nation of exploited factory workers, coal miners, and rural and inner-city poor. . . . Biblical scholars turned their noses up, calling it hysteria, theatrics, a faith of the illiterate. But in a place where machines ate people alive, faith had to pour even hotter than blood."

Even hotter than blood. The laws of the flesh were necessary in these impoverished agricultural communities, even if people could never live up to them, even if, as Bragg writes, "the preacher laid down a list of sins so complete it left a person no place to go but down." The church tethered the townspeople to a greater cause, which kept them plowing in the face of drought, faithful in the face of boredom, and sober in the face of hopelessness. It's no wonder they came to rely upon the laws, the preacher's voice cleansing their mean and bitter thoughts like fire cleanses refuse from a field, allowing sunlight to penetrate the soil.

My father would say I'm overthinking all of this. When asked about the song's origins, he focuses on the creative process—"pickin' my guitar and letting my mind go"—rather than on the lyrics. I think it embarrasses him that people have assumed he's an anarchist or ex-con. But think about it: my father needed money so he turned to art, writing a song about a guy who needed money so he turned to armed robbery. Both men longed for freedom: one from prison, the other from poverty, religion, and unending rows of cotton.

For my father, all those freedoms hinged on a freedom of mind (and in that sense, he was an anarchist, just as every artist is). Since he wrote his first song at age fourteen from the seat of his father's tractor, songwriting had been his exit valve, a way to escape the facts on the ground. That day he wrote a ditty about the moon. "Moon, moon, silvery moon, light up the heavens tonight," it began, self-soothing him like a lullaby. "Moon, moon, silvery moon, while I am holding her tight." There had to be a girl in there somewhere, he'd listened to enough country and western radio to know that much, though he knew little of romantic love, other than a schoolyard crush on a girl named Katherine who had once let him kiss her under the shade of an elm. Maybe he thought of that kiss as he wrote the song, or maybe he thought of Doris Day, the star of *By the Light of the Silvery Moon*, a film that had been released two years before. Or maybe he was just keeping his mind busy to escape the monotony of the field.

And just as he had that day, he felt the old rush of blood, the transformation from chaos to cosmos. The sand crackling against the screen door became a hi-hat drum. A nearby tractor drove a bass line through his gut. It was almost a rumble but not quite a song, not yet, but wait—breaking rocks, hot sun. The world transcribed into music.

We take the law for granted when we are young. We aim, as my father did that hot July day, in the direction of freedom, shaking off the bonds of family and place to form shiny identities. Now that I am the lawmaker for three children of my own, I find myself wistful for the days when others made the rules for me. *Watch your tone with me, put your napkin on your lap, off to bed you go.* There was comfort in those laws, in knowing people were watching out for me, conditioning me for this world. Not that I appreciated the laws when I was young, always ducking the rules, my teenage years a string of gleeful infractions. Now I see my oldest daughter weaving her way around the same obstacle course, her life like a corn maze. She can stray off course a bit, but there will always be someone nearby to guide her back on track, as there was for me.

That person was my mother. My father never bothered with enforcing household rules; he left that to her. Instead, he laid down his law in the form of lectures: on nutrition, history, personal finances, car maintenance, chord structures, on and on, without giving any thought to age appropriateness. He lectured me on interest rates when I was seven and bathtub safety when I was seventeen. His sermons were less apocalyptic than those of the country clergy of his youth, but perhaps he learned a thing or two in those humid tents, for once he started, it was hard to shut him down. His lecturing caused a rift with my mother, especially as I grew older and started leaving the dinner table early because I couldn't listen to him anymore. "Why can't you just talk to her like a normal kid?" I'd hear her gripe as I ascended the stairs to my bedroom.

Today my father's lectures are swept from my mind, though I can still make out the bleached ruins of a few: a rough chronology of the US presidents, an argument against the capital gains tax, Tippecanoe and Tyler Too. If my father was the law in my life, I didn't fight it so much as ignore it.

I wish I had known how to listen to him, and I wish he had known how to talk to me like a normal kid. But that is not how he was raised. And so, over the years, we've learned better how to abide by each other's laws. Or maybe we've just learned what my daughters do not yet fully know: that to be held to a law is often to be loved.

My father still lectures me, though less than he once did. Today he prefaces his laws with apology: "Far be it for me to give *you* parenting advice . . ." and I comply. *Thanks, Dad. I'll remember that.* What's the point of arguing? The future surges toward us in unrelenting waves, splitting the stars, eroding the earth. Now my dad is an old man facing down the ultimate law. Sure, that law will win one day, as it will for all of us.

But without it, what would we fight against?

CHAPTER 5

Civilized

Walk right back to me this minute
Bring your love to me, don't send it
I'm so lonesome every day...
—"WALK RIGHT BACK," WRITTEN IN 1960

He had the lick before he had the song. That was how he always wrote songs, the melody before the lyrics. Sort of like the way he entered the world: body first, name later. *Bum, bop, bum . . . bum ba-dum, ba-dum, ba-dum.*

He wrote it one day as he was futzing around with chord progressions on his guitar—first a major D, then the sixth chord, followed by the seventh, and back again. It was a catchy lick, a pop lick, a lick to usher in a bold new decade. The kind of lick that worms its way into your head and lends rhythm to your steps as you traipse merrily down the street.

Throughout the Crickets' springtime tour of England with the Everly Brothers, he hummed those ten notes of vim and vigor, his own little sunshine chorus of the mind. *Look at me now!* he must have thought more than once during that month, April 1960. A year earlier he'd been sleeping on his parents' couch in Meadow, and now he was performing on the BBC and picking sold-out auditoriums while standing behind the most famous singing duo in the world. "Cathy's

Clown" was the Everlys' biggest hit at the time, spending half that spring at number one on the English pop charts.

His association with the Everlys began the summer before in August 1959, six months after Buddy died. The brothers, Don and Phil, offered the Crickets a gig playing backup for them at a few shows out west, and J. I. had agreed on the condition they bring along my father, their new guitar player. The Everlys had toured with Buddy and the Crickets before the plane crash, and they probably felt sorry for the band in the wake of Buddy's death. The arrangement was a win-win. Relying on pick-up bands for backup was a headache, whereas the Crickets were a safe bet requiring no learning curve, a group of kindred musicians who already knew the Everlys' songs. The two bands had a lot in common, young men from Texas and Kentucky with Hank Williams roots and pop aspirations, all of them impossibly young. At twenty-two, Don and my father were the oldest in the two bands, Joe B. the youngest at nineteen.

The Everlys steered away from the glittery, pompadoured Elvis style and dressed like boys trying to make a good impression on a first date, in clean-cut tailored suits and skinny ties. They sang moony lullabies about high school heartache. What they lacked of Elvis's sexual swagger and Buddy's aggressive vocals, they made up for with choir-boy good looks and melding, ethereal harmonies that only immediate family members with the same genetic vocal timbre can achieve. The Louvin Brothers had it, and so did the Osmonds and the Carter Family. In the music industry, it's known as blood harmony.

England went crazy for the Everlys, and my father went crazy for the upside-down circus of England, a place where they drove on the wrong side of the road and sold whiskey out of vending machines. The Crickets stayed at the Cumberland Hotel overlooking the Marble Arch, the gateway to Buckingham Palace. Princess Margaret was about to marry a playboy photographer, and the city hummed with romance and gossip about the most daring royal. *Surely I'll never get the chance to come here again,* my father remembers thinking. He decided he would have to consume it all on that trip, all the lights and palace tours and cod wrapped in oil-splotched newspapers.

He was wrong and would return to England many times over the course of his life. By the time I was born, his years on the road had dulled his love of travel, but England never failed to thrill him, his speech forever peppered with favorite English expressions like brolly for umbrella and pudding for dessert. He and my mother took me there several times, and we always stayed in the same place: a walk-up flat on Hertford Street in Shepherd Market. We spent the winter break of my senior year in college there. One night at a pub across the street from our apartment, my dad bought a pack of cigarettes from the waitress, which was strange because he didn't smoke. When he offered me one in a hammy British accent ("Would you care for a fag, my dear?"), I gave him a look that said *Have you gone crazy?* "It's all right," he said. "Sometimes it's civilized to smoke." I thought of smoking as a trashy habit we had to hide from our elders, but the way my father casually flicked his hand to the side as he exhaled over his shoulder did, in fact, look elegant. I understood in that moment that my father was different in England, and that maybe the usual rules did not apply there.

I imagine my father held the country in his heart because it had loosened a tight knot at his core, if only for a month. With the Everlys, he could finally stop budgeting his lunch and relax a little, take in the sights. Midway through the tour, the band boarded an overnight train to Edinburgh. My father remembers how the porter gently nudged him awake, presenting him with a silver tray bearing tea, scones, and a newspaper. *Now this is living*, he thought.

On the train, they met Lady Lucy Lambton, who would grow up to become a BBC broadcaster and well-known British historian. But on that journey, she was just a posh teenage girl with an irreverent sense of humor. "When you get back to London," she told my father and the band, "you simply *must* attend a party I'm throwing for some friends who summered in Paris with me." The boys loved Lady Lucy, her highbrow accent and clever jokes, the way she teased Joe B. for

CHAPTER 5

talking like Huckleberry Hound. They did attend her party, where my father remembers her friends as "uppity but polite." After all, he was playing with the Everly Brothers. He was a star in their eyes, not some West Texas hayseed. He was civilized.

Finally he had the life he'd dreamed of on that winter day in Clovis when Norman Petty teased him with a Crickets slot. Beautiful girls winking from the crowd, silver-domed room service trays, autographs and cocktails. The good road. But whenever my father brushed too closely to fame, tragedy had a way of announcing itself like a warning siren. This time, that siren was Eddie Cochran.

A young, California-based rock 'n' roller best known today for his jangly teenage bop, "Summertime Blues," Eddie was also in England, touring with rockabilly singer Gene Vincent. The Crickets had played on Eddie's most recent recording session, which included "Three Steps to Heaven" and the raucous "Cut Across Shorty." J. I. was especially close to the star, and soon after the Crickets checked into their hotel, they headed over to see Eddie and Gene at Gene's apartment in the St. James district. It was early morning, my father remembers, the sun just beginning to burn off the London fog when they saw the two rockers, still up from the night before, drinking Jack Daniels and strolling the street in high spirits. The budding songwriter Sharon Sheeley, Eddie's girlfriend, slept off the night inside.

A few weeks later at the end of their tour, Eddie, Gene, and Sharon would rent a cab back to Heathrow after their last gig in Bristol, to fly home to L.A. The cab was traveling down a two-lane village road when it skidded and slammed into a concrete lamp post. The front seat passengers, the cab driver and Eddie's manager, wore seat belts and escaped unharmed. In the backseat, Eddie, Sharon, and Gene did not wear seat belts. Sharon and Gene walked away with their injuries, but Eddie, thrown from the car, was not so lucky. He was rushed to the nearest hospital in Bath, where he died hours later. He was twenty-three, one year older than Buddy had been at the time of his death.

The Crickets had just walked offstage after a gig in Leicester when they heard the news. Coincidentally, they were scheduled to play

Bristol, where Eddie had performed his final show, the next night. On the way there, they stopped by the hospital. A distraught Sharon asked them if they wanted to see Eddie's body and J. I. shook his head. It was a mere fourteen months after Buddy's death, and the Crickets had a front-row seat to the second big rock 'n' roll tragedy—a tragedy, like the first, with no moral takeaway, no villain to hang their grief on. *The driver was speeding, reckless*, someone at the hospital muttered, *going over sixty miles an hour. Threadbare tires*, someone else said. J. I. wanted out of the place. What did it matter? Another friend gone, another fallen star. No, he did not want to see the body. He'd seen enough.

I once asked my dad how Eddie's death affected him, especially coming so soon upon the heels of Buddy's. He told me he'd been too young to give it much thought. But I don't think that's true. I think my father did think about Eddie's death, and just as he had with Buddy's, he buried it in the past and leaned forward into the soft, open palm of his own future, because he'd been raised to trust God's plan no matter how brutal, and the fact *he* was spared must have meant he was spared for a reason, and that reason must have been music, because what else could it be? And so he tried to make good on his fate. He said he was sorry and walked out of the hospital. He drove north with the Crickets until they hit Bristol. He played his heart out. He taught himself to forget.

Bum, bop, bum, . . . bum ba-dum, ba-dum, ba-dum. He was still humming it to himself as he stepped onto the jetway, boarding the plane home from England. The Everlys had booked another tour in Australia, and after that they would return to L.A., where the two bands would cut an album together. His life was unfolding petal by petal, like a sun-starved flower finally kissed by the spotlight.

During a layover in New York, he called his mother, Violet, who cried out upon hearing his voice. "Sonny boy, thank God you called! The Army's been lookin' for you!"

"The Army?"

"Sonny, you gotta get down to Lubbock. You've been drafted."

CHAPTER 5

A month later, in June 1960, while the Crickets and the Everlys began recording their new album in L.A., my father reported for basic training three hundred miles up the shoreline at Fort Ord, overlooking Monterey Bay. I imagine him existing in a strange duality, a shadow of the real Sonny, the one sitting in the recording studio strumming his Martin, the one tipping a beer at the Palomino Club. The shadow Sonny narrowed his eyes and tried to transport himself to that world as he and his fellow recruits ran the tank trails to the ocean and back each morning, the powdery dirt so finely ground by tires, it coated his sweaty face like the chicken legs Violet floured before frying.

Bum, bop, bum, . . . bum ba-dum, ba-dum, ba-dum. The lick sounded like a taunt now. He wasn't exactly traipsing anywhere—privates were required to run every time they left the barracks—and he wasn't practicing either, his guitar not allowed in basic training. But one free Sunday afternoon, he discovered a dried-out Harmony in the corner of a barracks common room. It was a cheap, terrible guitar, hardly tunable, but soon enough he closed his eyes and summoned the diesel smells of London, the roar of the crowd, the taste of Earl Grey and freedom.

Bum, bop, bum, . . . bum ba-dum, ba-dum, ba-dum.

It needed words, he supposed. A month before he might have written happier lyrics, but on that day his loneliness seeped into the song, and he sang instead about heartbreak—country lyrics set to a pop lick. "I, I, I'm so lonesome," the song repeated like an incantation. The chorus issued an order: "Walk right back to me this minute." A bossy line, maybe not the best approach for winning back a woman, but the lyrics didn't matter much. The lick was strong enough to carry the song on its back. He titled it "Walk Right Back."

That week the recruits underwent the rifle qualification course. Out of 200 recruits, only six fired expert that day, the highest designation. My father was one of them. He'd never had any formal target practice, though when he was a kid his father taught him to shoot jackrabbits, which ran rampant in those post–Dust Bowl days, tearing out what little grass remained. Maybe it was dumb luck he was such a deadeye that day on the rifle course, or maybe it was something more preternatural. The gun was ubiquitous in his youth. It was the steel-bellied rattlesnake in the corner of his father's bedroom (*Touch it and you might get bit, Sonny boy*), the BB gun his brothers passed down to him, the hours spent playing cowboys and Indians after school, spaghetti Westerns at the drive-through if he had any money. It was his Grandfather Will's permanently clenched fist, a grim souvenir from the Arkansas gunfight that killed his brother.

Because he fired expert, he was granted a three-day pass while the other recruits caught up on target practice. He hopped the Trailways bus to L.A., where J. I. and Joe B. had rented a one-bedroom ranch house tucked in the hills behind Hollywood Boulevard, overlooking Gene Autry's Continental Hotel. My father had briefly lived there too, before he'd been drafted. At night he would stand on the balcony gazing out over the cold lights of La Cienega. On a clear day, you could see all the way to Catalina Island. The view was lofty and beautiful and it made him ache for the flat plains of Texas, for the simple glow of a coal oil lamp.

The Everlys were also in town, staying at the Hollywood Hawaiian Hotel. J. I. drove my father over to see them in his forest green Cadillac DeVille (such was the simple equation of success for J. I. and my dad: you made a little money, you bought a Cadillac). The brothers were seeking new songs for their album and J. I. suggested my dad play them his. Soon the brothers were strumming along, forging their silvery harmonies. The problem was, my dad had only written one verse. If he'd write a second, they said, they'd cut it.

The week after basic training wrapped up, my father jotted down a second verse. The day after he put it in the mail, he received a letter from J. I. "Hey Sonny," the first line read, "the Everly Brothers cut your song yesterday."

Yesterday? He read the letter a few times, but couldn't make sense of it. So the Everlys hadn't received the second verse? J. I. couldn't be wrong, but how do you cut a song with only one verse? he wondered. They must have used the song as a filler, he decided, some B-side

CHAPTER 5

bastard child. So that was it. He pushed the song to a corner of his mind and focused on learning Morse code, and practicing again. After basic he was transferred to signal corps school at Ford Ord in Augusta, Georgia, where he was allowed to bring his Martin D-28 on base. It must have felt good to hold his old lover, to press its tight strings beneath his fingertips and run his hand along its familiar curves. He played every night before bed, his mind still vibrating with dots and dashes, strange signals dispatched to faceless listeners.

In January 1961, he began his final tour of duty at the Jeanne d'Arc army base in Toul, France, a small, medieval town in the northeastern region of the country. But when he arrived on base, he learned there'd been some kind of bureaucratic mix-up. Jeanne d'Arc was a military hospital with no use for a signal corps private. The company commander called around France to find a better fit for him, but nobody wanted to train a draftee with less than two years remaining on his tour. He was an annoyance, unworthy of anyone's time. After some back-and-forth, the Toul commander agreed to let him remain on base, performing odd jobs for the sergeant major and delivering letters to Verdun—in other words, a gopher.

If this were fiction, here I'd concoct a story about my father haplessly stumbling upon some Cold War plot, maybe intercepting some shocking Morse code meant for a higher-up. It doesn't take Graham Greene to imagine such a scenario. That year tension was mounting between Soviet leader Nikita Khrushchev and the US allies, including France. The first year my father was stationed in France, the Berlin Wall began construction under Khrushchev's orders, dividing the Western European allies from the Eastern ones. Also while he was there, France began testing massive nuclear weapons in the Algerian desert, establishing themselves as the fourth nuclear power after the US, the USSR, and the United Kingdom. The tremors rippled outward. Across Europe, lines were being drawn in the sand.

But this is nonfiction. Though he would undoubtedly take issue with my opinion, my father's stint in Toul strikes me as one of the most tranquil military tours of duty on record. Not only did he avoid any semblance of war, he was able to keep performing. When word of his musical background got around, he was hired by a talent scout named Jack Babcock who organized shows to entertain the troops. My dad spent months traveling around France performing a nightly act on his guitar that included his hero Chet Atkins' "Poor People of Paris." Occasionally he starred in Babcock's plays, including one in which he was cast as a detective—possibly the most intrigue he ever saw in the Army.

In his downtime on base, he fell in love with the Toul library and its sprawling, second-floor music section, where he spent his weekends camped out on the plush armchairs, reading about Mozart and jazz theory. He made a few good friends, including a wine enthusiast from Pennsylvania named Richard Kooken. Alcohol was prohibited on base, but Kooken assembled a covert bar above his footlocker, which he stocked with French red wines. "Can you believe it?" he'd say. "The best wine in the world and it's right at our fingertips! And cheap!" His awe was infectious. Every night after dinner, my father and a few other guys would head to Kooken's room and listen to the Armed Forces Radio broadcast from Luxembourg while parsing the differences between Burgundies and Bordeaux.

Kooken also introduced my father to one of the great loves of his life: "Ahhh, it was Kooken who taught me how to make a martini," he tells me one day over the phone, his voice growing dreamy. My mom and I used to joke that my dad was on a lifelong quest for the perfect one, a quest he had to abandon after cancer surgery. I used to hate when my father drank more than one martini. He became belligerent, prone to picking arguments over the smallest perceived grievances. Yet he loved them so, I felt bad when he had to give them up. Maybe he never did improve on Kooken's martini, or maybe his quest was not so much for the perfect martini as it was for the feeling of discovery he got the first time the icy elixir flowed through his veins. Perhaps it was the memory of that beauty he sought to recapture throughout his life—the beauty of the martini, sure, but also the beauty of the Toul library's sweeping vista, the beauty of youth, the beauty of enlightenment.

"He was a terrific old boy," my father sighs, as if conjuring the memory of his old friend evokes his upper-crust speech as well. Of course I don't know how Kooken talked, but I like to cast him as James Stewart, another patrician military man from Pennsylvania. *Try some of this pinot noir, old boy. It's really top drawer.*

One March day three months after he arrived in Toul, my father strolled over to Kooken's room after lunch, a half hour left on his break. Kooken was dozing on his bunk, listening to the radio. Kooken's roommate was out, and my father plunked down on his empty bunk and shut his eyes. He had no courier job that day, no three hours to spend daydreaming in a cramped Citroën en route to Verdun and back. There were only two years of limbo stretching before him, as narrow and useless as the barrel of an unloaded rifle.

He was halfway to sleep when the announcer's voice came over the radio. "And here's the Everly Brothers with their brand-new hit, 'Walk Right Back.'"

He opened his eyes.

Bum, bop, bum . . . bum ba-dum, ba-dum, ba-dum, bop, bum . . .

He jolted off the bed as if he'd been shocked. "This is my song! I wrote this song!"

Then he remembered the second verse, and shushed Kooken to listen. The Everlys repeated the first verse. Apparently if you were an Everly Brother, you *could* record a song with only one verse.

When does life arrange itself in such epiphanic fashion? In that moment—the span of a radio pop song—my father's life changed, and he knew it immediately, the same way he could tell time in West Texas by the slant of the sun rays on the prairie. It was as if he'd tripped upon a moving walkway, speeding the tempo of his

(L–R): Phil Everly, Don Everly, Joe B. Mauldin, J. I. Allison, and Sonny playing the *Alma Cogan Show* in London, April 1960. (From author's collection.)

life's trajectory. Worries healed like wounds. In the flick of a dial, he'd made it.

He was discharged in May 1962, just days after he turned twenty-five. The boat sailed into New York Harbor at night, the city lights painting the water gold. As it passed below the Statue of Liberty, a brass band broke into "Stars and Stripes Forever," and even the toughest guys on board grew weepy. After they docked and received their official freedom on paper, my father and a friend bought celebratory bottles of vodka and orange juice, then took a cab to the Forest Hotel, a finger-snappers joint from the olden days—a real muso hangout. He'd stayed there a few years before, back when he was desperately peddling his songs to New York record labels while Buddy burned up the charts.

CHAPTER 5

When he awoke the next morning, he called Violet first, then J. I., who ordered him to take the first flight out to L.A., where the Crickets were cutting a new album. "Get here by yesterday!" J. I. barked. My father showered and changed into summer civilian clothes, leaving his Army greens hanging in the hotel closet. He taxied to the airport and bought a one-way ticket to L.A.

CHAPTER 6

Countrypolitan

Girl, you should see my little nest in the West
It ain't much, I confess, just a mansion
Swimming pool and a cocktail bar
And the maid is a movie star in the moonlight
Westward ho, follow the sun
Shoot that gun, have a little fun
You ain't had none, ain't you the one?
—"GIRL OF THE NORTH," WRITTEN IN 1968

She stood in the doorway slim and golden as a flute of champagne, her laughter the sound of bubbles rising. His chest bubbled. She held herself at an angle, like she didn't quite know how to stand. He could tell she was tall, but she slouched her shoulders as if she weren't proud of her height. *She should be proud*, he thought. Maybe she was embarrassed about her pants. God, her pants were ugly. They were the ugliest pants he'd ever seen, bellbottoms with patchwork and fringe. Why did women insist on wearing those darned things? He missed capris, kitten heels, pants that showed the curve of a woman's leg. But it didn't matter, not really. She was still the most beautiful girl he'd ever seen, and in that moment he forgot himself, forgot the girl beside him, forgot Texas, forgot his own name.

CHAPTER 6

He rose to greet her with an outstretched hand and she fixed her blue gaze on him, her ugly pants flapping. Turning the room on with her smile.

Where my father was conceived from dirt and born under the earth sign of Taurus, my mother was birthed by water under the water sign of Cancer. She was raised on a lake in the town of Stoughton, a suburb of Madison, Wisconsin, her early aesthetics carved by currents and washed in a haze of celadon. Her father Stener was descended from Norwegian immigrants who had settled the town before his father drank away their fortune. The family somehow managed to rescue the lake lot. Stener grew up determined to be different from his own father. As a young man, he served as a colonel in WWI before taking a banking job in the tony suburb of Darien, Connecticut. There, he married a young socialite named Margaret; my mother claims they ran in the same social circle as the billionaire tobacco heiress Doris Duke. But their rosy life together ended when Margaret died giving birth to their twin daughters. Both babies survived.

It was unheard of for men to raise children on their own in the 1930s, so the girls were sent to live with their aunt in Nebraska. Initially, Stener moved there to be close to them. Blinded by grief, he took a job with the FDIC, traveling around the Midwest to insure banks still reeling from the Great Depression. On a trip to North Dakota, he met Lottie, a teacher twenty years his junior. He proposed almost immediately, and the couple relocated to his hometown of Stoughton, where they raised three daughters together: Mary, Martha, and my mother, Louise, the youngest, born in the summer of 1946.

How much PTSD did Stener carry? He had survived an alcoholic father, trench warfare, the stock market crash, the death of his first wife, and the separation from his twin daughters. Others in his situation dealt with such traumas by drinking or beating their wives, but Stener turned inward. He was a kind but distant husband and father, his ghosts felt but rarely seen. My mother remembers how, in the winters after he returned home from his accounting job, he would lace on his skates and spend an hour etching figure eights around their frozen lake. Through the window, past the naked trees, my mother could make out his solitary figure whirling round and round, his scarf whipping behind him. He skated in that old-fashioned way with his hands clasped behind his back, leaning into the future, or away from the past.

By standard measurements, my mother's childhood should have been happy. Her family was solidly middle class. She and her sisters were lake kids as opposed to town kids, a badge of honor in Stoughton. Her parents loved her. But my mother has painful memories of her youth that cloud her nostalgia. School was torture, especially math. Today she would likely be diagnosed with a learning disability in the subject, though back then she was just considered dumb. It was a stereotype her mother reinforced, labeling Mary the smart one, Martha the pretty one, and my mother the ditzy one. But my mother was also pretty, tall like her mother, with high cheekbones and guileless blue eyes. And she was not dumb. Dumb people aren't curious about the world, and my mother was always hungry for books. When I was growing up she didn't so much read them as devour them, across genres—fiction, nonfiction, and poetry, highbrow and low. She loved a twisty narrative (literary mysteries were her favorites) but hated symbolism, books that made her look too far beneath the surface of the plot. The only genre she refused was short stories. She liked the heft of a novel, the faith it required.

She graduated high school in the spring of 1964 and was accepted at the University of Wisconsin, the alma mater of her father and sisters. Though tensions between the US and the North Vietnamese had been simmering for over a decade, that summer marked the official start of combat. As my mother packed for college that August, President Lyndon Johnson ordered air strikes on North Vietnamese patrol boats in the Gulf of Tonkin, resulting in two US aircrafts being shot down. Johnson responded by deploying the first combat troops. Later, the University of Wisconsin at Madison would transform from a bucolic lakeside college into one of the most radicalized campuses in the nation. But that year, it was still possible for families to keep the nightmare at bay, or at least away from the dinner table.

One brisk day that fall, my mother walked out of her French class to find a pre-med student named Rodney leaning against the wall outside the classroom waiting for her. She knew Rodney, or knew of him. He'd graduated Stoughton High School a year before her, where he was one of the most popular boys in his class. Back then, he'd barely spoken to my mother, who struggled socially as well as academically, her 5'9" stature rendering her gangly and awkward among her classmates. Now here he was, tracking her down for a date.

She gave Rodney her number and a vague promise. But something didn't feel right. When she returned to her dorm, she took a long look at herself in the mirror. She was wearing her daily uniform: a Peter Pan–collared dress with beige nylons and flats. Over her dress she wore a red tailored coat and matching red beret. Clothes her mother had bought for her, the only kind of clothes she owned. She saw in that moment how they attracted boys like Rodney, boys who would become doctors and bankers, move back to their hometowns to raise strapping young sons with their bridge-playing wives. My mother decided then and there that she didn't want that kind of husband, or that kind of life. Not only would she not call Rodney back, she would stop dressing like Doris Day. It was turtleneck sweaters and jeans from now on, she thought, tossing her nylons in the trash.

She flunked out of Madison after one year. Her parents were disappointed, but what did they expect? She always *had* hated school, she reminded them. Couldn't she just become a stewardess like her high school friend Joanie Sveum? But Lottie wouldn't hear of it. The slightly prudish daughter of a German minister, she found the whole profession tawdry. "My daughter is not going to become some waitress in the sky," she said. Instead, she enrolled my mother at the University of Whitewater, a state school where she could major in education and become a teacher, as her mother and sisters had done. The path was well paved for her. All she had to do was follow it.

By this point, Johnson had increased the draft to 35,000 young men a month. The political was fast becoming the personal, the personal the tragic. When my mother fell in love for the first time at Whitewater with a boy named John, a cute, curly-haired art student from a conservative Catholic family, the pall of the draft hung low above their heads. John's best friend was sent home from the war in a body bag, and his own draft number was creeping up.

In 1966, the couple joined the local chapter of Students for a Democratic Society. They bought a clunker of a sedan to drive to Madison each week, where they took classes teaching them how to register as conscientious objectors. They joined the university Peace Club, holding teary candlelight vigils for their fallen friends—part activism, part grief support group. Unlike many SDS members, my mother was not rebelling against her family. Stener and Lottie were staunchly anti-war, even though (or perhaps because) Stener had served in WWI. Objector status required a letter of recommendation from a military officer, and Stener wrote John's letter. John's own father, a high-ranking Army doctor, disowned him when he found out.

John was accepted at the Parsons School of Design his senior year, his first choice for art school. My mother remembers typing his application for him, and how elated they were when his acceptance arrived in the mail. But conscientious objector status required an alternate civilian service, and art school was seen as a frivolity during war time. The government denied John's student deferral. That meant if he attended Parsons, he would still be in line for the draft. Choosing between his dream and his life, John chose life. He was assigned to teach in an inner-city school in Madison. But as Langston Hughes knew too well, a dream deferred has a cost. John resented his job and students, his bitterness corroding his spirit like poison in his veins.

CHAPTER 6

Everything in my mother's life felt heavy: the incessant war, her changed boyfriend, the long Wisconsin winters, and her dull education classes with those impossible math requirements. The only bright spot in her life was a summer administrative job she took at a foundry—the camaraderie of the older men, lifers who called her out of the office every afternoon to watch the fireworks explode as they poured the metal into the molds.

One day in the summer of 1968 after her shift ended, she walked to a burger joint called the Huddle House in a building the color of old teeth. Inside, she ordered a grilled cheese sandwich and beer while newsreels of Vietnam loomed on the TV above her head. To drown out the death toll, someone played "Hey Jude" on the juke box. It was her favorite song, a song about opening your heart. But that day the song opened something in her brain instead. When it ended, she ordered another beer and played it again and again, her plan coalescing before her like liquid metal taking shape.

My mother's sisters had both moved to California after college—Mary to San Francisco and Martha to L.A., where she and her new husband Richard were living in a small apartment in the Hollywood Hills, tucked in a eucalyptus grove at the end of a rutted dirt road. It was a time in L.A. when two teachers could still afford a North Hollywood bungalow, a time when everything smelled of marijuana and eucalyptus. Not everyone was a hippie, but most were escaping something—Vietnam, adulthood, their square nine-to-five parents who feasted nightly on meatloaf and Lawrence Welk like a false religion. A precipice of time before the Mansons, when people didn't think to lock the doors, when sit-ins still felt hopeful and kids mainly smoked grass, a time before the hard stuff took over, the stuff that inhaled your soul like smoke. My mother remembers the light.

"The light was just different in California."

"Different how?" I ask.

"It shimmered."

Maybe that's all bullshit, and it was only that way for a lucky few, the talented and the charming, the beautiful and the white.

When my mother flew to L.A. to visit Martha and Richard, she saw a monkey dangling upside-down from their apartment roof, the pet of a previous tenant. Occasionally a spotted ocelot prowled the grounds as well. The wildlife, the eucalyptus-scented air, and that shimmery California sunlight. To a kid from Wisconsin, it might as well have been the rainforest. Soon after her visit, she emptied her savings and bought a one-way ticket to L.A.

If I were to unspool the thread of my own story, my own genesis, I would unwind it to the pilgrimage that began that day at the Huddle House with two beers and a Beatles song. In my mind's eye, I see the moment the plan came together: my doe-eyed young mother floating in the sky, a pink carnation tucked behind her ear. She rests her cheek against the airplane window and watches her state's horizontal farmland evaporate like vapors in the contrails.

In L.A. she found a job as a secretary for Bell Records, where she worked alongside a young woman named Carlie McCummings. Like my mom, Carlie was a leggy, blonde Midwestern hippie, and the two women hit it off immediately. Carlie found my mom a place to rent in her apartment building, a basement floor walkout overhanging the North Hollywood Hills. My mom thought Carlie was the coolest. A production assistant by day and go-go dancer by night, she knew the hippest clubs and most off-the-wall boutiques, and she always had a purse full of weed. After graduating college in Indiana, she'd driven to L.A. seeking sunshine and escape from her wealthy, dysfunctional family. She was hired to dance at Gazzarri's, a popular nightclub on the Sunset Strip that launched the careers of such luminaries as The Doors and Van Halen.

It wasn't long before my mom and Carlie fell into a deep, sororal love. When they got off work, they would change into their shortest skirts and head to the Whisky to dance to bands like The Flying Burrito Brothers or their favorite, Otis Redding. It was the most freedom my mother had ever known, and possibly the most she ever would.

CHAPTER 6

A few months after my mom moved, her mother Lottie called to read her a wedding announcement from *The Courier Hub*, her hometown newspaper. Her high school friend Joanie—yes, the waitress in the sky—had married a man named J. I. Allison, the paper said, and the couple was living in L.A. Like my mother, Joanie was descended from Norwegian immigrants who flocked to Stoughton in the 1900s seeking jobs in the sawmills and warehouses. My mother had longed to flee that wintry landscape, but hearing Joanie's name stirred up a feeling of homesickness. It would be nice, she thought, to see a familiar face. She dialed directory assistance and asked for Joanie Sveum—no, make that Joanie Allison.

So here they stand, my mother and my father, meeting for the first time in J. I. and Joanie's living room, him smitten and a little buzzed, her wishing for once she'd worn a dress. After Joanie made the introductions, J. I. mixed up martinis and presented my mother with one on a silver tray. Her first martini, it began to cloud her brain after only a few sips. This Sonny guy was cute, she couldn't help noticing, with a smooth Texas accent and wry sense of humor, slightly fawning, unlike the self-absorbed Midwestern boys of her youth. But he wasn't free. Another woman, named Sandra, was there. As he sat on the couch, my mother remembers her kneeling at his feet, coiling her arm around his pant leg.

After they finished their martinis, my dad drove them to the Aware Inn, an organic restaurant on Sunset where you could order tropical salads and maybe catch a glimpse of Warren Beatty. Over dinner that night, my mom learned that Sandra was a production assistant from New York, and that she and my father had dated for seven years. She was a pretty brunette, my mom concedes, "but small, not tall like me. She wasn't as pretty as I was." At some point during her early twenties, a secret had revealed itself to my mother: she was gorgeous. Being the tallest girl in the room had its advantages, she was starting to learn, a trait she could weaponize. Clothes looked good on her, even ugly bellbottoms. In her world, pretty opened doors. It landed you the job, and the man. Maybe it soothed her ego after flunking out of college, to know there was something she did indeed excel at. Her social life began taking the shape of a pretty contest she could win.

Two weeks later, my father called my mother to see if she wanted to go with him to a Del Reeves concert in Pasadena. *Did she know Del Reeves?* he asked. Of course she did. She'd grown up next to a tavern that played loud country music, and it seeded in her a love of the genre, as well as a hazy longing for cowboys.

"Let me see if Carlie can come too," she told him.

"Um, that's not exactly what I had in mind," my father said.

That's when she got it. Sandra was out, and she was in.

Other artists around L.A. were channeling their frustration into protest songs, but my dad was better at evoking the misty-eyed promise of the era, pastoral melodies with an undercurrent of yearning, songs about seekers. He channeled that honeyed glow into a song he wrote in 1968 called "The Straight Life." Set to a breezy melody, it was a song about a man daydreaming of a wild life, chasing the surf in Mexico and feeding beautiful girls corn on the cob. The song gained traction when Glen Campbell cut it on his massive-selling album *Wichita Lineman*.

After the success of "The Straight Life," San Francisco ad execs representing Olympia Beer asked my dad to write a jingle that evoked the same idyllic feeling. That jingle led to another contract, and another. Before he knew it, he was working fifteen-hour days in the recording studio, composing and producing jingles with a partner named Don Piestrup ("a real jazzberry," says my dad). His secret weapon was his ability to turn on his Texan accent if need be, and need often was in the *Gunsmoke*-crazy sixties and seventies.

One day in the spring of 1970, my father received a phone call from his friend Doug, who worked for the talent agency that represented Mary Tyler Moore. *The Dick Van Dyke Show* had ended a few years before, and Doug told him the suits at CBS were trying to launch a new sitcom starring Moore, its breakout star. Reflecting the era's

CHAPTER 6

burgeoning feminism, the actress would not play a doting wife this time, but rather a single career woman living in a big city. The show needed a theme song. Would my father like to try his hand at it?

That day around lunch, a courier arrived at my father's house to deliver a four-page treatment. It was slim on details: girl gets jilted by her fiancé, moves to Minneapolis, takes an apartment she can barely afford, and finds a job in a newsroom. He looked at the clock. It was noon. How long did he have before other songwriters across L.A. got a look at this same treatment? But he had it first; Doug had given him a head start. He picked up his Martin and began stringing chords together. Once again, the lick came first, then the line, a question he'd spent years asking himself: *How will you make it on your own?* Around two that afternoon, he called Doug back. "Who do I play this thing to?"

By four o'clock, he was sitting in an iron-backed chair in a large, barren room at CBS's Studio Center. Across from him sat the show's co-executive producers, James L. Brooks and Allan Burns. Brooks wasn't especially friendly. He made it clear they weren't anywhere near the stage to choose a theme song, but he supposed they'd give it a listen. Besides their chairs, the room was empty except for a black rotary phone on the floor. Allan Burns would later recount this moment in a documentary about the show, describing my father as a "shit kicker." "He put his guitar down, opened the case, had some pages of lyrics, put 'em down on the guitar case, and played the song. He finished and we looked at each other: 'How did we get this lucky?'"

Brooks picked up the phone and dialed an *MTM* staffer to bring a tape recorder. He asked my father to play the song again. Afterwards, Brooks picked up the phone and summoned another staffer. This cycle repeated itself until the room was completely full.

In her book, *Mary and Lou and Rhoda and Ted and All the Brilliant Minds Who Made the Mary Tyler Moore Show a Classic*, author Jennifer Keishin Armstrong describes James L. Brooks's reaction to hearing the song for the first time. "Could it be this easy?" she writes. "How did a Texas farm boy understand their show about a modern Midwestern woman when they still couldn't seem to complete the script?" How indeed? When reporters ask my father what inspired the lyrics to "Love Is All Around," he repeats a variation of the same answer, that he keyed into the part of the synopsis about Mary Richards renting an apartment she couldn't afford. It makes perfect sense, actually. My father and the title character had little in common on the surface, but if there was one experience he knew intimately, it was being flat broke.

A few months later, on September 19, 1970, my parents attended the premiere party at Burns's house in Beverly Hills, where crew members, stand-ins, and cast spilled onto the manicured lawn, everyone giddy with cocktails and success. A few days before the party, my father took my mother to a boutique in the valley, where she bought a sleeveless brown minidress with a Mandarin collar. "I must have weighed 120 pounds at the time," she brags over the phone to me one day. "The belt was very wide and accented my thin waist, and the shortness of the skirt accented my goooorgeous legs. Your dad was always whacking me on the back when I slouched because he was so proud of my height. Well, I can tell you, I wasn't slouchin' at that party."

The show had been granted a primo Saturday nighttime slot, positioning it alongside network giants *My Three Sons* and *Mission: Impossible*. The pilot was titled after my father's theme song: "Love Is All Around." The producers had wanted to hire a singer more famous than him like Glen Campbell, but in a brash move, he told them they could only have the song if he sang it. They reluctantly agreed, and he laid down a velvety vocal track, zero percent Texas shit kicker.

By this point, my mother had moved out of her apartment and into my father's house in Studio City, a decision spurred by love and fear. After the Manson murders, she no longer felt safe living alone in a bottom-floor Hollywood walkout with a flimsy screen door. She assumed moving in with my father was a natural stop on the road to marriage. But in late fall of that year, she made a painful discovery—my father hadn't ended things with Sandra so abruptly after all. There

CHAPTER 6

had been some overlap, and he'd taken Sandra home to Texas with him the first Christmas my parents were together.

This time, the math came easily to her. She and my father hadn't been living together at the time, but they had been dating exclusively, at least in her mind. She thought of how long Sandra had hung on—seven years—and how little she'd been rewarded. She would never be Sandra, she decided, sitting on the carpet and clinging to the pant leg of a restless man. She moved out of my father's house and in with a friend from her record secretary days.

My father continued to call, and sometimes she agreed to meet him for dinner. But now she saw him for what he was. When Christmas came that year, 1970, she flew back to Wisconsin with little fanfare. If my father wanted to take Sandra home with him this year, she thought, just let him. When she told her parents about the breakup, they pressured her to move back home and finish her teaching degree at Whitewater. Of all her options, it was the most familiar, and possibly the most sensible. Reluctantly, she agreed to fly back to L.A. to retrieve her things and start planning her move to Wisconsin. California had been fun, even glamorous, but she was twenty-four now. It was time to grow up.

If my parents' romance were a Hollywood movie, this would be the dramatic climax. Again my mother boards the plane to L.A. Again she rests her cheek on the airplane window. Again she sees the farmland ripple below her, though this time it's a bittersweet vista, cornfields she cannot escape. When the plane lands at LAX, my father is waiting for her at the gate.

"What are you doing here?" she cries.

"What do you say we drive to Vegas and get married?" he asks. He has no ring or speech prepared. Only a question. Without thinking, my mother says yes. That's how she phrases it to me over the phone one day. "I didn't think twice. I just said okay. Okay, let's do it."

They were married just past midnight on December 30, 1970, at the Chapel of the Little Flowers on the Vegas Strip. My mom wore an

My mother in L.A. in 1969, the year she met my father. (From author's collection.)

orange bellbottom pantsuit with a Nehru collar, my dad a dark suit. In the one black-and-white photo that exists from that night taken at a steak restaurant, he grins peacock-proud, his arm slung around my mother, who smiles demurely at the camera under her blonde shag haircut. He has the bigger smile. They didn't have rings; not then, not ever.

CHAPTER 6

This is where the movie would end. It's the classic marriage plot slicked with a seventies sheen—the beautiful ingenue tames the wild man and in return, she gets to keep him as a pet. Viewers leaving the theater might roll their eyes and scoff, knowing the couple would never last in real life. They would label the heroine a fool for following her heart over her education. Were I the heroine, my own love story would never end this way. I'm not saying I couldn't forgive the man of his transgression, but I guarantee it would involve expensive therapy and an agonizing amount of consideration before I'd ever walk down the aisle with him. Who gets married without thinking? Cognition should be the minimal requirement for marriage. And even more bewildering, how can any marriage that begins this way have lasted over fifty years?

A modern-day retelling might end like this: my mother returns to Wisconsin, but instead of resuming her education degree, she becomes a leader in the anti-war movement. She pays a visit to her old boyfriend John, who has turned his life around and started painting again. In his studio apartment, he unveils a large oil portrait he's made of her face, her hair streaked with gold, a carnation tucked behind her ear. She smiles wistfully, recalling those aimless days. But that was long ago, and she's wiser now. She bids goodbye to John. They briefly kiss before she pulls away. *Stay a little longer,* he pleads. No, she can't. She has a march to lead. In the closing scene, my mother strides onto an outdoor stage, bullhorn in hand, mindlessly humming a lyric from "The Straight Life." *But suddenly all my silly thoughts disappear....* The crowd erupts in applause, drowning out the notes.

I like that ending better. Except that in that film, I don't exist.

CHAPTER 7

Burning Out

Give me that tranquilizing, hypnotizing, localizing in my vein
Think about compromising, sympathizing, anesthetizing my weary brain
Surely as my position, you can see the need to supply
The means to control my bad condition, give my soul an intermission
Get me straight, get me high . . .

—"SOUL FEVER," 1969

I was born nine days before the fall of Saigon in April 1975. The sixties had closed like a phantasmagoria, a theater of horrors, its images indelible on the eye. If California had once signified promise to young seekers like my mother, that promise was broken with Robert Kennedy's assassination in 1968, the Manson family's blood-scrawled rampage in 1969, and later that same year, the bad trip of Altamont, an event journalist Todd Gitlin called "the end of the age of Aquarius." A desperate charge crackled in the air. My mom remembers eating at an outdoor restaurant in L.A. while strung-out hippies circled her table like birds of prey, descending on her scraps the second she called for the check.

She suffered her own desperation after marrying my father. Though she had no problem getting pregnant, she kept miscarrying after the

CHAPTER 7

first few months. A friend gave her the name of a hotshot fertility doctor in Beverly Hills who ran some tests and determined her problem was hormonal, easy to address with the right cocktail of injections. Every time she started to bleed, he instructed her to drive to his office for a series of needles. Thanks to these magical shots, I navigated the treacherous terrain of my mother's womb.

I was my parents' miracle, and they treated me accordingly, feeding me blended organic produce before the term organic had caught on. My mother studied Ina May Gaskin and Dr. Spock and *The Womanly Art of Breastfeeding*; she didn't let my lips touch sugar until I was two. My parents had an avocado tree in their backyard that never bore fruit, but one day when I was starting to walk, I toddled into the living room clutching something in my hands. "A-vo-ca-do," I said, holding up a perfectly ripened specimen. My parents claim it was my first word. When I watched my own babies begin to form simpler nouns, I saw that story for what it likely was: a California creation myth, the day the sacred child discovered language.

But L.A. in the mid-seventies was no place to raise a miracle baby. The city hollowed people out. My mom's friend Carlie was one of its victims. She'd married Gene Clark of The Byrds, and the couple moved north to Mendocino, where they fell in with a hard-partying group of musicians. Now when Carlie came to town, she was always drunk or high.

One morning my mom received a phone call from a storekeeper at Holly Harp, an upscale boutique on Sunset. "There's a woman passed out behind my alley and all she'll give me is your number," the woman sniffed. My mother drove down to, as she put it, "scrape Carlie's sorry ass off the pavement." She was losing patience with her friend, and she suspected the situation was getting worse. Rumors were circulating that Gene was into heroin.

At 3 o'clock one morning shortly after I was born, my parents were awakened by a loud banging on their sliding glass bedroom door. My father twisted the blinds to reveal what appeared to be a giant yeti smoking a cigarette and pounding on the glass. My mother screamed, waking me up. Her eyes adjusted and she realized it was Carlie, wearing a full-length mink coat like a junked-up Cruella de Vil. My mother joggled me in her arms as she slid open the door. On the street behind Carlie, she could make out the headlights of Gene's car waiting at the curb.

Carlie, what are you doing here? It's three a.m.!
I wanna shee da baby!
No, Carlie, no. You can't do this anymore, my mother told her. *Things are different now. Now I have a baby.*

The list of musicians my parents knew who lost their minds or lives during those years is both horrifying and mundane, a well-tread reminder of the shadow side of fame. There was Bobby Fuller, the up-and-coming rocker from El Paso whose band The Bobby Fuller Four made "I Fought the Law" a hit in 1966. Bobby grew up idolizing Buddy Holly, his proof that a kid from Texas could strap on a Stratocaster and hit it big. He started covering Crickets songs as a cocky teenager, picking rough dance halls across the border in Juárez. When the band recorded "I Fought the Law," Bobby called my father into the studio to listen. He was sweet and respectful, a fellow Texas boy made good. Six months later, Bobby's mother would find his body sprawled across the front seat of her Oldsmobile, bloody and beaten and doused in gasoline. Though the facts pointed to homicide, the county coroner's office declared Bobby's death a suicide by asphyxiation from gas fumes and closed the case.

There was Ric Grech, a onetime bassist for the Crickets who would die of liver failure from heroin addiction and alcoholism at age 44. And there was Ric's close friend Gram Parsons, the country-rock guitarist for The Byrds and Flying Burrito Brothers. One fall day in 1973, he dropped by J. I.'s house to see his friend, Ric, before the band traveled to Nashville to record. My mother was there that day, helping Joanie cook meals for them to take on their trip. She still remembers how Gram's eyes were, as she put it, "vibrating in their sockets." Later

CHAPTER 7

that night he would pass out on J. I.'s couch holding a lit cigarette, setting the couch on fire. The next day, the Crickets left for Nashville and Gram headed to a party at the Joshua Tree Inn, where he would die of a heroin overdose.

But closest to the bone for my father was Jim Gordon, a young drum prodigy he met on a 1964 European tour with the Everly Brothers. Jim was fresh out of high school at the time, six foot four with a cherubic face and wild blond ringlets. He and my father hit it off straight away and became roommates and traveling companions. They rode the Orient Express through the verdant Bavarian countryside, past the Alps to Salzburg, where they visited Mozart's birthplace. When they arrived back in Munich, Jim said, "Man, that was so much fun, let's do it again!" The next week, they did.

Around his Texas buddies, my father was used to hiding his interest in classical and jazz, but Jim was curious too, a real muso. From Munich the band flew to Milan, where they stayed at the La Scala Hotel, spitting distance from the legendary opera house. The Everlys' road manager made a few calls, and my father and Jim found themselves sitting in a box a few feet away from Italy's prime minister, watching Rossini's grand opera, *Moses in Egypt*. After Milan they traveled on to Paris, Amsterdam, Stockholm, and London. It was a free classical arts education for two young men who had never darkened the door of a college, and the experience bonded them deeply.

By the late sixties, Jim was a member of the fabled Wrecking Crew, a group of roughly twenty elite sidemen (and one woman, bassist Carol Kaye) who performed on nearly every rock 'n' roll hit in the sixties and seventies. His sound was so electric, it even acquired a nickname: "the Gordon bounce." His drumming elevated tracks by the biggest stars of the day, from the Beach Boys to John Lennon to Joe Cocker. When Jim was available, which was rare, my father hired him to play on his jingles. But he was starting to notice a sea change in the drummer. On a road trip to Arkansas they took with some mutual musician friends, Jim sat in the backseat taking pulls off a bottle of brandy all day. The Jim he'd known had barely dabbled in grass, but that might have changed when he was hired to play drums on Joe Cocker's 1970 Mad Dogs & Englishmen tour, a bacchanalian orgy of sex and drugs. Another musician friend of my father's, a lanky bassist from Tulsa named Carl Radle, was on the tour. Ten years later, he would die of complications from heavy drug use at age 37.

But Jim remained sober for jingle sessions; he still hit the sweet spot on the drums; and he and my father still liked hanging out at Muso and Frank's after the day's work was done, talking their old muso love language. True, Jim had grown quieter, slightly strange, my father thought, and he worried Jim was succumbing to substance abuse like so many others. Doctors thought the same, treating him for alcoholism and missing the fact that substance abuse was a symptom of Jim's undiagnosed schizophrenia—the mechanism he was using to silence the voices in his head.

On the night of June 3, 1983, the voices won. Jim drove his Datsun to his mother Osa Marie's North Hollywood apartment, where he hit the 72-year-old woman several times with a hammer before plunging an eight-inch butcher knife into her chest. He was sent to a California mental institution, where he remained until his death in March 2023.

My father had met Jim's mother, even had dinner with her at their family home in Sherman Oaks a few times in the early days of their friendship. They were by all accounts a loving, suburban family. I'm not sure how he processed his friend's horrific act—I wouldn't have even known to ask about Jim had I not learned about their connection in an obscure interview with my dad I found online. "Must be a little bit chilling to know that you slept in the same hotel room as this guy," the interviewer asked.

"He was quite sane at the time and we got along great," my father answered. "We were just good buddies and it really saddens me."

My dad may have caught a break in the Army, drafted between two wars, but the music world had its own body count. What does it do to a person to watch so many bright young friends and fellow musicians die? I imagine it would calcify something inside you, keep you from getting too attached to people. I think about my phone calls with my father, how I've been trying to say "I love you" more before hanging up, and how he always says it back to me—*I love you too, Sweetheart*—but never first. And sometimes I can't bring myself to say it first, not because it isn't true, but because it seems hard for my father to press his feelings into words, like he's trying to forge metal with a rusty anvil. Sometimes I just let it go and say goodbye.

My parents weren't the only ones growing disillusioned and tired of living under the existential shadows of Vietnam, urban deterioration, drug abuse, and the growing amount of water pollution and smog, of which L.A. had more than its share. Music was changing to reflect the mood—people didn't want psychedelic space rock anymore; reality was unsettling enough. Even Bob Dylan needed a break from politics. In 1969, he released the album *Nashville Skyline*, abandoning protest music in favor of gauzy country ballads. Like Dylan, people yearned for—what? An Americana rooted in soil, truth, and beauty, along with something nebulous they couldn't place, maybe because it had never existed. But as *The Whole Earth Catalog*, the movement's bible, reminded readers in its mission statement, "We *are* as gods, and may as well get used to it." Clean air, green meadows, and a fresh start: an Americana they would have to build from the ground up.

The back-to-the-land movement of the seventies was luring thousands of young, mostly white, middle-class couples like my parents to the country, where they aimed to forge brave new frontiers. Though my parents knew other families doing the same, they did not see their move as part of a larger exodus; few did. Culture is the water we swim in, even if we can't feel its temperature on our skin. "Only afterward was it called a movement," wrote journalist Robert Houriet in his classic book on the era, *Getting Back Together*. "At the outset, it was the gut reaction of a generation." And maybe for musicians it was also an act of self-preservation, a way to separate themselves from the temptations of the industry, especially when couples began having children. People longed for the pastoral salvation of rural life, not recognizing that salvation too might be a myth.

Armed with this idealism and *Whole Earth* subscriptions, several of my parents' friends began making the pilgrimage from L.A. to land outside Nashville, where they could fulfill their farmland fantasies in close proximity to the country music publishing world. J. I. and Joanie left first, then bassist Joe Osborn, a former Wrecking Crew member. One day in 1976, Joe called my father in L.A. to let him know a farm had come up for sale on his street, Mt. Sinai Road. My father was scheduled to record in Nashville and decided to check it out on his trip.

The land belonged to a retired cattle farmer who drove him around one hundred acres of pastures that flowed into each other as melodiously as a ballad. It was spring, dogwood season, the air perfumed with vanilla and musk. Even the grassy scent of manure was a salve to my smog-weary father. Unlike the flat fields of his youth, this farm was rolling and lush with hidden treasures, like a two-hundred-year-old log cabin and a narrow river called the Piney that cut through the western edge of the property. My father found a perfect spot to build a new house set back from the road, tucked out of sight behind a maple grove. He could already see it in his mind: a house made of cedar and glass, earth and water. In the meantime, we could live in the farmer's small but habitable white farmhouse.

Like Moses delivering his new commandments from the summit of Mt. Sinai, my father called my mother in L.A., where she and I were holed up inside riding out a heat wave. I had just turned one. I imagine her balancing the phone on her shoulder and me on her hip as she looked out the kitchen window at her parched scrap of garden, my father's smooth Western drawl delivering tales of green meadows and babbling streams, promises of horses and vegetable gardens. It only took three days to break her.

"Oh, go ahead and buy it," she said back then.

"He hosed me," she says now.

My dad signed the deed and flew back to L.A., where he began the process of transplanting the three of us from a Hollywood bungalow to

CHAPTER 7

Everly Brothers tour of England, 1964. Jim Gordon is second from left, my father second from right in sunglasses. (From author's collection.)

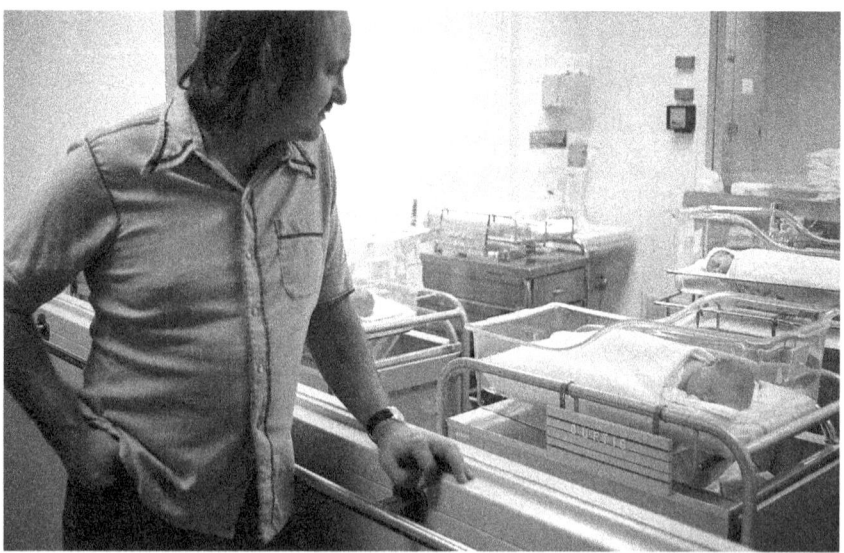

My father at the hospital after my birth. (Photo courtesy of John Livzey.)

one hundred snake-ridden acres on the outskirts of a rural Tennessee town called Dickson.

First he had his two Cadillacs to deal with: his black 1972 DeVille and a colossal, vintage pink model with fins. A few weeks before we moved, he convinced a friend to help him caravan the cars to Tennessee. I can see him now, sailing along the freeway in a pink Cadillac with the windows rolled down, tapping his hand against the steering wheel as he hums out a new song about his future home state he would name "Tennessee, I Love You." In his blissed-out imagination, "virgin dogwoods wear their bridal veil in spring" and children "whistle Dixie while they learn their ABC's" (possibly my dad's worst lyric ever). It may as well have been one of his jingles, a sell job for a moonlight and magnolias version of the South that never existed. An illusion from the start.

PART 2

Back to the Land

CHAPTER 8

The Glass House

Sometimes I imagine myself as a drifter,
Seeker of fortune, connoisseur of great wines
Dashing through meadows of yellow and green
Trying to catch the impossible dream
Leaving the straight life behind
—"THE STRAIGHT LIFE," 1969

The summer after I turned one, my dad flew us down to Nashville to see our new home. The first thing my mom noticed amiss was the drive from the airport to the farm took a lot longer than she expected, over an hour. The second thing she noticed was the town of Dickson was tiny, as was our new house. The third thing she noticed was raccoons were living in her attic. As she climbed the rotting stairs, she spotted a family of them balled in a corner. The fourth thing she noticed was the mice.

"Is there even a bathroom?" she asked, looking around at the shrug of a farmhouse. There was. It was outside on the porch. That was the fifth thing.

Run, I want to say to my mother at this point. *Don't do it. Put the place back on the market and come up with a plan B.* Instead, my parents hired a handyman while we rented a ranch house in town. I think my parents saw the move as an adventure. *If everybody had an ocean*, the Beach Boys sang of 1960s California. In the seventies and eighties—at least in my parents' circle—everybody had a farm. My mom's sister Martha and her husband had also left L.A. and bought a farm outside Milwaukee, where they were raising their three kids alongside a bevy of animals. Joanie and J. I.'s farm lay thirty minutes from ours in an even more rural community. They'd bought horses, beef cattle, and two cute but deplorable goats they named Samson and Delilah. As a child, I remember my mom spending long hours on the phone to Martha and Joanie, laughing and groaning over the pitfalls of farm life.

The man who rented us the ranch house was a local politician from a venerable old Tennessee family, a Kennedy by Dickson standards. As my parents unpacked, he stopped by the house to deliver a warning disguised as a welcome.

"I'm going to tell you right now, you'll never be accepted in this town," he said. "No matter what, you'll always be an outsider here."

My mom proved his point her first morning in town when she ran to the local Kroger for diapers and milk. With her shaggy blonde seventies perm, jean shorts cut high atop her long, tan legs, and a tank top that showed off the rose tattoo on her back shoulder, she faced a harsh initiation. "I felt like I had dropped off the moon. People were actually stopping in the aisles to stare at me. I kind of slunk home, put my bra on, tied my hair back, and found a shirt that covered up my tattoo. All I could think was, *What have I gotten myself into?*"

After we moved, my dad flew back and forth to L.A. for jingle work. He had not yet broken into the Nashville music scene, and now he had a child to support, a farm mortgage, and livestock and equipment to buy. Jingles kept us afloat. My mother, sick with loneliness, stayed back with me in her strange new homeland. One afternoon she noticed her next-door neighbors, an older couple raking leaves, and bundled me on her hip to introduce herself. She stood before them, stuttering to explain who she was, and why she was there. They never said a word. They didn't even look up.

Eventually we rid the farmhouse of the raccoons, and our cat Big Kitty took care of the mice. The handyman built a bathroom inside, and J. I. dropped by to help rig up a wood-burning stove, as fall was approaching. We moved into the tumbledown farmhouse, the place where my memories begin.

The journey from downtown Dickson to our farm ran fifteen minutes down a two-lane country highway, off of which branched Mt. Sinai Road, the center of my universe for sixteen years. Were you to turn down Mt. Sinai, you would wind your way past a few brick ranch homes and country farmhouses, up a wooded hill, to a Pentecostal church where people were rumored to drop to their knees and speak in tongues. Past the church, the road began its downhill descent and the sky opened, the world widening into green pastureland. Our farm was on the left, our long, gravel driveway snaking through an uncultivated field dotted with daffodils and Queen Anne's lace. Years later when I got married on a Tennessee hilltop, I tried to replicate the wildness of that pasture in my bouquet with lamb's ear, ferns, and Queen Anne's lace.

When I think back to being small on that big farm, the first thing I remember is the gates. Each pasture was fenced with its own metal gate in order to corral our beef cattle, large, lumbering Simmentals. Each gate led to a different pasture, and each pasture to a different world. When my parents took me for walks around the farm, they'd lift me to the top rung, where I'd dangle while one of them climbed over to help me down from the other side. I still remember the pride I felt the day I was able to climb those six metal bars alone.

A beaten trail past my father's pole barn led to a two-hundred-year-old log cabin. My mom and I roamed through it a few times, the air thick with dust and mold, the floor littered with shards of green glass. One day I picked up a cracked silver hand mirror with the backing peeled off and stared at my face in the scratched surface, at my round cheeks and pointy chin, the freckles sprouting on my nose. Everyone told me I had my father's face, though I wanted my mother's. I wondered whose hands had held this mirror last. An old woman? A girl the same age as me? Was she pretty? How had she died? I think the log cabin was my first introduction to the idea that time was more than the present moment, more than the buttercup I held in my palm, more than my mother's wet kiss upon my cheek. Time bent further back than I could ever reach.

Past the cabin, the trail led down to another gate, another pasture, where the Piney River made its slow crawl to the Gulf of Mexico. The family who built the log cabin also built a wooden spring house on this pasture. In our early days of discovering the farm, my mother and I peeked inside it one fall afternoon to find the ceiling thick with sleeping bats. So this is where they all came from, I realized, all the not-birds I saw winging low across the moon when we sat outside on summer nights. "That's not a bird," my mom would say with a shudder. The bats never scared me though, at least not like the spiders and the copperheads, my frightening fellow earth-dwellers. Bats were sky creatures. I'd witnessed them at their most vulnerable, these defiers of gravity who could sleep upside-down, their wings neatly folded over their tiny bodies. I never returned to the spring house, though I accepted the bats into my realm with the unquestioning awe a child accepts any mystical creature.

My mother taught me to believe in fairies, to look for signs of them, which were everywhere on the farm. On the forest floor beside our house, a lush carpet of mayapples sprouted every May, transforming our woods into Tolkien's Middle Earth. I called them fairy umbrellas, though my mom warned me if I poked under them I was liable to turn up a brown recluse as a fairy. She taught me to identify the spider by the guitar shape on its back, an alarming image for the child of a guitarist. On mornings after rains, I occasionally looked out my bedroom window to see a large, dark green circle on the yard, maybe ten feet in diameter, where the grass had grown taller. My mom told me they were pixie rings where the fairies had danced the night before. She didn't give me some scientific answer about underground fungi, as I would give my own children (she also didn't have the power of Google). She preserved my sense of wonder, my faith in the unseen. If fairies were real, and if they were *dancing under my window at night*, then surely the universe was wider than my mind.

My mom undertook her new role of farm wife with the plucky aplomb of an actress tackling an audition. My dad bought a used pickup truck for farm chores, an old brown rattletrap with no park gear, only neutral. Each afternoon, my mom loaded a tire in the bed for me to sit in, a seventies version of a child seat (I suppose she could have buckled me into the cabin beside her, but where's the fun in that?). First we'd gather hay from the barn loft, which she scattered around me in the bed like a real hayride, then we'd drive through the pastures distributing the bales. After we flung each bale, we'd tip back our heads and shout my dad's signature cowboy call: *Sewwwwww Cow!* It was my favorite part of the whole affair. Then my mom would scramble back into the truck as soon as the cows came running. No matter how hard she tried, there was little romance in her heart for cattle.

Pasture to pasture we'd go, feeding cows and opening and closing gates. That's what we were doing one sunny afternoon when I was three or four, my mom fiddling with a gate latch while I sat behind her in my trusty tire, eating a bag of Fritos. When she heard the wheels in motion, she turned around to see the truck sailing down a hill, heading straight for a culvert. She'd forgotten to put it in neutral. I can still see her racing behind the truck screaming "LIE DOWN!" But I had as much control over my body as one does on a roller coaster. Finally my adventure ground to a bumpy stop when the truck hit a sapling. Had it made it to the culvert it surely would have flipped, and that might have been the end of me. My mom reached the truck bed and promptly vomited in the grass.

"My Fwitos!" I cried, my lifelong affinity for salty snacks already evident. She wiped her mouth on her flannel sleeve and gazed up at me, this chubby creature scooping up corn chips oblivious to her mortality. That night at dinner, she told my dad he needed a new farmhand.

Soon after we hired a rangy older neighbor named Phillip to take care of the cows, and my mother's life became easier. Leathery and bowlegged, Phillip had a mild intellectual disability, or as my father put it, he was a bubble off plumb. Yet he could speak to animals. My dad might have been born under the sign of Taurus, but he was no match for our bull, an orange beast I named Rutherford B. Hayes after my favorite president's name (when he was acting especially bullish, we called him "Rutherford Behave"). Once when my dad tried to corral the wayward Rutherford, the bull charged at him. He managed to fling himself over a gate just in time to avoid being gored. He called Phillip, who looked the bull square in his big, dopey eyes, mumbled something under his breath, and sauntered away with the bull on a rope like a kitten on a leash.

Whatever notion of rugged individualism my parents had brought with them to the farm was dissipating. My dad was a gentleman farmer, but Phillip was the real deal, and we needed him to be our lifeline to this precarious patch of earth. We soon hired a second farmhand, a handyman named Clyde, who moved into the white house with his wife and son. Though we trusted Phillip and Clyde, we learned to avoid them at night, for both men were heavy drinkers—especially Phillip, who cracked his first can of Pabst Blue Ribbon at lunch and drank continuously throughout the day. My dad would joke that the rows Phillip bushhogged through the field were straight until around three, when they'd turn curly.

Ten years into working for us, Phillip walked into our kitchen one morning and told my dad in his signature Phillip style that he'd been diagnosed with "ferocious of the liver." But before the disease could claim his life, he died in an early-morning car crash. For a decade after his death, we'd find flattened Pabst cans throughout the pastures. *Oh look*, we'd say with fondness, *Phillip was here*.

Those years were prolific for my dad because they had to be. We survived off the breadth of his imagination. One morning when I was very young, my mom took me out of the house to go somewhere—maybe to Nashville to see a movie, followed by a trip to

Baskin-Robbins. Now I realize the outing was designed to give my dad the headspace to write. When we left that morning, he was sitting in a T-shirt and jogging pants at the kitchen table, playing his guitar and ignoring us as he penciled in sheet music with one of his sharpened Blackwing pencils. We returned early evening to find him sitting exactly where we'd left him, the house completely dark except for the light fixture above his head. "Oh Sonny, have you even eaten?" my mom cried as she flipped on the lights. *What was wrong with Sonny?* I worried. *Why hadn't he moved?*—but then my parents were laughing, and my dad said he had a new song to play for us, and I understood that everything was okay, that this was how our family life was meant to be, that it was my father's job to go somewhere in his mind where my mother and I could never reach, and it was our job to facilitate his journey.

Around this time, my dad and I had an argument about something and I threw a temper tantrum that inspired him to pick up his guitar and write a song about me. He originally titled it "It's Not Easy Being Four," but decided the age didn't carry enough stakes, so he changed it to "It's Not Easy Being Fifteen." A tender, painful rendering of adolescence set to a classical melody, it's undeniably one of the most beautiful songs he ever wrote. For years, my mom would request he play it on stage or in living room concerts, and he would introduce it by saying he wrote it for me. *It's not easy finding out who / lives behind that face that everyone knows is you,* the song goes, and my own face would burn as every eye in the room turned to me to find the answer. To this day, I have a hard time listening to that song for the memories it stirs. It reminds me of my own adolescence, which my father could only envision when he wrote it, but it also reminds me of all those awkward concerts when everyone in the room would believe they had a window into my heart.

My dad had given up a promising jingle career in L.A. and now with the exception of occasional Crickets gigs, he was on his own.

CHAPTER 8

So when Waylon Jennings called J. I. to ask if the Crickets wanted to open for him at a few shows in Arizona, it felt like a gift from an old friend—one who happened to sell out 20,000-person stadiums.

My dad had known Waylon since his early DJ days at Lubbock's KLLL. They were both products of the same hardscrabble West Texas world, born one month apart into poor cotton-farming families. Waylon spent his early years in a dirt-floor shack in Littlefield, fifty miles north of my father's dugout. Waylon and the Crickets had seen each other through failed dreams and reversals of fortune, and shared more than flimsy stages and greasy truck stop suppers on the road; they shared a cultural shorthand. Maybe Waylon sought to ease the loneliness of fame and road life by surrounding himself with men who spoke the familiar language of home. Being with the Crickets also helped him heal the primal wound of Buddy's death. It's now the stuff of legend how Waylon relinquished his seat on Buddy's doomed plane to flu-ridden J. P. Richardson, and how he and Buddy ribbed each other afterwards.

I hope your ole bus freezes over, said Buddy.

Well I hope your ole plane crashes, said Waylon.

Those were the last words they ever spoke.

Where my father had honed his pop, jazz, and classical sensibilities in L.A., Waylon was factory-made to be an enormous country star. He had the kind of craggy baritone country music stations hungered for, and he looked like the romantic lead in a Western; or maybe more accurately, the handsome villain, the rogue cowpuncher who would seduce your wife.

The Arizona gigs went so well, he hired the Crickets for more shows, then more, and soon, my father found himself living on the road. And so my memories of him fade nearly as soon as they begin, arriving in glimpses, fragments, broken verse. Black jeans and Lucchese boots, T-shirts embossed with a cartoon eagle in the shape of a W. Time to fly. Two weeks on, one week off. Flagstaff, Chicago, East Coast tour, we'll meet up with you in Louisville. Packing, packing, my mother always packing for my father, my father always patting his pockets, always "in a fizz." He was in charge of his guitar, she took care of the rest. *Bus leaves at noon, I'm in a fizz, Louise! Goodbye, adios, I love you, I'll miss you, I'll be back before Easter, your birthday, Christmas. Be good, be careful, I'll call y'all from the road. Take it easy, greasy, you gotta long way to slide.*

When my dad came home from the road, there was a new tension in the air between my parents. The farmhouse was too small for them to argue in private; even if they went behind closed doors I could hear the vibrations of their angry voices. One argument from that time stands out most of all. In my memory, I'm clenched in a tight ball under the coffee table, listening to my parents scream at each other. My mom hurls a final insult before she retreats to their bedroom off the living room. As she tries to shut the door, my father reaches in and grabs her arm. She yanks from his grip and manages to slam the door. Now my father is really yelling. I cup my hands over my ears but can still hear my father's fists beating against the door, my mother no longer yelling but crying now, her voice ravaged by tears as she begs him, *Please, Sonny, I'm tired. Just go away.*

It's a frightening memory, made more frightening by the fact that it is perhaps my first memory, as if my parents' warfare summoned my very consciousness into being. During a phone call about those years, I summoned the courage and asked my mother about it. *Ohhhhh yeah*, she says. *I remember that fight. I'm sorry you remember it too.*

It was after Dean's funeral, she said. Dean, the middle Curtis brother, died of a sudden heart attack in his forties, leaving behind a wife and three young children. Five years older than my father, Dean was his best friend growing up. He invented country games to play with him for hours on end, building boats out of sticks or tying strings to June bugs' legs and flying them around like tiny kites. Most older brothers would have found these games babyish, but not Dean, my father once told me. He never acted frustrated or bored. *He was just the best big brother in the world.* Growing up, Dean had been a talented fiddle player and a close friend of Buddy Holly's, but he'd abandoned music to support his family, farming the land alongside their oldest brother Pete while my dad chose a different route. When Dean died, a part of my dad died too, a severed link to the earth and people he'd left behind.

After Dean's funeral, my parents and I made the long drive from Texas to Tennessee, arriving home exhausted. J. I. came over that night to offer his condolences, and the men had too much to drink, my mother says. I was owly from travel and she wanted them to shut it down so she could go to bed, a fair enough request. My father was heartsick and wanted another drink with his friend, perhaps equally fair. My mother finally snapped and kicked J. I. out. A fight ensued.

My memory aligned with my mom's story. And while it answered long-held questions, it also made me sad. How vividly had the memory of that fight colored my perspective as a child, led me to choose allegiances at too young an age. Good guys and bad guys, the present, golden mother pleading for peace and the moody, dark-haired father who refused to grant it.

When I was two, my mom suffered her final miscarriage. Dickson didn't have a liquor license back then, much less a hotshot fertility doctor. She was five months pregnant, so far along her own health was threatened, and she spent days recovering in the hospital. My shaken father, home from the road and terrified at the prospect of raising me on his own, announced from my mom's bedside that they were done trying for another baby. Per his way, he spun it into a joke. "Hey man, I got five siblings. Trust me, they're overrated." I can imagine my mom laughing weakly as he squeezed her hand. The matter was settled.

So she was dealing with grief, not only for a lost baby but for her future plans as a mother of siblings. I also think she felt my father dropped his end of the deal in some way, stuck us in the middle of nowhere then left without giving much regard to our day-to-day existence. A few years ago, she and I were standing in my kitchen chopping vegetables for dinner when she blurted out that my dad wouldn't have even heated our home without J. I. shaming him. Our first autumn in Tennessee, the Crickets were about to leave for a gig when J. I. learned our house was unheated and insisted we buy a wood-burning stove. My father apparently hadn't considered the upcoming frost.

"He didn't care about anyone but himself in those days," she said, stabbing a celery through its heart. "He wasn't as sensitive as he is now."

I set down my knife and excused myself to my bedroom, where I lay staring up at the seventies popcorn ceiling above my head. I hated that ceiling. But not as much as I hated hearing that my dad didn't care if his wife and child froze while he was off performing for adoring crowds. Suddenly I was a child again, torn between my parents, weighing evidence like a judge. Who sticks a wife and toddler on a remote farm and leaves without ensuring their basic needs? One point for Mom. But couldn't she have bought the stove herself? One point for Dad, who may have put his career before us, sure, but wasn't that his own form of caretaking, a wrenching drive to support his family and never be poor again? And why did my mom even tell me this? What good does it do me now?

I didn't need to adjudicate every old slight between my parents who were, at this very moment, downstairs engaged in pleasant conversation. The past is the past, however much it shadows the present. They could have separated when I was young but they did not, not then and not ever, for over fifty years. Their marriage was infinitely more complex than a simple tally. Like any long-term relationship, it was a breathing organism that evolved through time, callous and tender, bitter and sweet, always adapting to the facts on the shifting ground.

The Waylon years ushered in a new version of my father: Sleepy Sonny. In a photo taken on Easter Sunday in 1978, he naps stretched out on our narrow picnic bench, his arm flopped on the lawn, his beard long and hair unkempt. I stand looking down at him wearing a dress printed with red apples, my mouth open mid-sentence. A silver can of Stroh's beer sits on the picnic table. To an outsider, the image

CHAPTER 8

startles: a cherubic toddler about to awaken a wild, possibly drunk, creature of the woods.

In one of my earliest memories of him from this era, I am trying to watch *Sesame Street* while he naps on the couch behind me. My mother is in the kitchen clanging pots and pans, that percussive prelude to dinner. "One of these things is not like the others, one of these things doesn't belong," a high-pitched children's chorus sings on TV. The halting rhythm of my dad's snores drowns out the song, but I've seen this one before. It's obviously the square.

My mom has warned me never to wake my dad—*Let him rest, Sarah, he's fried*—but I am three and bored. And so I ignore her warning and climb the hill of his stomach, nestling between him and the couch cushion, its nap as scratchy as his dark beard. He does not stir.

"Wake up, Sonny," I whisper, prying open his eyelids.

"What's goin on?" he mumbles.

"Look, star!" I say, pointing through the window at the first light winking in the dusky sky.

He squints his eyes to see what I am pointing at, then shakes his head and closes them again. "Nope, that's a planet."

"Not planet, Sonny! *Star!*"

He forms a shotgun with his thumb and index finger, points it at the sky and fires. "Sarah, that right there, *click*, that's Venus. Remember our song? *Mary Very Easily Makes Jam. S-U-N spells sun, and then there's Pluto.*" He had devised the mnemonic for the planetary order during Pluto's stint in the pantheon. What I am looking at is the V in Very, he says. The E stands for Earth. That's us. *Stars, moon, planets, sun.* They were the first definitions his parents had likely taught him as well, imposing order on a lawless sky.

He explains how the hours in a day corresponded with the Earth's rotation on its axis. If I want proof of this, I can track the sun's movement throughout the day. As I eat my lunch, it will be right above my head. The sun can tell me where I am too, what direction I am going. I begin to tune him out. *Mary very easily makes jam*, I hum.

"Are you listening?" he asks, poking me in the belly button. "Well," he sighs, "it comes in pretty handy to know where you're goin'. Let's say you're lost on the farm . . ."

"I won't get lost!" I cry. I had memorized the gates.

"Well, you could. While you and Mommy are off feeding the cows. You have to be careful." So many dangers to learn on the farm.

A rich smell wafts from the kitchen, the meat sizzling in the pan as my mother sings Joni Mitchell's "Both Sides Now." As usual, she's sharp.

An idea dawns behind my father's eyes. "Hey, you wanna hear something neat?" He explains how the Earth is spinning twice, rotating and revolving, at that very minute. I close my eyes and try to feel the sway.

"Why aren't we falling off the couch?" I ask. He laughs and gives me a squeeze. There is something invisible around us, he says, something called gravity. It's a law, and it even though we can't see it, it will always hold us down.

Around the time I started kindergarten, construction wrapped on our new farmhouse, the one my father envisioned that day he first saw the property. We moved out of the small white house and into my father's dream, a house made of wood and glass—earth and water, just like my parents.

The first thing that hits me when I close my eyes and summon the glass house is the scent: the warm, herbal base notes of Western cedar. The bedrooms and bathrooms were mostly drywalled, but the rest of the house was made of exposed wood and glass. The house wasn't big but it was tall, three stories if you counted the walk-out basement. The guest bedroom and bathroom were located on the bottom floor along with a living area where my father kept his dartboard, stereo, guitars, and record collection. This was the place where my parents' parties ended up, with raucous dart games and Clapton on the turntable.

CHAPTER 8

To remind them of their honeymoon in Maui, my parents wallpapered the guest room with a Hawaiian mural of palm trees lining a frothy beach. When we were in seventh grade, my friend Jennifer and I took Polaroids of each other posing in front of the mural wearing bikinis, then brought them to school and told people we'd vacationed in Hawaii over the summer. A cute sixth grader nicknamed Jon Boy saw them and passed a note to me in the hall with his number above the words "Call if you like wang." I was grossed out by the note, but also a little excited by it. Jennifer and I had taken the photos as a joke, jutting our hips and pouting as we'd seen models do on the cover of *Mademoiselle*. I had no idea that we were casting a line when we brought them to school, a line that could hook a fish.

The living room on the second floor had glass walls that rose all the way to the rafters. When my parents stood the Christmas tree in the corner each year, the glass walls reflected three Christmas trees, a mirrored hall of Christmas trees, and it almost made up for the lack of snow. The room opened out to a wraparound balcony, my father's favorite spot in the house. After dinner, he might grab his guitar and pick us something new he'd been working on. Sandy would laze happily at his feet gnawing a steak bone, if he was lucky. For all the house's flaws, that balcony remains idyllic in my mind, as perfect as any child's first refuge: the emerald canopy of leaves above my head, the cows mooing from the rolling pasture, the chirrup of a bobwhite perched on the rail.

Inside the living room, a floor-to-ceiling bookcase required a ladder to reach the top. On the highest shelf stood the bronze statue of Buddy, a relic collecting dust on a shelf none of us could reach. I preferred the reference books at the bottom—an *Encyclopedia Britannica* set and my favorite, a series of books on the seven wonders of the world. When I was young, I'd sit cross-legged on the carpet and flip through the photos of the Taj Mahal and the Hagia Sophia, places so far away they seemed accessible only by magic carpet. I never knew what I might discover in the bookcase, each title a code I wanted to crack, and as I grew older I did. Between my father's nutrition books and my mother's Jane Austen collection, I learned where to find Erica Jong.

Next to the bookshelf, a pocket door partitioned off my father's office, another guest bedroom, and the bathroom we all showered in, since our shared bathroom on the top floor held only a clawfoot tub. My parents originally installed the shower with a glass greenhouse overlooking our back lawn and pasture. Showering in a greenhouse! It must have seemed such a refreshing idea in smoggy L.A., but in practice the greenhouse was leaky and cold and my mother never managed to keep the plants alive, so finally she gave up and we were left with a shower on full display to the backyard and anyone who happened to be there. The scenario went like this: I'd step into the shower, lather my hair, then glance outside to see Phillip riding by on a tractor. I'd reflexively drop to my knees below the greenhouse, where I'd hunch over the drain for the rest of my shower. When I became a teenager I gave up and started showering in the basement guest bathroom, which attracted wolf spiders but no farmhands at least.

The glass walls giveth, and the glass walls taketh away. During the day we lived in the forest, but at night we lit up like a factory and the world beyond the glass went dark. The tall trees that cloaked us in the daytime became useless. Occasionally Sandy would bark, and we'd look out to see a car's headlights peering back at us, its tires crunching down the driveway. There was nowhere to hide. My heart would ice over, though it was usually just a wrong turn or a neighbor coming to tell us our cows were loose.

But once when my father was on the road with Waylon, the headlights belonged to our least favorite neighbor, a reclusive salesman rumored to have put a hit on his ex-wife. I was in bed when he showed up. He greeted my mother under the pretense of a farm matter, but grew leering when he found out she was home alone with me. She noticed he was slurring his words—something about his ex-wife getting what she deserved?—and began to wish she hadn't invited him in. Sandy pricked up his ears at the changing cadence of my mother's voice and lunged, baring his teeth as the neighbor bid a quick goodbye and ducked into the night.

CHAPTER 8

A little past the salesman's house, the tree line thickened and Mt. Sinai crumbled into a dirt road. There, perched on a hill, sprawled the A-frame farmhouse belonging to Joe Osborn, the bassist who brought us here in the first place, the one who'd called my father in L.A. to tell him about our farm for sale. Joe and my father were around the same age, both dark-haired and bearded, but where my father had jovial features, Joe resembled a sad bear, with round, brooding eyes. Back in L.A., he'd been a member of the Wrecking Crew, a "first call" bassist who played on some of the biggest hits of the sixties and seventies: Ricky Nelson's "Travelin' Man," Simon & Garfunkel's "Bridge Over Troubled Water," and The Mamas and the Papas' "California Dreamin'," just to name a few. That part halfway through The 5th Dimension's "Aquarius/Let the Sunshine In" when the hippies stop yammering about mystic crystal revelations and the song explodes into euphoric funk? That's Joe Osborn.

I didn't know Joe's impressive resume growing up, but I knew my father admired his didn't-give-a-shit attitude. Joe was not a people-pleaser like my father. Once a powerful L.A. record executive shunned Joe at a Hollywood party, only to stop him at the studio a few days later. "Hey man, I didn't know you were Joe Osborn when I met you the other night," he fawned. "I'm a big fan."

"What are you, some kind of part-time asshole?" said Joe. My dad loved that story. "Part-time asshole" became a permanent part of his lexicon to describe any mercurial person. My mom, however, thought Joe was a full-time asshole. She told me he had a dark side, that he'd made some enemies in L.A., enemies with clout.

Joe and his wife Gwen had four children, two boys and two girls who were all older than me by an average of ten years. When I was a child, the boys were long-haired, rebellious teenagers whom I feared and loved in equal measure.

We were friendly with the Osborns, but not close friends. My father often visited Joe to drink a beer and discuss farm life or the music business, but my mom avoided him, and she pitied Gwen, who in my mind is forever bent over the oven taking out a casserole dish of bubbling enchiladas. My mom also thought the Osborns let their kids run wild, though that didn't stop her from hiring the older daughter to babysit me when I was three, an arrangement that ended when she was arrested for being an accessory to murder.

As the story went, the young woman's boyfriend convinced her to drive the getaway car while he robbed a convenience store, but the robbery went awry. The attendant fought back, and her boyfriend pulled out a gun, fatally shooting the man while she waited in the car. She went to jail for several years after that, though my parents always spoke of her as if she were the victim, not the perpetrator.

When my mom asked me to make the Osborns a Christmas card shortly after the murder, I drew each member of their family as a smiling stick figure, with thick, black bars in front of the older daughter. "Oh no, we can't send them that," my mom said, wincing.

You'd think my parents would have ruled out the Osborns' babysitting services after that, but instead they hired the younger daughter, a painfully shy teenager with cystic acne and Coke-bottle glasses. I felt sorry for her. She reminded me of a fragile mollusk shell curled in upon itself, her back hunched as if she were trying to protect something breakable at her core, as if she were bowed under the weight of her family's troubles and aggression. She ended up babysitting me for my entire childhood.

The glass house was beautiful and dangerous, hiding us by day and exposing us by night. My father kept several rifles under his bed, and the pistol in his bedside table loaded. For years after moving away, I had home invasion nightmares about the glass house that always began the same: the sound of tires on gravel, two headlights peering through the dark.

The glass house felt singular and mythical, but of course it wasn't. On the half-hour drive to the neighboring town of Franklin, my parents and I would pass another house almost identical to ours. My father would ease his foot on the brake, explaining how the owners

CHAPTER 8

My father and me on Easter Sunday, 1978. A holiday break from Waylon's tour. (Photo courtesy of Joanie Allison.)

had used similar blueprints. "I like ours better," my mom would say, and he'd agree. While they parsed out the similarities and differences, I sat in the backseat imagining the people who lived there. I always saw them as an older, childless couple. I didn't think the house was fit for any child but me, a child as singular as Robinson Crusoe, the only girl who'd managed to thrive on my own remote island, a house made of cedar and glass, earth and water.

CHAPTER 9

The Last Waylon Party

And when he played his guitar, the tone was deep and rare
And they lined up at the stage door just to touch his raven hair
—"COWBOY SINGER," 1980

"Now remember," my mother began, "Waylon will be there, and you know how he is, how much he *loves* children." (*Yes*, my father agreed, *he really does love children*.) "If he asks you to sit on his lap and you're feeling shy, you don't have to. But what you *do* have to do—"

"Is be polite," my father cut her off.

"Because he's your father's boss, you know," my mother added.

This always went on too long. "I know, I know!" I said, pretending it was no big deal, that Waylon didn't terrify me. I knew he wasn't an actual monster, but he sure looked like a man halfway through a werewolf transformation. And then there was the way he talked—fast, in a road language I couldn't begin to decipher, though my father spoke it, as well. I think even as a child I understood his power, a strong undercurrent that held everyone in its grip. Or at least it did me.

CHAPTER 9

The year was 1982, and I was seven. My father and the Crickets had been touring with Waylon for nearly five years, almost as long as I'd been forming permanent memories. My mother rarely took me to see the concerts—they were no place for a child. But I do remember one concert she brought me to when I was three, maybe four. In my memory she holds me safely in her arms offstage, barely hidden behind the velvet curtain.

It is the country music outlaw era, and we are flanked by actual outlaws, Waylon's bodyguards Deakon and Boomer—hulking Hells Angels who, for some reason, do not scare me. Maybe because my mother tells me they are my protectors. What scares me is the swell of faces beyond the curtain, the sea of screaming fans glowing red under the house lights. A demonic pit of adoration.

Wave to Daddy! My dad stands beside Waylon, the portion of the show when Waylon and the Crickets perform together. He winks clownishly and shoots a trigger finger at me as if to say *I see you!* Then Waylon turns to see me too. Waylon, hair black and oily, skin glistening with sweat and drugs. Waylon, the eye of the storm, his eyes on me. "Come on out here, darlin'," he says, motioning me onstage with a bearded smile.

No! I shriek, burying my face in the nape of my mother's neck. Her hair smells of cigarettes and Calèche, the perfume my father buys her at Duty Free on his travels home from far-flung tours. "Honey? You want Waylon to introduce you?" she whispers in my ear. I bury my head deeper. "Oh, but you look so pretty!" she pleads. My mother traffics in pretty. She has dressed me in a smocked jumper and patent leather Mary Janes, always preparing for my debut.

In the seventies, Waylon felt constricted by the slick, heavily arranged Nashville Sound, as it was known. In the 1950s, producers Owen Bradley and Chet Atkins had intentionally pivoted away from country's hayseed roots toward more orchestrated arrangements, replacing steel guitars and fiddles with soaring string sections, for example, in order to better compete with rock 'n' roll. Waylon wanted to form a rawer style. This was what the outlaw movement represented at its heart, music truer to country's honky-tonk and rockabilly roots. In line with this shift, Waylon abandoned rhinestone Nudie suits and started dressing like a real cowboy (albeit one with a leather fetish). The substance of the music was rawer too. He sang introspective songs that spoke to a search for freedom, while recognizing that freedom comes with loss. "Mammas Don't Let Your Babies Grow Up to Be Cowboys" chooses an outlaw life over capitalism, even though capitalism is painted as the happier route. "Surely you know my heart is wild," begins "Destiny's Child," a song my father wrote for him in the late sixties. Waylon's heart was very wild.

At that point in my life, I couldn't remember a time when we weren't inside Waylon's force field. He was the reason my father left for two-week stints and returned home lifeless. Touring was different back then. Today when a band goes on the road, the tour is finite, spread over the course of several weeks or months, longer if the band is famous, but eventually the gigs end and the band goes home, gets some rest, and records new material. This was not the case in the seventies and eighties. Musicians toured constantly at the record labels' behest. My father was on the road with Waylon for five solid years. They would take breaks—two weeks on, ten days off—but the tour never stopped. Often gigs would be added while the band was still on the road, their breaks canceled at the last minute.

How did they do it? They took pills. The wheels of the music business had been greased by amphetamines for almost as far back as my father says he can remember. In Nashville, every muso on 16th Avenue was popping fistfuls of Desoxyn and white crosses, including my dad. He was partial to Jack Kerouac's favorite, Benzedrine, or bennies, as everyone called them. And then there were the fabled L.A. turnarounds, a potent dose of the amphetamine Obedrin that musicians joked could keep you awake long enough to drive from Nashville to L.A. and back again. Popping pills was accepted, ubiquitous, and legal. As Waylon wrote in his autobiography, he believed there were drugs and then there were prescriptions: two separate categories, one addictive, one not. Doctors and pharmacists issued no warnings as they handed over scripts. Booking agents passed them out like aspirin.

Every music hub had its own Doctor Feelgood, and in Nashville it was the aptly named Dr. Landon Snapp, a pasty older man whose East Nashville office "looked like a goddamn Grand Ole Opry meeting every Monday morning," the singer Don Bowman once told a biographer. A lot was accomplished under the Snapp administration. Gigs were booked, and someone was always awake enough to take a turn at the wheel after the shows. Songwriters could pop some bennies and stay up writing or recording for days at a time. The seventies were arguably some of Music Row's most creative years—they were certainly Waylon's most prolific. That's the inconvenient truth about drugs. They work, until they don't.

In 1977, Dr. Snapp was convicted on twenty-three counts of illegally distributing amphetamines and sent to federal prison for twelve years. Suddenly a lot of musos found themselves itching for speed and turning to tainted street drugs to score a fix. Where pills had been plentiful, recovery options were stigmatized in this culture built on hardscrabble, working-class values. When addicts "twisted off," as my father put it, they had limited options. They could quietly check into a sanitorium or spend a week in Parkview, a gritty psych hospital on the outskirts of Nashville that Johnny Cash memorialized in his song "Committed to Parkview." Not coincidentally, Snapp's conviction aligned with the advent of cocaine, as musicians like Waylon turned to the drug in order to kick their pill habits, without fully realizing they were revving up a more powerful addiction.

Waylon's coke habit had become a beast more powerful than the Hells Angels he'd hired to be his bodyguards. Of course, I didn't know this on the drive to that party. At age seven, I had no clue what cocaine was or what it could do to a person. That a giant country music star could be overtaken by a white powder that looked like my mother's laundry soap. That our very universe, our livelihood, could be upturned by it. My mother knew, and so did my father; of course they did. But in the backseat of their Buick, I stuck to my directives, laws I wouldn't question. How could I? I looked to my parents like I looked to the sun and the moon, my vision of the world filtered through their light, and their darkness.

The party was at J. I.'s farmhouse, a half-hour drive from the glass house, down a winding rural highway outside Nashville. When we pulled into J. I.'s driveway, I saw a few burly bearded men tossing horseshoes on the front lawn and drinking cans of Stroh's. My parents greeted them by their entourage nicknames: Jigger, Crank, Boomer, Joe Beautiful. And then there was Deakon, Waylon's head bodyguard, a hulk of a man with a wild gray beard (I have only the blurriest memory of Deakon, and when I asked my mother to remind me what he looked like, all she offered was, "like a scary motherfucker"). Waylon may have been a country music outlaw, but the Hells Angels were some of the most notorious outlaws in America, their violent counterculture mythologized in books of the era by Hunter S. Thompson and Tom Wolfe. Waylon and the Angels were a natural fit.

We entered the house through a narrow mudroom, its brick walls glinting with gold Buddy Holly records. Inside the kitchen, a few of the musicians' wives and girlfriends sat gossiping around a breakfast table, body-permed bees in the center of the hive. Like my mother, they wore cowboy boots, 501 Levi's, and oversized sweaters. Their hair was loosely tousled; their faces, lightly kissed by makeup. They didn't have to try too hard. They weren't groupies.

My dad often dreaded these events—offstage he was an introvert, and parties placed him in what he dubbed "the conspicuous zone." Music parties were my mom's domain, the places she most truly came alive, flitting from room to room and greeting everyone with a little high-pitched shriek, all the while mining the room for gossip. Parties gave her material to entertain her through the week. On the drive home or on the phone with friends the next day, she polished her gems. From the next room, I'd listen to her dish about some musician's latest fortune or foible, honing her delivery. Her gossip taught me that life giveth twice: once in the living and later in the telling.

CHAPTER 9

Sounds from the adjacent living room flowed through the house in constant, heavy waves—the men's explosive laughter and the reverb from the stereo. My father headed in that direction while I hung back with my mother in the kitchen. There, the music was lighter, safer: the women's languid Southern vowels, the hiss of the soda as it hit the ice, the highballs clinking merrily. *Cheers.*

My mother poured me a Coke, forbidden in our home, and I gulped it down greedily. Soon, I grew bored listening to the women's gossip, veiled references to people I didn't know. My mother, perhaps eager to be rid of me so she could talk freely, suggested I go see Samson and Delilah, the billy goats that J. I. and his wife Joanie kept penned beside their barn. But first, she added with a raised eyebrow, it would be nice if I said hi to Waylon.

I paused under the arched doorway to the living room while my eyes struggled to adjust to the shadows. Above Roger Miller's nasal vibrato rising from the turntable, I made out the sound of my father's laughter and stumbled half-blindly in the direction of his voice. He sat on the couch, telling an old rock 'n' roll story.

"Hey there, li'l sweetheart," he said, pausing his conversation to pull me onto his lap. My father never acted anything less than thrilled to be interrupted by me, whether he was in the middle of transcribing a song or telling a joke. He rarely came to me; I had to seek him out, as I do to this day. But when I did, his eyes would register a sudden mixture of surprise and relief, as if he had recovered a lost treasure, a crumpled hundred-dollar bill in the pocket of some old Wranglers. Something wonderful he'd forgotten he had.

"Who's that pretty girl?" Waylon boomed. He knew me, of course.

"Hi, Waylon." I twisted my lips into a smile.

"Come on over here, hon."

I wound my way to the end of the room where Waylon sat shooting dice at a card table in the corner, his shoulder-length hair stringy with oil, his back to the wall. It would have been where Don Corleone chose to sit—a place of power and visibility. He ashed his cigarette and threw a flannel arm around my shoulder.

"You're gettin' prettier every time I see you, you know that?" He held me at arm's length while he examined me. That was Waylon's style, to relate to women through flattery and objectification. Sizing me up was how he began every conversation with me, whether I was seven, thirteen, or twenty-six, the last time I saw him, when I visited his tour bus before catching one of his final performances in Chicago, where I was living at the time. As I grew older I understood that he was more than a little sexist, and also that sexism was how he expressed admiration for women. *After all the shit you gotta put up with in this crazy world,* his attitude seemed to suggest, *how do you still manage to look so fine?* I'd be lying if I denied the boost his words, his gaze, sometimes gave me. Especially when I was thirteen, with pimples and new glasses, which, over dinner at a Chinese restaurant with my parents, he said suited my face beautifully and which I then began wearing to school with pride.

"Can you believe this pretty girl belongs to Ol' Son?" he asked the men at his table, who politely laughed, emitting a cloud of stale beer breath. It didn't come from Waylon, who never had a taste for alcohol. He smelled of something different, sweat and smoke mixed with a sour perfume I did not like. "You know I've known your daddy since we was kids?" he asked. "Ain't he a good guitar player?"

"I guess," I said with a shrug.

"What do you mean, *you guess?*" asked Waylon.

I did not know what I meant. Waylon laughed and squeezed my shoulder.

"Well, it sure is good to see you, beautiful. I feel sorry for your daddy. Those ole nasty boys are gonna be beating down your door soon." *Boys? Ick.*

Waylon chuckled and patted me goodbye. "We know who her daddy is," he said as I felt my way back through the dark room. "Still tryin' to figure out who's her mama." Behind me, the men erupted in laughter at this familiar Waylon joke, one I'd heard him make before about other musicians' kids. Today, I better understand his brand of comedy, how he liked jokes that turned the usual syntax on its head, but back then I wondered why it was so funny to pretend nobody knew our mothers. Maybe that was part of the joke as well, to exclude through language, to draw a tight circle around the living room, or the tour bus, or whatever space Waylon occupied. The inner sanctum: you were either in it, or you were out, and aside from Jessi Colter, Waylon's wife and fellow musician, women were out. Sometimes, even Jessi.

Outside, a car pulled up and a member of Waylon's entourage got out along with her young daughter Allie. I'd played with Allie before at an earlier Waylon party, where we'd bonded over our deep affection for Joan Jett. Though I was thrilled to see another kid my age, something wasn't right. Despite the crisp fall weather, Allie wore no coat over her flimsy pink princess dress, the kind you find in the toy aisle of a drugstore. She was knuckling her eyes, which she had rimmed in cornflower blue, the crayon I used to color in skies. It looked as if she had colored outside the lines of her face, smeared red crayon in wide circles around her mouth and cheeks. After a few seconds, I realized it was lipstick; she'd gotten into her mother's makeup drawer. Her mother had gotten into the liquor cabinet.

"I let Allie dress herself!" she shrieked to the horseshoe players before weaving off to mingle.

Allie stood alone, a lost clown. After a few beats, a guitarist's wife named Pat, a friendly woman with straw-colored hair to her waist and a gravelly smoker's voice, approached her. "Come on, honey. Let's go wash your face," she said, taking the little girl by the hand and leading her into the house.

It was Allie who broke through my mother's carefully constructed wall of denial. It wasn't the Hells Angels and their threat of head-breaking carnage always bubbling below the surface, or the partygoers lurching in and out of the bathroom, eyes afire, or even Waylon's sweat-drenched mania. It took a blameless child to do the job. Seeing Allie was "a turning point," my mother later told me, and in that moment, she made a decision: there would be no more Waylon parties for me.

There weren't many left for Waylon either. The following year, 1984, his addiction would nearly eat him alive. When he began missing shows because he was too high or sick, he and Jessi retreated to her home state of Arizona, where he would dry out for good, though his health never fully recovered.

After Waylon got clean I saw that, stripped of his drug-addled werewolf persona, he had a tender side. The summer after I graduated college, I attended a barbecue at the home of the Crickets' bassist Joe B. It was a small backyard party, maybe ten family friends, and at some point Joe B. and his wife put on fifties rock 'n' roll and everyone set down their paper plates and broke into the jitterbug. I didn't know how to jitterbug, and so I sat on the patio next to Waylon, the only other person not dancing. He was battling complications from diabetes, though even healthy, Waylon wasn't the jitterbug type. As we watched the dancers, he asked me about my college experiences, my career plans, and of course, because he was Waylon, why I didn't have a boyfriend. Waylon was trying to be real with me, but I found it impossible to be real with him, rotating the conversation back to him at every turn, wondering, *Why in the world would Waylon Jennings want to hear about me?*

I've never liked meeting famous people. My parents tell the story of how, when I was four or five, they took me to J. I.'s house for a barbecue hosting Keith Richards and his then-girlfriend Patti Hansen, who were staying in his guesthouse (J. I.'s house has always attracted a spectacular array of wayward musicians). Despite the sweltering July heat, the couple was dressed head-to-toe in black leather. I stayed close to my father's side, burying my face in his hip and whining for him to take me home until he eventually scooped me up and made an excuse to leave. My mom says I was frightened of Keith's strange clothes and kohl-rimmed eyes, and that is probably true. Though I wonder if even then I sensed an electricity surging through the muggy air, a molecule shift I've always been able to divine when I enter a famous person's space. It's not that I'm afraid they'll disappoint me, or I'll disappoint them (though I don't like being cast as a perv, or worse, a melon). Exchanges between the famous and the non-famous just feel so contrived, so performative, everyone's roles predetermined before we open our mouths. I don't like fame's power, the way it thrusts people in its orbit like those nightmarish Gravitron rides at the county fair. I find myself unable to breathe. I say stupid things, then hate myself for saying them, then hate myself most for hating myself. I don't like the person I become around the famous, a glommer-on whose morals, I suspect, could be easily compromised. I become something worse than a perv or a melon, fans whose motives are at least authentic. I become a fraud.

My dad once told me that as a young musician, he wanted to be famous more than anything on Earth. And yet, as the years passed, celebrity began to assume the dark pall of a curse. "Fame destroys people," I've heard him say, and he's seen the body count to prove it. But did fame destroy Waylon? Maybe what fame destroys is the normal currents of human interaction, the tidal rhythms of friendships and love affairs reversing direction around a star, flowing in but rarely out. Maybe what fame destroys is gravity itself.

What transpired during those Waylon years, what my father witnessed (or participated in), is a question he skirts, one I've tried to answer by reading primary sources about the era—in this case, co-written celebrity autobiographies: Waylon's 1996 *Waylon*, Jessi Colter's 2017 *An Outlaw and a Lady*, and the most sordid of the three, 2016's *Waylon: Tales of My Outlaw Dad*, by Waylon's late son, Terry Jennings.

Here's what I've learned, or at least what's been published. By all three accounts, Waylon was an insatiable womanizer and adulterer. On the road, he booked multiple hotel rooms for his mistresses, even if Jessi was on tour with him. According to Terry, if he had his sights on a groupie who was with another member of his entourage—even his son—he would call the man's room and tell him to "pass the biscuits." He called his groupies "snuff queens," which one online dictionary defines as a sex worker and another as a woman who trades sex for cocaine, which sounds about right. Waylon was arrested by the Feds for cocaine possession and conspiracy to distribute in 1977, the year before my father took the tour gig. A powerful lawyer who had worked for Robert Kennedy eventually got him off. But "one thing the bust didn't do was slow down my drug use," Waylon wrote in his autobiography. He liked to cut McDonald's straws in half and pump them full of cocaine and crushed-up speed, then keep the straws in his shirt pocket where he could snort them every fifteen minutes. He gave straws to his older kids, instructing them to snort out of both nostrils to avoid feeling "lopsided," which has to be the saddest fatherly advice I've ever heard. But if you always get what you want in life, what incentive do you have to be a moral human being? Absolute power corrupts absolutely, and unless you're born with the soul of a saint, the same can be said of fame.

At the height of Waylon's addiction, he was blowing through $1,500 a day on coke. By 1981, his drug abuse and financial mismanagement had landed him two and a half million dollars in the hole. To avoid bankruptcy and dig his way out, he fired much of his entourage and stepped up his tour schedule, and that tour involved my father. "The newly trimmed version of the Waylon Jennings traveling carnival, featuring the Crickets . . . hit the road," Waylon wrote. "Slowly, show by show and month by month, I put money aside for the debt." In other words, paying off Waylon's cocaine debts was partially the reason my father was on the road so much during my childhood.

Calling my prudish father to ask him about this depravity is, shall we say, "delicate," but I do it anyway one crisp March afternoon. I ask him if he read Terry's book first, because Terry thanked him in the acknowledgments. He hasn't. "Should I?" he asks, sounding nervous. I tell him he can skip it, and give him a sanitized version of the highlights, or rather, lowlights. No, the irony is not lost on me, that I'm sugarcoating a toxic music scene to a man who actually lived it, but how do you ask your eighty-two-year-old father if he remembers said biscuits being passed?

I skip the snuff queens and focus on the drugs. He admits he was no angel, but says he tried to care for his health, despite the temptations. He clung to the hippie wisdom he'd found in the aisles of L.A. health food stores, our kitchen cabinets always stocked with wheat germ, kelp, Bragg's vinegar, and shelves and shelves of supplements. One night on the tour bus, he sat next to Waylon and tried to persuade him to take vitamins. "I said, 'Waylon, if you're gonna do bad things to your body you gotta put something back. Don't just do damage, take some vitamins!'"

"Thanks, Hoss," said Waylon. "I'll think about it."

Besides swallowing fistfuls of supplements every morning, my father had another hard-and-fast rule, he tells me. "After the show ended at eleven or midnight, you're keyed up and it's hard to go to sleep. There was generally a party on one of the buses or back in the hotel, and I'd stop by for a few drinks. But I learned early on DO NOT STAY UP WITH EVERYBODY ALL NIGHT LONG. There's a gig tomorrow! I want to feel good for the gig! And so I had a personal rule." He pauses for effect. "Four o'clock was my bedtime. I never stayed out past four."

"*Four?*" I ask. I say that's still pretty late . . . or early.

"Well!" he says with a huff. "I thought four o' clock was suitable."

Such were the monkish laws laid down by my father, arguably the most disciplined member on one of the most debauched tours in country music history.

On a springtime visit to my parents' house, I ask my mother if she knew Waylon's tour was a drugged-up orgy from the start. We've finished eating sandwiches for lunch, and my two youngest daughters have left the table and moved into the family room, where I can hear them singing a goofy song, rhyming *waiter* with *tater*. "Well yeah, I guess so," she admits. She describes meeting a road manager in Waylon's entourage early in the tour. Like Waylon, he kept a baggie of cocaine and a straw in his shirt pocket, often pausing his conversation to take a snort. "They were all into it," she says with a bemused laugh as she rises to clear our plates. "But your dad didn't want anything to do with the groupies. He didn't like hookers. Well, maybe as a teenager he went to Juárez a few times, but that was different. Everybody did that."

"Juárez? Wha—uh, never mind. What I'm asking is, if you knew all that about Waylon's tour, why did Dad take the job?"

"Are you kidding?" She looks at me as if I asked why water is wet. "It was the height of Waylon's career. We had just moved here from L.A., and your dad was trying to reestablish himself as a songwriter in a new town. We needed a steady income. And, you know, it was the good road."

The good road. I've heard my father use that term before. Before (and after) life with Waylon, the Crickets schlepped their own gear from gig to gig, highway hotel to highway hotel, through smoke-filled casinos, and down congested city sidewalks. They set up their own sound checks before the shows, adjusted their own amps, and traveled in a rickety RV sold to them by an aging Grand Ole Opry star (when he saw they'd replaced his stained carpet, he said, "Why'd you do that? You probably threw out a hundred pills!") That was the bad road.

The good road was different. Even "newly trimmed," as Waylon put it, his entourage included two eighteen-wheelers for the sound equipment and three large buses—one for Waylon, Jessi, and their bodyguards, one for his band the Waylors, and one for the merchandise—along with a smaller RV for the Crickets they nicknamed "the weeniemobile." Instrument techs and sound engineers managed everything; all my father had to do was show up. Every time he walked onstage, a roadie would sling his guitar strap around his neck, his instrument already tuned, his strings replaced. He found the microphone perfectly positioned to his height. After he performed, he'd hand his guitar to the roadie to tune for the next show, then stroll into the night to find a town car waiting to take him back to the hotel. That was the good road. For my father, anyway.

I consider my mother's rationale as I watch my daughters singing in the living room, laughing themselves delirious over their song. *I really wanna date her, but I'm just a waiter, servin' up fried po-taters.* Even at eight and ten, they're starting to learn the score.

CHAPTER 9

The good road, circa 1980. (From author's collection.)

Seventies party. (Clockwise from left): My father, J. I., Joe B., Don Everly, Joanie, my mother and me, Karen Everly. (From author's collection.)

As I watch their unburdened faces, I think about the family dysfunction I hide from them, the violent news stories I switch off before they can hear, the barriers I construct to wall out the messier parts of their world. I think about mortgage payments and sacrifices, choices and complicity. I think about how my youngest is eight, the same age I was at that last Waylon party.

"Yeah, I get it," I say. It isn't a lie to smooth over the moment. I do get the witchery of fame. And though I would have made some different choices than my parents, if Waylon's traveling carnival had offered me a ride, I might have climbed aboard. Scratch might. The truth is, I would have done the same thing.

CHAPTER 10

Sonny Comes Home

*That road out there goes everywhere
But I can't seem to find my way back
To where I used to be*
—"EAGER FOR THE EDGE," 1980

Many people remember the day their father left. I remember the day mine came home. It was a Saturday morning when I was eight. The glass house was so camouflaged in the trees, songbirds frequently flew into the windows before falling like stones to the second-floor balcony, where they'd sit cockeyed for an hour before shuddering their wings into flight. When I awoke that morning and walked downstairs, I found my father sitting on the couch drinking coffee, looking as stunned as the birds.

My father's dazed expression after coming off Waylon's tour bus was nothing new to me by then, so I took little notice. Opposite him on the chaise lounge, my mother slumped deflated in cotton pj's, raking her fingers through her bangs, a nervous habit that stood them on end. Usually when I entered a room, she greeted me like the second coming. This morning, she barely looked up.

Other than their tableau, I don't remember much—not the season, nor the weather. There was sunlight of course, as there always was in the glass house, but I don't recall whether it was a bright summer glare or a bloodless winter sky. I don't remember the color of the leaves flickering past the glass walls, or if the trees were bare. I only remember the emotional weather in that living room: cloudy. *Bad vibes*, as my mother would say.

Before I could turn on Bugs Bunny, my mom asked me to join them. I plopped down on my father's Casio keyboard bench and started hammering out "Hava Nagila" on harpsichord, full volume. My mother shushed me, and that's when I knew something serious was afoot. "Hava Nagila" was her favorite. "We have something to tell you," she said, her eyes fixed on my father. "Your dad is going to be home a lot more from now on. He's off Waylon's tour."

I turned to my father. "Why?" I asked, but he appeared to be busy reading his future in his coffee grounds.

My mother chewed her thumbnail for a minute, then launched into a curious story: Waylon was on a European tour that didn't include the Crickets, though he had brought along J. I. on drums. But he and J. I. had fought for some reason, and J. I. quit the tour, leaving Waylon without a drummer. It was a drastic move on J. I.'s part, one that immediately severed the chance of the Crickets ever touring with Waylon again.

In that moment, the full weight of J. I.'s action had not fully settled on my parents' shoulders. They looked like they'd witnessed their basement being flooded and were trying to figure out how to suction up the water before they could assess the damage. One question stood out to me above all others—a childish one, though the answer was childish too. "What did they fight about?" I asked.

My mother rolled her eyes. "Oh, you know ... cards," she said.

"Cards?"

"Yes," she sighed. "Cards."

My dad had recently taught me to play gin, and each time I retracted a card I'd just laid he'd bark at me: "They'd cut off your hand in Vegas for that!" The image of a bloody stump where my hand used to be popped into my head every time I reached to withdraw a card, and made me reconsider. I wondered if that's what J. I. had done wrong. Still, it seemed a stupid reason to break up a band.

It's a question I tried to resolve over thirty years later on a visit to my parents' house.

"I told you *what?*" my mother asked.

"You said they broke up over cards. That's what I thought for, well, forever."

My mother threw her head back and let loose a full-throated laugh. "Oooooh boy, I don't remember that," she said. "I guess I didn't want to say cocaine."

Back in that cloudy 1983 living room, she tried to lighten the mood. "Won't it be nice having your dad around more?" she asked, her voice rising a half-step above its mark. Sharp, my father called it. I knew not to trust that tone. And I wasn't sure I wanted my dad around more. He'd been gone so long my mom and I had grown used to his absence, to eating takeout pizza, or chop suey out of a can, or Hungry-Man dinners on TV trays while we watched *Family Feud* and then, if we were too lazy to change the channel, *Hee Haw*. We made fun of *Hee Haw*, though my dad had guest-starred on it in 1980 (if you achieved any country success in 1980s Nashville, sooner or later you'd have to jump out of the Kornfield).

My father didn't want to eat frozen chicken in front of *Hee Haw*. He wanted the table set and a martini poured. He wanted his ribeye cooked medium rare and his salad served on a separate plate. He didn't care much for school gossip as my mother did, but preferred to tell cornball jokes and old rock 'n' roll stories. And in the months leading up to that day, he'd begun asking me to call him Dad. I'd always called him Sonny, which he thought was cute until my teachers started asking questions. *Is Sonny your father?*

A coke-fueled card fight was a bad way to say goodbye, but it was probably time for the tour to end and us to become a family again. If only we could remember how.

I wonder if every family has an era when they feel the most harmonious, a time when they can look back and agree, *that was it, our happiest time.* I wonder this when I see photos from my children's toddler years, their sweet faces rapt in everyday awe at butterflies and fireworks. *We were happiest then and I was too exhausted to know it.* Now they are older and more independent. They speak their minds and hold me accountable for my sins. But I love their minds. I enjoy their company (for the most part). I've softened into a familiarity with motherhood. Maybe one day I'll look back and realize that this era is actually our happiest time. At times I can see glimpses of it, after the school conferences and driving lessons and volleyball games, when the sun sinks beneath the pines and the day's work is done. *This is it,* I think, *you must remember this, o happiest of days.* But as Mac Davis sang of growing up in Lubbock, sometimes happiness is clearest in your rear-view mirror.

If I were to pinpoint the happiest time with my parents, it would be those post-Waylon years. My mother was slowly settling in to her new community. She joined the PTA, as well as the board of a nonprofit for disabled adults. She began dressing more modestly, in long flowered skirts and blouses that covered her tattoo. She made friends with a tall, gregarious woman named Judy, whose youngest daughter Martha was my age. Judy was a stay-at-home mom whose husband owned a local insurance company, his wide smile plastered on a billboard overlooking Dickson's main highway. The family lived in a comfortable ranch house where they employed a full-time housekeeper, a soft-spoken Black woman they called Nanny who had also been Judy's nanny when she was a girl. My mom told me Judy had grown up in Nashville and attended private schools. That tracked. I wasn't sure how she'd ended up in Dickson, but it was clear Dickson did not deserve her.

If I could have drawn the perfect mother, I would have drawn Judy, colored in her auburn helmet of hair (she had a standing Saturday "wash and set" appointment) with burnt sienna, chosen green and navy for her pleated pants and matching sweater sets. She wore Etienne Aigner loafers and monogrammed sweaters and she used the word *accessorize* a lot. Judy's matching clothes, her lilting

Southern accent—Martha was *Mahhh-tha*—the unflappable ease with which she managed her surroundings. She was a chef's kiss: perfection in my book.

Judy had a lot of friends and imitators, so I wasn't sure why this goddess of a woman took my mother under her neatly feathered wing. Maybe she felt sorry for my mom, with her bohemian wardrobe, Midwestern accent, and long-haired husband who was never around. Not that Judy's husband was around much either, or rather, he was there in the way my friends' fathers all seemed to be, ignoring us from another room, an ancillary cog in the household machinery.

When my mom met Judy, my life improved in measurable ways. First, Judy clued her in to a sneaky way to privatize the public school system. On an assigned day each spring, parents could stand in line at five a.m. to choose their child's teacher for the upcoming school year. My kindergarten teacher Mrs. Robertson had been a sadistic, beehived matron who paddled five-year-olds with glee in her eyes and menace in her heart (she even claimed to have an "electric paddle" under her desk for the worst offenders), but post-Judy, my elementary teachers were kind and professional, and I always had the same core classmates, mostly white children of doctors, lawyers, bankers, and educators.

When summer rolled around, Judy convinced my mom to let her sponsor us for a pool membership at the Dickson Country Club. Summers on the farm were miserably hot and buggy, and there were only so many days my mother and I could spend roaming the library checking out the same James Michener and Beverly Cleary books. I made more friends at the country club, girls whose mothers dressed like Judy, in polo shirts and culottes. The moms didn't wear swimsuits because they never got wet. How I loved their honeysuckle accents, the way their vowels swayed midair. *Hello, Miss Say-rah!* They had Reagan/Bush '84 stickers on their station wagons and Jacqueline Susann novels in their Lands' End boat totes. They didn't have boats but they sure had anchors, children and churches and ruddy-faced husbands who golfed. They were small-town royalty, perfectly jello-ed in their molds. Why couldn't my mother be more like them?

My mother sat in the shade of an elm, reading Paul Theroux's snarky take on the *Orient Express*. She wore a tropical-print tank suit under a lacy cover-up. She thought Reagan was a moron and Jacqueline Susann wrote trash. But the thing that made my mother perhaps the most different was this: she swam.

When she got too hot, she'd set down her book, fling off her sunglasses, and saunter past the watchful mothers, down the baby steps and into the water where she'd unfurl like a jellyfish, her legs frogging out behind her as she dipped below the rope. Near the end of the pool she'd emerge and float belly-up, her face relaxing in ecstasy. Sometimes she'd let out a loud sigh. A few feet away, I'd be playing Marco Polo or underwater tea party with my friends. I pretended not to see her, but she was hard to miss.

Does your mom have a tattoo? A friend would always notice. Every time.

It's with wonder and some respect that I realize now how little my mother cared what the other mothers thought of her. I don't remember her ever getting hurt feelings about being excluded—why would she? She didn't want to be included. She would have preferred a stomach flu to a chicken salad luncheon at the club. The one and only time my parents ate dinner there, guests of Judy and her husband, the evening ended awkwardly when Judy's husband announced his past support for Vietnam. But it didn't matter, not really. My parents had only accepted the invitation as a friendly gesture. They had no interest in participating in the Dickson social scene. They had the luxury to make that choice. I did not.

That's not to say my mom didn't like some of the other mothers; she did. But they were acquaintances, not friends. Nashville was her social universe, not Dickson. She had her real best friend Joanie nearby, her sisters a phone call away, my father home to help out more around the farm, and, most importantly, she had me. Oh how my mother loved having me home with her during school breaks! The saddest I remember her being in those years is when I returned to school each fall. I was her "Merry Sunshine," as she liked to call me, after the nickname Ramona Quimby's mother gives her. My job was to be happy for my mom, to relay school gossip for her each afternoon like a spy, to add excitement and sunlight to her life.

When I was eight or nine, I figured out that if I wanted to fit in with the other kids in my school, a few things needed to be different. My mom needed to stop packing me tomato and cheese on sprouted wheat and start packing me ham on white. She needed to stop buying her clothes at a Mexican import store in Nashville and start shopping at Talbot's like Judy. And most especially, we needed a church.

Dickson didn't have a Lutheran church, my mom's childhood religion, so she decided the next best thing was St. James Episcopal, a small building a block away from the massive Walnut Street Church of Christ, a brick superstructure where many of my friends attended. By this point, she'd sussed out a few Democrats in town who'd given her positive reviews of St. James's thirty-something minister, Father Mauldin. When my mom and I attended one Sunday, we were instantly smitten. Father Mauldin was dynamic and nerdily handsome, with a kind presence that relaxed me like a glass of warm milk before bed. Children are natural telepaths when it comes to vibes, and I could feel the grown-ups around me vibrating with love each time he took the pulpit. As for my mom, she adored Father Mauldin and his pretty blonde wife so much, she did something out of character for her in Dickson and invited them to our house for dinner.

I can't remember the meal or the conversation that night, but I'm guessing Father Mauldin asked my dad why he never came to church with us, and my dad told him about his Pentecostal upbringing and his hang-ups over organized religion, and Father Mauldin, because he was Father Mauldin, probably said something reassuring and profound. After dinner, the adults retreated to the living room with their glasses of wine and that's when I did something inexplicable, something that still makes me cringe.

First, I took wooden sticks from my mom's pasta drying rack and arranged them in my hair in a kind of demented Kabuki theater getup. Then, I performed a mime act I'd rehearsed in my afterschool acting class where I was stuck in a box. My parents laughed (my dad loved it when I hammed it up, a performer to his core), and Father Mauldin and his wife pretended to find it enthralling. Now I wonder: Why? Why the pasta sticks? Why any of it? In front of our *minister*? But I'd been trained to see performances as offerings, and I think this was my little pearl of vulnerability for Father Mauldin, this magic man who made my mother so happy each Sunday.

Maybe we should have seen it coming. A minister as good as Father Mauldin doesn't last long in a run-down church in a small town, but still when he announced he was moving on to a bigger church in Florida, we were crushed. My mom took to her bed with an old-school case of the vapors. I ceased my confirmation studies, never to return to them. Nothing gold can stay.

Father Mauldin could not be replaced, but replaced he was by a towering man named Father Wood. Unlike Father Mauldin, he didn't see my mom and me as a self-contained unit, but rather a three-legged stool missing a leg. When he found out my mom was married, he made recruiting my dad part of his mission. "We'd love to see Sonny here next week," he'd purr as we made our way out of each Sunday service, giving my mom a lingering, two-palmed handshake. She'd reply that my dad didn't exactly "do" church, her eyes darting toward the parking lot. Father Wood would cock his head and ask another question about my dad, and my mom, because she was my mom, would answer honestly—*because he's traumatized by organized religion*—which only delayed our freedom. My stomach grumbled and my tights itched, but Father Wood stood between us and the outside world like a sentry whose weekly riddle we had to solve in order to pass through his gates, and it became clear to me, if not my mom, that trashing organized religion was not the correct answer.

On the last Christmas we attended St. James, Father Wood got his way. He must have caught my mom in a benevolent mood, warmed by the holiday spirit, for she agreed to direct our congregation's nativity play and felt no nepotistic shame in casting me as Mary. Maybe it was my debut acting role that lured my father in, though he came as a performer, not as a congregant. He sat in the pew nearest the exit strumming "What Child Is This?," his guitar both his sword and his shield, his entrée into and physical buffer against the world. From the altar, I cradled my plastic newborn and felt aligned with the universe in a way I rarely did. Here we were, a family like almost every other family in our town: one together at church on Christmas.

After that Christmas, my mom and I took a few years' hiatus from church. She seemed relieved, but I missed the ritual. Sure, church was boring, but at least it had been a way to break up the monotony that was a Sunday on our farm. After *Siskel & Ebert* was over, nothing came on TV until my parents ordered pizza and watched *60 Minutes*, and between the two programs lay one long stretch of listening to my dad practice his guitar while I watched dust particles float through the air and the cat twitch in her sleep.

When I was thirteen, I convinced my mom to give church another try. She refused to go back to St. James; the Presbyterian church downtown was the obvious choice because it was the only other church where Democrats attended. I was on board because so did several cute boys from my school. One summer day, I looked out the window to see a sedan rambling down our driveway kicking up dirt clouds. It parked in front of our house and a tall, beefy man with a full head of silver hair got out. My mom introduced him to me as the minister of First Presbyterian. "Call me Preacher Bill," he boomed, delivering a crushing handshake. I excused myself to read in my bedroom, but Preacher Bill's pulpit voice carried, distracting me from the *Dawn Treader*'s voyage.

I could hear him telling my mom of his former college football career at the University of Tennessee, to which she made zero attempt to feign interest, and then they moved on to discuss novels in the living room bookshelf, more familiar terrain for her. After an hour at the kitchen table eating coffee cake and schmoozing my mom, Preacher Bill hollered goodbye to me from the bottom of the stairs.

"He was nice enough," my mom reported after he left. "Kind of pompous. I told him I don't buy predestination. But he promised he won't pressure your dad into coming, so I guess we've got a new church."

Being off Waylon's tour was clearly good for my dad's health. His mood improved, and he had more energy. He was home a lot more, for he hadn't just left Waylon's tour; he'd also left the Crickets. There were many reasons for the split, some I know and others I can only speculate about. My father and J. I. loved each other as brothers, and they could fight like brothers. They were sick of each other, sick of performing the same old Buddy Holly hits night after night. So the Crickets hired a replacement lead singer while my dad and J. I. retreated to their respective pastures to lick their wounds inflicted by years spent stage-wired and road-weary, strung out on fame and tour bus cocaine.

Our family life assumed a comforting rhythm. I went to school, my mom took care of the house and lawn, and my dad plowed the fields and wrote songs. Being away from the Crickets allowed him to focus on composing and producing. He signed as a songwriter with Tree Publishing and spent his days writing in a closet-sized room he rented on Music Row, capping off his day's work with other songwriters over a beer at Brown's Diner. In the evenings when he wasn't in the studio, he played us his latest arrangements. I liked his faster songs; my mom preferred his ballads. She was thrilled about his career shift into songwriting and loved the new muso friends he made at Tree, a few of them ex-hippies from California like her. They hosted a backyard barbecue for their new friends, mostly jolly, middle-aged men with beards and flannel shirts. Among the guests was Harlan Howard, Nashville's patron saint of songwriters, the legendary composer who coined the phrase that a good country song is "three chords and the truth." Nobody disappeared into the bathroom to snort straws. Nobody got high and neglected their kids. Everyone took their casserole dishes and left at a reasonable hour, because the drive back to Nashville was long and dark.

My parents grew especially close with a slightly younger couple during this period, Jim Haber and Cheryl Ebarb. Jim was a lanky piano prodigy from New York who'd performed with Waylon and the eclectic Western swing band Asleep at the Wheel under the stage name Floyd Domino. His new wife Cheryl was an actress fresh off a stint playing the original Shy on Broadway's *The Best Little Whorehouse in Texas*. Beautiful and unaffected, she wore her long, auburn hair slightly unkempt and dressed in jeans, baggy sweatshirts, and no makeup, which was refreshing in the South. After Cheryl gave birth to a baby boy, my mom and I would sometimes drive to Nashville to visit them while my dad and Jim were working. We'd lounge around the living room passing the baby back and forth while Cheryl regaled us with the most amazing stories in her sleepy Texan accent. She told me about anorexic ballerinas she'd known in New York City who lived on nothing but ice cream. There was an ongoing saga about a Hollywood actor who was cheating on his megastar wife with Cheryl's naïve, also famous, actress friend. But my favorite stories she told were of growing up in a haunted house in Texas where mirrors bounced off walls and antique lace dresses floated off their hangers. Like my mom, Cheryl lacked a filter when it came to children, or she understood that children crave good stories. I thought she and Jim were the coolest couple on Earth.

When I was seven or eight, Cheryl gave me a VHS tape of Paul Reubens' original Pee-wee Herman stand-up special, and immediately I became a ground-level Pee-wee fan. I spent the next several years perfecting my imitation of him, so much so my third-grade teacher wrote on my report card, "We enjoyed having Pee-wee in class this year." A lot of parents would have found this annoying, but unlike my dad's parents, mine adored all of my shows, even the mime acts. Soon, my dad and I fell into a nighttime routine. He would come home from his day on Music Row and imitate the characters there, especially one who called himself Cowboy and spoke with a lateral lisp. I would imitate Pee-wee. Sometimes we'd conduct whole dinner conversations pretending to be other people, my mom our loyal audience of one.

I grew to know my father better during this period, his sunshine and his shadows. I learned, for one thing, that he hated winters. Even the glass house did not provide enough sunlight for him, so he built himself a tabletop light machine out of plywood and fluorescent bulbs. He propped it on the coffee table behind whatever sheet music he was transposing in his meticulous handwriting. A pencil sharpener sat beside him, and every few bars, he'd jam his Blackwing pencil into it, keeping the point as sharp as a scalpel, the box's glare casting an eerie silver aura over his face. One day I asked him what the box was for and he told me the winter gave him the blues. Later I'd learn other things that gave my father the blues: overhead lighting, Sunday afternoons, brown liquor, and amber-tinted sunglasses that made the world look "like a Texas sandstorm."

Gone was the father who slept all day, replaced by one who couldn't sleep at night. His sleep was a limited resource in our house, slippery as a shadow. He blamed his insomnia on the fact that his parents hadn't enforced bedtimes in the shack, one of the only crimes I ever heard him lay at their feet. Because of his sleeplessness, my parents kept separate bedrooms—my mother slept in the guest room on the second floor and my father in the master, down the hall from me. At night he would soothe himself to sleep at night with *The Andy Griffith Show*, followed by whatever old Western was on. When I woke in the middle of the night to use our adjoining bathroom, I'd see the blue light flickering under his door, the muffled clip of horse hooves beating a dusty path across the expanse between us.

When I was a girl, I once asked my mother if my father had wanted a boy, a question maybe every girl wonders at some point. She said no, he'd wanted a girl because girls love their fathers so much. It was a curious answer (don't boys also love their fathers?) but one that made an imprint on me. I knew then that my job was to adore my father, and he adored me back. He didn't teach me how to tie a knot or ride a bike. He rarely made it to my school events or ballet recitals. But his love was like gravity, invisible and strong.

Where my mom's go-to compliment was pretty, my dad told me I was smart, the smartest kid in the world, that maybe one day I could even be a president myself. Or at least a politician. That was my father's not-so-secret dream for me: that one day I would make the laws of the land, that children would study my name in books. I knew my worth at home was tied to my grades, that making straight A's drew my dad's attention in the best way. When my fourth-grade teacher told me I was raising my hand too much in class, he demanded to set up a meeting with her. It did not go well. He told her I was to raise my hand as much as I damn well wanted. I can see him now, his eyes narrowed, his index finger jabbing the table with each word. What's more, he said, if she treated me differently in any way after this meeting, he would get his lawyer Steve involved. Steve Gladstone was a tall, suave man who wore gray suits with cowboy boots and called me kiddo. My father threw his name around our house like his personal avenger: *They don't want me to get Steve on the case!* According to my mother, the meeting ended when my teacher cried. My father meant well, but at times he used a hammer where a flyswatter would suffice.

Those years were a blessed between-time: after the tumult of Waylon and before the political fragmentation to come. Back then, my parents got their news from the same source: PBS's *The MacNeil/Lehrer NewsHour*, Jim Lehrer's detached, grandfatherly voice rendering each crisis as boring as a passing cloud. My parents' arguments passed more quickly too, for the most part. I learned to accept them as I did Tennessee thunderstorms. Flash floods or steady rains, they were usually over in a day.

Vietnam and Watergate had jaded Baby Boomers like my mother, but my father was part of the Silent Generation, a smaller cohort born amidst the defeat of Nazism and the fallout of the Dust Bowl and Great Depression, mass tragedies that required the aid of the American government. They'd been conditioned to work within the system, not against it, thus earning them their nickname. Like many of his generation, my father held politicians in high regard. He might have disagreed with his locally elected officials, but the presidents were as untouchable as gods—so much so, I confused the two. On a road trip I took with my parents when I was around five, my mother bought me a coloring book filled with creative drawing prompts. One page asked me to draw my image of God, and without hesitation, I drew the bust of George Washington I'd seen on the one-dollar bill. There was no question in my mind: George Washington was God. They were one and the same, their hair and ruffled collar made of clouds, lording over us from sea to shining sea. When my mother looked at my drawing, she laughed and assured me they were two separate entities. But that wasn't right. *In God We Trust*—it said it right there! Right there under his face!

To pass the time on long car trips we took to visit family in Texas or Wisconsin, my father taught me to recite the presidents in order. I don't remember him teaching me much about their actual politics (except, weirdly, when it came to Teddy Roosevelt—I was the only third grader who could opine on the flawed premise of the Bull Moose Party). Instead, he taught me their myths and machinations. By age nine, I knew that Pierce was a sad drunk and Taft was too fat for the bath and William McKinley adored his epileptic wife. When McKinley was governor of Ohio, he checked on her by waving his white hanky out his office window to her bedroom window across the Capitol courtyard every afternoon at three o'clock. After McKinley was assassinated, she continued to wave hers to the air. I was deeply affected by this story's mixture of romance and tragedy. But my father preferred stories involving guns, especially duels—his favorite between Andrew Jackson and a man named Charles Dickinson.

The happiest time. (From author's collection.)

Dickinson had publicly insulted Jackson's wife Rachel, calling her a bigamist because the couple married before the ink was dry on her divorce. Jackson challenged him to a duel, killing him. Later accounts indicated he fired twice, a breach of duel etiquette, but no matter, my father was squarely on Jackson's side. I think he liked that story because it involved some ancient gentleman's code he'd learned as a boy in West Texas, and because a hero from our fair state of Tennessee had won. Years later, I would learn Jackson was no hero. But I don't remember my father telling me much about the Trail of Tears. He leaned into stories that took on the mythologies of Westerns, cowboy heroes protective of their women, white hats versus black.

Also on those long car trips, my father taught me to sing two-part harmony. He would sing the root notes, and I the upper third. We filled hours this way, the dashed highway lines whizzing by like beats on a metronome, my mother dutifully clapping after each song. Over the years, we developed a repertoire that included Cole Porter and Peggy Lee and old cowboy campfire songs. Our specialty was a version of "Red River Valley" my father made up:

Come and sit by my side if you love me
Do not hasten to bid me adieu
Just remember the Red River Valley
And the cowboy who tore half in two

We sang that song so much the absurdity wore off, though it never failed to make my mom laugh. I didn't know how the cowboy had managed to cleave himself, but I did know that the ugliest image could be made beautiful by harmony, and that harmony could not be expressed alone. Later in life, a voice teacher would tell me mine was "mezza mezza," but my dad said it was pure. We weren't the Everlys, but we made our own kind of blood harmony.

CHAPTER 11

Frog Song

I came to Nashville a long time ago
People said that I'd be a star
But all I remember is loneliness and hunger
Whoa, I sure didn't get so far...
　　—"THE LAST SONG I'M EVER GOING TO SING,"
　　WRITTEN WITH J. I. ALLISON IN 1969

A football field's distance from the glass house down a sloping, uncultivated hill lay a large crater where my father once tried to dig a pond. His goal had been to keep the cattle hydrated, but the excavation men he hired dug too far and broke through the water table. And so the pond was destined to be dry. For decades, it was a thorn in my dad's side as he watched his beloved Simmentals mill around dumb and spiritless in the ankle-deep mud. Once he tried sprinkling a white powdery chemical on the hole, but it did nothing except hang in the air for a month doing God knows what to our lungs. My father did not have a way with water.

In the spring, rains would raise the pond's water level along with his hopes. Then the cicadas would screech the summer into song, drought baking the pond dry. Blessed rains would wash the air clean and refill the basin, a silver breeze gentling the grass. Afterward the air would sparkle and shine. On these firefly nights we might eat outside on the balcony drinking in the impermanence, knowing tomorrow's sun would resume its hot slap and today was but a breach, a window of sacred within the profane. The days would grow shorter, the air turning crisp and lemony, and the empty pond would fill with dead leaves. My hours too would fill with homework and ballet and petty schoolyard dramas and new television sitcoms at night. For the next two seasons the pond would be forgotten until spring came roaring back, the rains once again turning the farm into a cathedral of green and my father, sipping his coffee, would look out the kitchen window and say, "Hey look, the pond's filling up."

My father's career ebbed and surged just as mercurially. The wind had picked up his dream seed of being a Big Nashville Country Star and redistributed it, but I believe a part of it always stayed with him, Nashville his white whale. For a brief period in the late seventies and early eighties, that dream was rekindled when he signed a deal with Elektra Records. He cut three Elektra albums, a mishmash of old hits, intricate ballads, and country tropes—songs about barroom romances, cheating men, and the loyal women who stuck around. Songs that were originally pop like "Love Is All Around" were given the country treatment with steel guitars. My father was countrified too, the album covers all variations on the same theme: him standing on our pasture looking rugged and unshaven in a flannel shirt and cowboy hat. All that was missing was a hayseed between his teeth.

The albums didn't sell well. Elektra released a few turntable hits, meaning DJs played the songs but the label didn't market them. Looking at the albums now, I can see why they didn't have mass appeal. His persona seems forced. I hesitate to call the covers inauthentic—he was a farmer, and those were his shirts—but it would take more than steel guitars to drown out his love of pop, jazz, and classical. In his downtime, he was more likely to listen to Andrés Segovia than Johnny Cash (he admired Cash but found his music too simple, as he did a lot of country). Three chords and the truth didn't work for him. He could pose in front of hay bales and jump out of the Kornfield on *Hee Haw*, but he couldn't change his Mozart-inspired chord structures or mellifluous voice. Ernest Tubb only became a huge country star after a botched tonsillectomy roughened up his singing; there was a lesson in that. Nashville didn't want silky vocals. It wanted the shit-kicker my father had left behind years before. The irony: a man born in a Dust Bowl dugout, no longer country enough for country.

After a merger in the early eighties, Elektra closed its Nashville office and let all its acts go. Jimmy Bowen, the head of Elektra and a fellow Texan, called my dad into his office to deliver the bad news. The meeting was so short, my dad remembers that a secretary brought him a cup of coffee and he didn't have time to take a sip.

"Just leave it," Jimmy said, waving him off.

My dad hustled a lot in those years, either in the studio or on month-long solo tours around Great Britain. After being let go from Elektra, he formed his own label with his personal avenger Steve Gladstone. He still had his songwriting contract at Tree, and his friends there often pitched him songs to record. And he focused more attention on his growing fan base in England, Brits being his favorite pervs in all the world.

Yet even when he was home, he was largely absent from my life. We'd grown slightly cold toward each other. He'd loved my company back when I was a cheerful girl willing to memorize the presidents, but he didn't know how to relate to me once I became a teenage girl who wanted to go on car dates. Like him, I was starting to get the blues too, days when my heart felt as heavy as an overfilled water balloon. My mom's blues were on the cerulean spectrum between anxiety and malaise, but my blues were indigo like my dad's—a paranoid, nihilistic edge that manifested itself as surliness.

I have a clear memory of an argument I had with him around the time Elektra let him go that has always stayed with me, though I can't remember what caused it. There's no telling. I had a sharp tongue and sometimes he did too, especially if he'd had a martini before dinner. I'm guessing I said something nasty to him before retreating to my

CHAPTER 11

room. I imagine my father, downstairs at the table, staring down his dregs of cabernet. *How dare that kid?* he must have thought. I have a teenager myself now; I know the resentment well. *After all I've done for her.* My mother would have tried to calm him as she rinsed the dishes, reminding him I was a good kid but yes, I could definitely be an asshole. Probably he poured himself two fingers more of wine and stewed over it as he sat in the living room after dinner, watching the news.

How dare that kid?

Probably he thought about it as he headed up the cedar staircase, then paused at the top, deciding whether to turn left to my bedroom or right to his. He turned left and opened my bedroom door.

"Do you know who I am?"

I looked up from my textbook. What a strange question. Did I know who he was? Sleepless Sonny who lay in bed all night channel surfing Westerns? Tractor Sonny who plowed endlessly out my bedroom window? Awkward Sonny who always wanted to take a French leave from parties? Stage Sonny who introduced "It's Not Easy Being Fifteen" as *my favorite song I ever wrote because it's about my daughter, Sarah?* Distracted Sonny who could never find his wallet, keys, or guitar pick? Martini Sonny who twisted conversations into arguments? Couch Sonny who strummed the same curving notes for hours at time? Generous Sonny who every year invited me to a fancy restaurant with him and my mother on their anniversary because *where in the world would we be without you, Sarah?*

There were a lot of possible answers, but not the one he was looking for.

"I'm a *star*."

Hearing this announcement, my mother stepped out of the bathroom into the hallway, where she stood rubbing cold cream on her face in tight circles.

"Oh my *God*, Sonny," she said before returning to the sink.

My adulation may have been my father's goal in that moment, but his words had the opposite effect. I pitied him, standing there in his jogging pants and faded T-shirt, and saw him a little differently afterward. Chasing stardom had never been his outward brand. Musicians who bragged about their hits, opening acts who overstayed their welcome onstage, stars who acted like, well, *stars*—these were some of his biggest pet peeves. But perhaps *in vino veritas*. His words pierced my surly teenage bubble because I knew he had unwittingly entrusted me with a deep insecurity. In that harsh hallway light, I had witnessed the burden of his naked ambition. From that moment on, a part of me carried it too.

The truth was, my father's star was waning. Yet he was able to support us by making art and performing on his own terms—no small miracle in the music business. And then, out of nowhere came a sudden ebb. One (ironically sunny) Nashville afternoon, he and his friend and sometime co-writing partner Ron Hellard wrote a country song called "I'm No Stranger to the Rain." They pitched it to an up-and-coming singer named Keith Whitley who released it as a single. Whitley's haunting baritone made him a perfect match for "Stranger," a song about a man who's lived through some bad weather, a man still battling the demons in his life. I was twelve at the time. My dad still likes to remind me that when he first played it for me, I said, "That's a hit." And I was right. The song hit number one, where it spent the entire month of April. That year the Country Music Association voted it Single of the Year.

Less than a month later, on May 9, 1989, my father's fifty-second birthday, while the song was still burning up the charts, while my dad rode his tractor through our pasture cutting the first hay of the season, maybe even knitting the lyrics to a new song in his mind—on that sunny spring day when my father was riding high, Keith Whitley, alone in his Nashville home, drank himself to death.

Certain observations, however cliché, never fail to startle me. That babies grow into children, and children into teenagers. That people vote against their own self interests. That spring defeats the most brutal of winters. Add to that list: that fame does not make people happy. We see proof every day of celebrities' Faustian bargains—the failed marriages, the overdoses, the public meltdowns and subsequent stints in rehab. There's even medical evidence to suggest that famous musicians live shorter lives. A 2007 study led by British health researcher Mark Bellis examined North American and European musicians who had performed on any album, across musical genres, on a list of the All-Time Top 1,000 albums. The study found that the musicians were 1.7 percent more likely to die young than the general public. It's perhaps fitting that Whitley's last hit was "I'm No Stranger to the Rain," a song about the darkness within us all. We expect our heroes to articulate our pain for us, so why are we surprised when that pain eats them alive?

"I'm No Stranger to the Rain" was my dad's last songwriting hit. He kept writing and plugging songs for a few years after it charted, and then without fanfare, he quit. Quit plugging but also quit writing. The shift was imperceptible in our house at first, but at a certain point in my late teens, I noticed an absence. Gone were the pithy hooks I used to find scattered on slips of paper throughout the house, bon mots written in my father's blocky capital letters: *MY WORST ENEMY (IS ME)* or *YOU ARE THE LESSON I NEVER LEARNED*. Gone were the impromptu concerts he would play for my mother and me before dinner. I had taken those concerts for granted growing up, and now I missed them.

It's normal, necessary even, to recalibrate our dreams in middle age, to ask ourselves which ones are worth pursuing and which to let go. To give up the dream of Big Country Music Star was a mature decision for my dad, one I don't think he regrets. But why did he quit writing songs? What artist quits creating at age fifty-two? He was no longer a young man, but he wasn't old. I've asked him, and I've asked my mother, and the answer they give is that he was tired of the hustle, of having to pitch his songs to bigger stars when he wanted to sing them himself on his own label. "Pitching songs," he once told me, "is a young man's game."

There's a line I love from the poem "Famous" by Naomi Shihab Nye. "I want to be famous in the way a pulley is famous, or a buttonhole. Not because it did anything spectacular, but because it never forgot what it could do." My father didn't need to chase fame anymore. But why did he abandon what he could do? A part of me will always wonder about the artist he could have been. Songwriting was his state of flow, the way he'd transcended reality since he was a teenager driving his father's tractor. Maybe he could have kept at it had he been able to separate the writing from the pitching. I wish he had, but as a writer now myself, I get it. There must be a relief in setting down the pen and escaping the wearying cycle of pitching and rejection. But just as writing nourishes me, songwriting nourished him, and by extension, my mother and me. When he quit, a light turned off in our house and a door to a beloved room slammed behind us. Sometimes I would knock on that door, present him with a hook of my own, some clever turn of phrase I hoped would be brilliant enough to convince him to write something new.

"Huh, pretty good," he'd say, and change the subject. There was no use. That door was locked forever. It would be years before I'd learn to open a door of my own.

While my father was molding his identity to fit the shape of Nashville, I was doing the same in Dickson. To quote Kurt Vonnegut, "We are what we pretend to be, so we must be very careful about what we pretend to be." I grapple with that quote, with the notion that we have immutable selves and all else is costume. We've managed to survive this long as a species because we're masters of adaptation. Where does pretense end and adaptation begin? I've spent years thinking and writing about the question my father posed to me that night in my bedroom doorway. *Do you know who I am?* But who was I?

When I try to summon my teenage self I can only pull up disparate prototypes of a young woman pretending her way toward adaptation, but suffice it to say: I was a girl who went along with things.

CHAPTER 11

Dumbing myself down to attract friends or boyfriends, tolerating bigoted remarks from friends (or their parents), smiling politely when the assistant football coach, my chemistry teacher, began pulling me out of business law class to complain about his marriage: these actions churned my internal waters. I couldn't reconcile certain aspects of my identity. I needed friends. I was becoming a sexual being. I could neither deny nor abandon these truths, nor could I pretend, at least to myself, that it was okay for a friend's dad to use a racial slur over his dinner plate, or for a married father of four to hit on his student. I went along with so many things back then. But each time, I churned.

I dated country boys. Boys who liked to cruise back roads and drink Bud Light under pink moons. Boys who wore flannel shirts that smelled like the earth after rain, boys who went hunting with their dads on weekends and ranked bucks via a point system. I liked the feeling of their hands on me after bonfires, lying on blankets in the flatbeds of pickup trucks, our mouths slicked with beer. It felt exciting to be wanted. Throughout elementary and middle school, my self-worth had depended on my good grades and ability to memorize facts for quiz bowls. But high school pedestals are formed from flimsier substances: beauty, hormones, a good throwing arm. In order to thrive in my new environment, I needed to shed that old honor student like a frog outgrows her skin.

Being a girl in Dickson felt as perilous as balancing my bike down our gravel drive. To be pleasing to boys, tough around the girls, smart but not a nerd, sexually appealing but not promiscuous. All that identity shifting will wear a person down, make her forget her fragile boundaries, and maybe that's by design. As for Coach X, it never went further than those coerced therapy sessions, but not all girls were so lucky when it came to certain coaches. Sexual affairs between coaches and students were open secrets in our town, like a perk of the job. When the coach began calling me at home, I told my mom. She was horrified, as I knew she'd be, but I made her promise to wait until after I graduated before she complained to the school board. *Please,* I begged her, *please just let me get out of this town first.* She kept her promise, and the following year the coach announced he was stepping down to spend more time with his family—classic harasser subterfuge.

I don't think my mom ever told my dad about the coach, and I definitely didn't. For one thing he was gone a lot, but even when he was around we protected him from subjects that might keep him up at night. He was an anxious parent, always lecturing me on freak occurrences like slipping and hitting my head in the bathtub or accidentally electrocuting myself with my hair dryer. He misidentified the dangers of being a girl, and my mom and I shared an unspoken understanding to safeguard his innocence.

My last spring on the farm the pond rose again, but my father was touring England and no longer swayed by its mercurial charms. We'd sold off most of the cattle by then anyway. After Phillip died, the cows became too much work. My mom started complaining more about her long drives into Nashville, and I knew it was a matter of time before my parents sold the farm. But that last spring, the pond was an orchestra pit for a symphony of crickets, owls, coyotes, and frogs.

I had hardly ever ventured down the hill to stand at its banks, but one spring night my boyfriend Jay convinced me to go frog gigging, a gig being a narrow, eight-foot pole with small tines at the end for spearing frogs. I had no interest in killing frogs but he seemed excited about it, and anyway, it was something to do. Which is how I ended up trailing Jay down the unplowed pasture, through the tall grass into the murky abyss. When we reached the muddy bank, we sloshed around for a few minutes, observing our prey. There were frogs, that much was certain, frogs everywhere, their croaking so loud I could feel their vibrations under my skin. Mating season.

Jay had bet me I couldn't gig one so I was determined to prove myself, though my stomach wavered. I was psyching myself up for the act, plotting the arc I'd make with the gig before plunging it into the frog's—back? Eyeball? I shuddered imagining where one gigs a frog. That's the question I was asking myself when I heard the gunshot.

CHAPTER 11

I reeled from the source and gradually registered the sight in front of me. Jay had pulled a black pistol out of his jacket pocket and was pointing it at a bloody tangle on the ground that I realized must have, a moment ago, been a bullfrog. *Frog blood runs red?* I thought, watching him blow up another. I'd dissected a bloodless frog in biology once. Had I assumed that "cold-blooded" meant frog blood ran mineral blue, or sickly green? He shot another, then another. *How strange*, I thought, *it's red, just like my own.*

Finally, Jay stopped shooting and looked at my stunned face. A few seconds of silence passed between us as he gauged my reaction to his amphibian genocide. Would I scream in horror or signal acceptance, waiting out the night as dumb as the cattle this pond was designed to serve? It didn't feel like much of a choice. I wasn't the one holding the gun.

"Here, hold this open," Jay ordered, tossing me a white plastic trash bag. I did as I was told. I was getting better at playing the part of the willing girlfriend. Jay resumed shooting, stopping every so often to collect his kills and throw them in the plastic bag, though they didn't seem worth saving to me. Finally he finished shooting and we stumbled up the hill in silence, with me still holding the bloody bag. He seemed distant, even angry, as if shooting the frogs had not made him feel as good as he hoped. After he left, I tiptoed through the quiet yellow kitchen, hoping that my mother was asleep, that she would not come downstairs and see what the harsh bathroom light revealed: my face ghostly pale, my jacket and jeans spattered with frog entrails. Red like mine.

I've always wondered why my mom didn't hear the gunshots that night. Maybe she did and assumed they were coming from a neighboring farm. Or maybe the shots were drowned out by the crying of the frogs. I never realized how loud their calls were until I returned home from college on holiday visits. By that point, I'd begun the long process of discovering what I was as well as what I wasn't, and what I wasn't, I decided, was that town. I was separate from those people. I would slip their bonds, erase them from my mind, and they would never, ever claim me.

But sometimes at night, I'm awakened by the shrill blast of fire trucks leaving the station down my suburban street and I think about that farm, our farm, sold off over twenty years ago. The smells and the symphonies, the dullness and the rapture. It all comes back to me, the green meadows and repeating guitar chords, the bullfrog nights and long cicada days that, even as the sun was slipping west across the pasture, I was sure would never end.

Sometimes my dad's unwritten songs worm their way into my subconscious and I dream of the younger me, lying on my bed staring at the lavender irises tendrilled across my wallpaper and wondering when my life will begin. I hear an unfamiliar melody drifting up from the living room below. The tune is catchy, more bluegrass than country. A little fingerpicking. A heavy downbeat. Not many lyrics yet, just a hummed chorus. The lick, not the hook. Body first, name later, like its composer.

I walk downstairs, past my father playing guitar on the living room couch and into the kitchen, where my mother is forever standing over the sink peeling potatoes.

"What's Dad playing?" I ask.

"It's something new he's working on," she answers, eyes alight. "Isn't it great?"

"It's a hit," I say. I was no musician, but I could often tell a hit when I heard one, knew it in my blood. The way you learn to when you're the daughter of a songwriter.

CHAPTER 12

Miseducation

*It's not easy finding out who
Lives behind that face that everyone knows is you*
—"IT'S NOT EASY BEING FIFTEEN," 1978

- Age 7: A boy named Wally bullies me. He follows me around the playground, yelling that I'm the dumbest girl in school, that my face makes him want to throw up. I tell my mother. *That means he likes you*, she says.
- Age 9: "How are you so thin?" Veronica asks Betty over the phone.

    Cut to Betty, dressed in jeans with a bandana wrapped around her head. "Ronnie, do you want to know my secret?" she whispers.

    "Yes, please!" squeals Veronica. "I'm dying to lose five pounds for the homecoming dance!"

    Betty pulls out a mop and duster. "Housework!"
- Age 10: My ballet teacher tells our class our stomachs are too flabby. He assigns uniforms of black leotards with pink ribbon belts, the better to track our disappointing circumference. We scrap the usual routine and spend the hour doing sit-ups. If we really want to be ballerinas, he tells us, we should forget about Mikhail Baryshnikov and study Jane Fonda.
- Age 14: My history teacher Mr. Hudson assigns an essay on Belle Watling, an old-timey sex worker in *Gone With the*

Wind: "Is Belle a lady? Explain your answer." The question doesn't seem to have anything to do with the lessons I'm supposed to take from *Gone With the Wind*—the romanticism of slavery and rape and so forth—and I write, "Can you define the word 'lady'? I'm not sure I know any ladies."

Later, Mr. Hudson flings my essay back at me with a red X over my answer and the words, "Well maybe you should meet a few!"

- Age 16: During an initiation into a Dickson social club called Sub-Debs, older girls blindfold us and seat us in a circle, where they douse us with cat litter, raw eggs, and condiments, and make us roll in cow manure in front of the most popular boys in school. They wrap diapers on our heads Sharpied with mean phrases and make us read them aloud. Many of the girls cry. The reward for this suffering is an annual Christmas dance at a public park.
- Age 17: Coach X, a married father of four, tells me I'm the only person in the world he can talk to about his marital problems, and can I skip my business law class to talk some more, and after school can I drive him to the field house to talk some more and can we talk over the summer, *can we can we can we?*
- Age 18: My AP English teacher Mr. Jones is shocked at the logic unit scores. "Sarah Curtis scored the highest? Didn't see that one coming!" The boy next to me laughs, but I don't get the joke. I smile and collect my test.
- Age 19: A Massachusetts boy I meet at college orientation tells me he's already figured out Southern girls are easier than Northern girls. I remember Mr. Jones's logic unit and picture women as a scatter plot, their sexual availability a cluster of dots ascending in proximity to the Mason–Dixon line.
- Age 20: My boyfriend from Spain tells me American girls are easier than Spanish ones. Now I picture women as a Venn diagram, with American and Southern making up the slutty center oval, the place where I am located.

- Age 21: The film student I am dating writes a screenplay about a young couple in love. It is very romantic until the end, when the couple is swimming and the man suddenly pushes the woman's head underwater and drowns her (reader, I kid you not that he told me this *while we were swimming in a pool*).

    "But why does he kill her?" I ask. "There are no warning signs."

    "Don't you see? *That's what gives the scene its power.*"

Growing up, my worldview was a meadow of garden-variety sexism and gender inequity, my parents' marriage the ground beneath me. It was a fragile ecosystem predicated on a system of subterfuge and coercion, bills split between credit cards, shopping bags left in the trunk, brought inside when my father wasn't around. My mother repeated certain mantras about gender which I accepted without question. If you wanted to convince a man to do something, you needed to make him believe it was his idea. If you wanted a man to apologize, guilt worked better than anger. Tears before yelling. And of course, if you look good, you feel good! Beauty was a woman's currency. "Were you the prettiest one there?" she asked each time I came home from a party, as if my life were one big pretty contest.

As I grew older, I learned the story of my parents' elopement like it was my own creation myth: how my father had a seven-year girlfriend, how my mother issued something called an ultimatum ("If you ever issue one, be prepared to follow through," she lectured me darkly), and how the saga culminated in a romantic airport proposal and a Vegas wedding. It was the perfect marriage plot, one I still find romantic, if problematic. My father's ex-girlfriend seemed a narrative obstacle rather than a flesh-and-blood human—she gave their romance teeth. Without her, the plot turned conventional. She was the thing my father had to relinquish in order to prove his love, the sacrificial lamb. And why did the lamb have to die? Because my mother was prettier. I owed my very existence to her beauty.

"What made you fall in love with Mom?" I asked my dad over a dinner at my parents' house a few years ago, just the three of us finishing our meal under the yellow glow of their fruit chandelier. Across the table, my mom eyed him with a sly smile.

"Because she was the most beautiful girl I'd ever seen," he said in a tone that implied *Well, duh.*

"Yes, of course she was beautiful, but why else?"

He raised his eyebrows in a way that suggested my question was harder than I believed it was. "I dunno. She was just so beautiful."

"Even in my ugly pants?" my mom teased.

"Yeah, your pants were pretty ugly." They both chuckled. This was their storybook narrative, but I was no longer a storybook reader. I was an adult woman who wanted my dad to dig deeper into his affections. My young mother could turn the room on with her smile, but she was also goofy and well-read and committed to social justice. When she and my father met, they bonded over their love of the same country songs and artists. She could sing every lyric to the murder ballad "The Long Black Veil," a sexy party trick that always brought the house down. She was magnetic and free, a loyal friend, a nurturing soul. My father could have given many reasons for loving my mother. But beauty was the only one he chose that night, and my mother didn't seem to mind.

Those were the values I was raised with. I didn't question them or wish for another worldview because I didn't know there was one; I woke up each day, plastered on a smile, curled my hair, and wore the proper footwear for the field. That was about to change.

On the curb in front of my new college dorm in Memphis, my dad swooped in for a quick hug. Though it was cloudy, he kept his dark wraparound sunglasses on, unwilling to let me see him "tune up," his euphemism for crying. "You give those other kids a chance now," he said, his signature first-day-of-school line.

My mother wiped away tears and clung hard to me. "I'll be alright, Mom," I tried to assure her, but in truth I worried more for her than for me, for the lonely hours she would spend in the glass house while my dad was gone. Inside their Jeep my mother gave me one last shaky wave as they pulled away, our tight little trio no more. I stood there long after their taillights had blended into the traffic on University Street, my feet rooted to the ground. Their car could be any car now, just as they could pass as anyone's parents. My dad had cut his hair, and my mom no longer bought all her clothes at the Mexican import store. Living in a small town had sanded their edges.

My new college campus was a Gothic fever dream of mosaic sandstone, a factory for the production and distribution of Southern royalty. With few exceptions, my new hallmates in the dorm had all graduated from elite Southern private schools. Unlike the hairsprayed, heavily made-up girls of my high school, they wore their hair in messy buns, their faces scrubbed and shiny. They spoke the same language and knew the same people. I envied their bonds. Almost all my high school girlfriends stayed around Dickson after graduation, dating the same cadre of country boys.

My new hallmates felt like the friends I was always meant to have. I loved how lightly they took themselves, how comfortable they seemed in their skin. They teased me for my small-town makeup and big hair, but they did so affectionately. In Dickson, teasing could result in a credible threat of violence. But there was no competition among my hallmates. Then again, they'd never had a scarcity of resources. The world had unfolded before them like a plush carpet removed of obstacles, cars bought and paid for, college tours booked in advance, recommendation letters signed and delivered. In return, I mirrored their values, dialects, and style. Sometimes I wonder how much of my identity is even mine and how much is jerry-rigged from a small group of bawdy, white, private-school girls.

CHAPTER 12

The college had its share of pearl-wearing Southern belles, but my hallmates were different. They smoked cigarettes and weed and introduced me to bands like the Pixies. We tried to harmonize like the Indigo Girls, who channeled our sadness, and scream like Courtney Love, who channeled our rage. By midyear, we got wind that some boys had nicknamed us the Hell Quad, and we brandished the nickname with pride on a sign we hung in the hallway. One Friday after class, a few of us ventured to a head shop where we bought a short green "hall bong" we named Bobbitt after the recently castrated husband of Lorena Bobbitt.

We looked out for each other, and we were in need of protection. Over the course of my four years, two of my close friends were violently raped by older frat boys who went on to graduate with honors while my friends both transferred colleges to pick up the pieces. The media called these experiences *date rape*, as opposed to actual rape, as if being assaulted by a boyfriend were a lesser crime than by a shadowy assailant on the street. The college began to feel like a landmine, and eventually if you were a woman you learned where to step. You avoided certain men, certain fraternities. If you needed a date for a party, you chose from a list of pre-approved "safe dates," as we called them. You traveled in packs. You made friends with bartenders who watched your back.

The onus fell on young women to monitor the signals we gave out. I doubt many young men back then were given lectures before college like the one my mother gave me before I left for school, sitting on the edge of my bed—to be careful not to drink too much at parties, or something terrible could happen to me as something terrible had happened to her. The conversation was tinged with shame, so I didn't ask questions. I understood the message, and packed it away as I packed my toiletries and bedding. Sexual assault was a woman's burden, along with periods and childbirth.

Enter Women's Studies 101. The class was dual taught by Faber, a stocky history professor with a short swoop of black hair who dressed like a greaser in black jeans and motorcycle jackets, and Marshall, a tall, elegant Shakespeare scholar who wore cashmere sweaters and ballet flats. I loved them both and studied them like a detective, noting everything they wore, everything they laughed at, and everything they disdained (sometimes, I suspected, each other). Where Faber spouted her opinions forcefully and often profanely, Marshall's words exited her mouth as polished as beveled diamonds. Like the best teachers, she practiced the Socratic method, layering question upon question until we all revealed ourselves as fools. The very first class, I must have looked too cheery because she called on me to define feminism (oh, I see you now, Marshall and your perilous inquiry). I sputtered something about how feminism meant the sexes should be treated equally. This was not a sufficient answer, I realized as soon as Marshall began her terrifying cross-exam. Equal for *whom*? Equal in whose *eyes*? And how did biology play a role in my so-called *equality*, hmmmmm?

But despite my twice-weekly mortifications, I looked forward to Women's Studies like no other class. Not only was I in love with Marshall and Faber, I was in love with feminism, the way it made sense of my life. Women's Studies 101 knew me better than I knew it. It knew I was malnourished from a diet of pop culture and familial patriarchy, from Barbies to Archie comics to a father who called the shots. It knew about Coach X, and it taught me of the power abuse inherent in his actions. It knew about the older family friend who gave me some vile red hooch at a party when I was seventeen, and it taught me that what happened next wasn't entirely my fault. Feminism didn't cure me, but it gave me a pretty accurate diagnosis.

That fall, we were assigned to read Adrienne Rich's 1979 essay collection *On Lies, Secrets, and Silence.* In the chapter, "When We Dead Awaken: Writing as Re-Vision," Rich writes:

> Most, if not all, human lives are full of fantasy—passive day-dreaming which need not be acted on. But to write poetry or fiction, or even to think well, is not to fantasize, or to put fantasies on paper. For a poem to coalesce, for a character or action to take shape, there has to be an imaginative transformation of reality which is in no way passive. And a certain freedom of the mind is needed—freedom

to press on, to enter the currents of your thought like a glider pilot, knowing that your motion can be sustained, that the buoyancy of your attention will not be suddenly snatched away.

The problem, she goes on to explain, is that a glider pilot cannot get off the ground if she is with a man "in the old way of marriage," if she has diapers to change and dinner to cook, traditional gender roles "in direct conflict with the subversive function of the imagination."

I still have the book, with that passage highlighted in faded yellow, a penciled star beside the line *in direct conflict with the subversive function of the imagination.* I can still remember where I was when I read it—back in the glass house on Thanksgiving break, lying on my childhood bed. I can still touch the page and remember how the air shifted the moment I read those words, how a surge of understanding rose within me, twisting its way up my spine. How I read it again and again and again. Downstairs, my father played his guitar on the living room couch, repeating a lick—*an imaginative transformation of reality*—while my mother banged pots around the kitchen—*in direct conflict with the subversive function of the imagination.* Places, everyone. They knew them so well. And, by extension, so did I.

I saw in that moment that the solitude my father's artistry required was built on a platform provided by my mother, who undertook all the day-to-day operations of the house, the child-rearing and the housework and even the balancing of bills, despite her math phobia. Freedom of mind comes with a cost, Rich showed me, and my mother was clearly the one paying it.

Still, I missed them. I'd forgotten how pretty the glass house was, like a jewel sparkling through the trees. When I visited, my mom would cook my favorite dishes—roast beef with Yorkshire pudding, stewed okra and tomatoes, cornmeal-breaded catfish and rice. My dad and I put aside our bullishness and forged a freer, looser connection (maybe because we started drinking wine together at dinner). He made me laugh with his funny lingo I'd taken for granted growing up. If he liked something, it was "a groove," or "double-clutching e-flat."

If the day turned unlucky, he had "more problems than a man on the wrong train." A traffic jam was "a state fair bog down." A "country squire" was a man with a bad toupee. Sometimes his lexicon required long explanations that were flat-out ridiculous: to miss a belt loop was "to Burl it," which he coined after performing on a TV variety show with the singer Burl Ives, who'd skipped a loop on his belt. A "Webster" was a stand-off between two people who aren't on speaking terms, a story too long and frankly mundane to untangle. And then there were weird Roger Miller jokes that nobody understood. Perhaps no musician had a greater influence on the Nashville lexicon than Roger, the singer-songwriter and comedian who would go on to write numerous country and pop hits including "King of the Road." He and my dad had met when they were both young and broke, starting out in Nashville. As my dad wrote in his memoir to me, "[Roger and I] had a whole lot in common. We came from the same neck of the woods and had music biz dreams bigger than the West Texas sky." I loved my dad's treasure trove of Roger Miller stories, especially the early memories, before Roger became addicted to alcohol and pills.

But despite these happy reunions, a storm was brewing in the glass house. When I was growing up, my parents had always voted Democrat—for Jimmy Carter and Walter Mondale over Ronald Reagan, then Michael Dukakis over George Bush Sr. For twelve years, they lost. This is what I knew about Democrats as a child: they cared more about poor people and they always lost. Then Bill Clinton came blowing in like a Southern victory breeze. We were mesmerized by Clinton. He spoke more like a preacher than a politician, and we claimed him like a new religion. For the first time in my life, I felt politics transcend my father's history lessons and take on a thrilling immediacy.

I cannot pinpoint the exact moment the political winds started to shift direction for my dad, but to paraphrase Hemingway, it happened gradually then swiftly. Today when I ask him what did it, he says he started thinking deeper about his taxes—not exactly a sun bolt on the road to Damascus, but the devil is in the details. In the early 1990s, he subscribed to the conservative newspaper *Investor's*

Business Daily. That led him to read *Basic Economics* by Thomas Sowell, a libertarian scholar who worshipped at the altar of the free market. Sowell advocated for decriminalizing drugs, which appealed to my dad as an ex-hippie, and guns, which appealed to him as a Texan. Welfare reform? Please. He'd clawed his way out of a dirt hole into a glass house three stories above the earth. Granted, he was white, and male, and born with an innate musical talent in a community that fostered that talent. But he used himself as an example of how the world should work. And then there was Tipper Gore. When the vice president's wife started slapping parental advisories on rap labels, my dad decided he'd had enough of the Clinton administration. He leaned libertarian and was staunchly anti-censorship of any kind—after all, censored Black artists helped lay the foundation of his career.

As my dad turned against Clinton, my parents entered a new phase of warfare. Dinnertimes were the worst, their anger still festering from whatever they'd seen on the nightly news. If I could describe their fighting style, I'd say my dad skewed belligerent and my mother patronizing. They both resorted to easy insults and personal attacks—neither would be much good on a debate team. If he'd drunk a martini, my father might smash his fist on the table, rattling the silverware, my cue to clear my plate.

I missed them, I loved them, I needed them like no other humans on Earth. But I was increasingly glad to leave them behind. They could yell all they wanted. Nobody would be around to hear their discordant duet.

If it weren't bad enough that my dad now voted for my mom's sworn enemies in the Republican Party, in the summer of 1994 he officially rejoined the Crickets. My mom was not happy about the decision. He'd been making inroads on his own record label, his shows in England were drawing bigger crowds, and after the success of "I'm No Stranger to the Rain," top-tier Nashville songwriters were clamoring to co-write with him. She thought he should stay solo, that he'd moved past the old Buddy Holly song and dance. But after years of forging his own path, the Crickets must have felt like a soft landing—the camaraderie of his oldest friends, the post-show beers, the old rock 'n' roll stories they never tired of repeating to each other, though their wives were sick to death of them.

The fall of my sophomore year, my mom showed up to Parents' Weekend looking sallow and thin. My dad was traveling around Sweden with the Crickets on their first tour back together. She'd gone along in the beginning but flew home early. The tour had been terrible, she told me over dinner at a Chinese restaurant in midtown Memphis. She hated Sweden, with its punishing darkness and drunken audiences, the suicide hotlines printed ominously on every hotel medicine cabinet. And what's more, she said, the Crickets had grown rusty from my dad's absence and their shows were God-awful. The tension of the trip weighed so heavily on her, she threw out her back in Stockholm and collapsed on the sidewalk while pedestrians stepped over her. "What a miserable experience," she said, finishing off her pinot grigio.

"That sounds awful. Are you sure you don't want an appetizer, Mom?" I asked through a mouthful of shrimp. I was used to my mother's drama, but it was weird for her not to order food in a restaurant.

"No, I'll just have another glass of wine." She raised a finger to summon the waitress. "You don't get what I'm saying, Sarah. I'm done being a Cricket groupie. I'm leaving your dad."

I'm leaving your dad. This was new. I'd never heard my mother use those words before. *Pack a bag, we're going to Wisconsin for a week*—she'd told me that a few times over the years after fighting with him, though she never followed through. *We're leaving for a week*, that one I knew. Not *I'm leaving your dad*, full stop.

On the car ride back to campus, I looked out my window at Beale Street's distant neon lights switching on and imagined what my parents' divorce might mean for our family, what lights it would switch off. "Mom," I asked, "don't you love him anymore?"

"*Love*," she snarled. "You know what love feels like to me, Sarah? Love feels like a burden around my neck."

Despite this strange metaphor (was the burden that she felt love or didn't feel it?), I knew there was a lot of affection between my parents. I didn't necessarily want them to divorce, though a part of me could see how divorce might be a relief, an end to all the discord. I spent the next week talking to friends and hallmates whose parents had divorced, mentally preparing myself for the next phase of our family life.

After my dad returned from Sweden, I called home for an update. My mom answered, back her old chatty self. "Mom, stop," I finally said. "Did you tell dad you're leaving him or not?"

"Oh geez no, we made up. We're fine now," she acted as though she'd forgotten our entire conversation. "I'm sorry I told you that! Menopause is really screwing with my hormones. My doctor is putting me on estrogen. Medicate, not meditate, I always say!"

So that was it, another passing tempest. I hung up feeling like I should be relieved, but mostly I felt irritated. Irritated at my mother's glibness and thoughtless transparency (Did she have to tell me *everything*? And on *Parents' Weekend*?) I felt as though I were the parent, and they the squabbling children. I was growing up, and instead of seeing my parents as guide stars I was starting to see them as humans following their own flawed patterns and mythologies.

I'd begun noticing myths all around me ever since Professor Marshall assigned Roland Barthes in a literary theory course. In his 1957 essay collection *Mythologies*, the French philosopher argued that our culture confuses nature and history, draining ideas of their actual meaning and repackaging them as bourgeois myths. He examined a wide range of pop culture elements, from wrestling to detergent ads to striptease, and deconstructed them to reveal their deeper meanings.

Mythologies changed how I saw my world, the steady diet of myths I unconsciously ingested and regurgitated on a daily basis. My father's Texas gunslinger legends, my mother's Hollywood fables, the moonlight-and-magnolia version of the South, even the steak on our dinner table. All myth. Myth, myth, myth, everything in my life was a myth—unnatural, man-made, spurred by a cultural will to belong. For my seminar thesis, I took a page from Barthes and wrote a takedown of my own sorority handbook I titled "Greek Mythology." That year I deactivated in a fit of literary passion. Marshall encouraged me to submit it to the college literary magazine, but I never did. While writing brought me joy, it didn't occur to me to take it seriously like my father did. That was the domain of real artists, usually men. Who gave them the permission? This was a question I never asked myself. All I knew was I didn't have it. I wasn't trained to be an artist; I was trained to be an artist's fan.

A few months before I graduated college, a friend who interned for the Memphis Blues Commission invited me to an annual awards ceremony as his plus-one. He had work to do backstage before the show, so I headed to the bar alone. That's when I noticed a long-time friend of my father's I'll call Robert, leaning against the bar wearing a beige suit and joking loudly with the bartender. Robert was tall and loose-limbed, with a handsome grin and the blocky physique of an aging football star. The son of an old-timey country music star, Robert was visiting Memphis from Nashville, where he served as a vice president at BMI. He and my dad went way back; not only were they friends, Robert had published several of my dad's songs. But they went back even further than that. His father had given my dad one of his first jobs, a gig on his tour in the fifties. I hadn't seen Robert in years and approached him hesitantly to introduce myself, wondering if he'd remember me.

He greeted me with exuberance—everything Robert did was exuberant—as if I'd been on his mind for years. What was I doing after graduation? he wanted to know. I said I was still trying to figure that out. Then he uttered the most beautiful sentence I'd ever heard: "Why don't you come to Nashville and see if we can wrangle you up a job at BMI?"

I should have paid attention to context clues: his glib delivery, his wolfish grin, the bourbon on his breath. But I was twenty-two and inexperienced, and wasn't this how the world worked? Other college friends were relying on family connections to get jobs; why couldn't I? The following week, my internship supervisor told me Robert had called her for a recommendation and she'd given me a glowing one. The job, it seemed, was a sure thing.

When I called my dad to tell him about Robert, he was thrilled—not only at the prospect of bumping me off the payroll, but by the symmetry of the situation. *His dad gave me my first job, and now he wants to give you yours!* All hail the venerable Music City gatekeepers! How lucky I'd been to run into Robert—thank goodness I bellied up to that bar, ha ha! I'd been so anxious about lining up a job, but it turned out I didn't need to worry. Life was easier than it appeared, and to my credit, I'd worked (fairly) hard in school, so didn't I deserve it? Yes, yes I did!

Suffice it to say, it was not a shining moment for the former champion of Mr. Jones's logic unit. Can you look past my jackass entitlement and notice the flaw in my reasoning? If the universe was testing me, I failed. I failed to ask basic questions ("Gee Robert, what *kind* of job?"), I failed to perform due diligence, but most importantly, I failed to remember one of the cardinal rules of my childhood: sure things don't come easy in Nashville.

CHAPTER 13

Dead Awakening

And I'll put this cloud behind me
That's how the man designed me
To ride the wind and dance in a hurricane
    —"I'M NO STRANGER TO THE RAIN," 1989

The girl sitting across from me etching lines of coke onto a mirrored tray did not look familiar, though I had known her once.

"You know who that is?" my college friend Brooke whispered to me. I shook my head. "It's Allie."

Allie? I gazed through the cloud of cigarette smoke and tried to remember the last time I saw Allie, dressed like a macabre princess at that long-ago Waylon party. In our house, her name had been a warning synonymous with bad adult behavior, and here the omen was realized before me. Once a pretty wisp of a girl, she looked bloated and somehow hardened, though I thought I could see a flicker of her former self in her round, heavily lined eyes. The coke carved to her satisfaction, Allie leaned over and helped herself first.

We were sitting in the upstairs VIP room at an after-hours club located on an industrial stretch of downtown Nashville. Brooke had brought me here to hang with a group of her high school friends, kids who ran in the same private school circles. They'd returned home to

CHAPTER 13

Nashville after college where most of them worked for their family businesses. Two guys with shaggy hair and rumpled khakis sat perched on the arms of our couch like bookends, gossiping over my head about people I didn't know. Beside me sat Catherine, Brooke's friend from Memphis, the only other outsider in the room. I squirmed each time our arms brushed.

"Allie!" Brooke called out. "This is Sarah. Remember I told you about her? Her dad played with Waylon?"

Allie looked up from the tray at me. Suddenly I was rendered visible to the room, as if I had apparated out of the cigarette smoke. "I remember you," I said. "We played together a few times when we were little."

Allie did not return my smile. "Who's your dad?"

"Sonny Curtis."

She gave an irritated half-shrug that conveyed two messages. One, she did not know my dad. Two, she could not care less. She bowed her head, returning to the task.

"He . . . he plays with the Crickets, um, the lead singer? They were on the road with Waylon in the '80s. So I remember you? And your mom?" *Oh God, why was I still talking?*

"Uh-huh," said Allie, not bothering to look up. "Where'd you go to high school?" The part where I always hit the wall.

"Dickson."

"*Dickson?*" one of the guys said. Someone made a joke about rednecks or flatbeds and I disappeared back into the beige couch cushion, my stupid grin fading last like a sad Cheshire Cat.

High school alliances reigned supreme with this crowd. It was a familiar Nashville dynamic I hated, but still I went where they invited me, still I waited in vain for one of the private school boys to talk to me, and still I accepted whatever drug they passed my way. At college parties, I had only seen weed and psychedelics, but in Nashville, the drug was always cocaine.

After college I'd packed up my life in Memphis and moved into a bare-bones apartment building in Nashville. Because the apartment complex had no sign in front, my friend Shelley called it the Apartment That Dare Not Speak Its Name. My first week in town, I called Robert to set up a meeting and his secretary took a message. The next week, I left another message. Then another. And another. A summer passed while I worked a series of temp jobs calling Robert on my lunch breaks, but each time his secretary headed me off at the pass, her dismissals growing more and more sympathetic. When I did manage to get through to him once or twice, he issued vague promises and apologies, his words dripping with *honey* and *sweetheart*.

Eventually I stopped calling Robert and took a job as an admissions officer for a Catholic college, where I reported to a rigidly conservative sect of Dominican nuns. They dressed in layers of long, white robes with black trim, their habits covering everything but their eerily youthful faces. A month into the job, the head nun wrote me up for wearing too short a skirt. The job felt like a punishment, though if I'd adjusted my lens, it was a better gift for a young woman with writerly inclinations than a job at BMI. Every day I was given an opportunity to observe a fascinating culture, but I was too consumed with self-pity to see it. How could Robert *do* this to me, I wondered, and by extension to my dad, supposedly his friend? Why had I moved to Nashville without getting the job in writing? I could have stayed in Memphis, where at least I had internship connections. How could I have been so stupid? These were the questions I asked myself night after night, bottle after bottle of cheap merlot that left my mouth tasting like dried blood.

Sometimes when I couldn't bear another weekend in my indifferent new town, I drove to Memphis to visit friends who'd stayed in the city. I missed Memphis, with all its funk and swagger, its pace as languid as the Mississippi River crawling south under the M bridge. Memphis and Nashville were different not only in terms of music, blues versus country, but in terms of landscape, economy, and vibe. A long-standing rivalry existed between the cities. Memphians

CHAPTER 13

disparaged Nashville, for, as Peter Taylor wrote in his novel *A Summons to Memphis*, "its vulgar, ugly, plastic look." Nashvillians often looked down on Memphis for being poorer, "unsafe" (that pervasive white euphemism), and slow-moving. I preferred Memphis, or maybe I just felt more welcome there, though being back in the city depressed me, every intersection spurring a memory of a party, or a friend who'd moved on to better things.

After one of those weekend visits, I stopped at my parents' house on my way back to Nashville. I always left Memphis in a gloomy mood, likely hungover, and I'm sure that was my mindset when I arrived at the glass house while my mother was setting the table for dinner.

Now that I was an adult, the house seemed smaller than it used to. But it held the same comforts and conflicts. The same cozy yellow kitchen, the knock-off Tiffany fruit chandelier over the dining table bathing the kitchen in amber light. A glass of cold white wine for me, a martini for my dad. The glass walls growing darker and darker until they became mirrored reflections of the three of us gliding from kitchen to living room like figures in a dollhouse. And as usual, another toxic verse in my parents' never-ending duet. I can't remember the exact argument that night, but it's safe to assume it involved Clinton.

"Please, you guys," I pleaded, "not tonight." But they continued to argue as if I weren't in the room. That's when it dawned on me: I didn't have to be. I didn't have to retreat to my bedroom to avoid their warfare. I could just *leave*. I stood up from the table and grabbed my bag. Suddenly, my parents startled to my presence.

"Please don't go!" my mother cried. "I'm sorry your dad is being such an asshole!" She looked at my dad as if to say, *Do something!* But I was already out the door.

Back in my Ford Probe, I lit a cigarette and wound my way down the dark two-lane highway away from the glass house, past the familiar pole barns, past Tice's Springs country store, past the ranch homes of school friends I'd lost touch with years ago. On the radio, Jim Croce was singing about having a name, a song, a dream. But what was my dream? My problem, I saw, was that I didn't have one. I had a blurred vision of the life I desired: a job that involved writing, a prettier apartment, a boyfriend who called me back. But I didn't know how to achieve these things, and every decision felt weighted by doom. I'd felt such a sense of belonging in college, but now I felt untethered from my friends, my culture, even my own family.

I was happiest that year on weekend mornings when I allowed myself to lie in bed for as long as I wanted and read. Sometimes I'd lie there all afternoon, drinking lukewarm coffee and forgetting to eat. After four years of being assigned novels, I gravitated toward nonfiction. The summer before, a friend had loaned me her pool-stained copy of Joan Didion's *The White Album* and I'd devoured it in one gulp, spending the rest of the summer scouring Burke's Book Store on Poplar Avenue for everything she'd written.

If Roland Barthes once cracked a window in my brain, Joan Didion was like the hot Santa Ana winds blowing it off its hinges. This revelation is cliché in writerly circles, as the nonfiction writer Meghan Daum once observed: "There is nothing more Basic MFA Bitch than saying Didion changed your life." Yet change it she did. At an age when my own emotions felt messy and hard to articulate, Didion's detached take on the world was a cool salve on a burn. It wasn't that she didn't have emotions; she claimed them and rose above, like when a hippie offered her acid in "Slouching Towards Bethlehem" and she turned him down because she was "unstable." How easily the word slipped off her tongue. She wasn't there to let loose or fit in; she was there to document the chaos, to sell people out, as she famously put it. That, to me, is the primary reason Didion was so revolutionary for young women trained to be the passive object of the patriarchal gaze. She not only claimed that gaze for herself, she turned it on the very men who had shaped American culture and mythologies: John Wayne, Howard Hughes, Jim Morrison. I wanted that kind of agency. I still do.

Didion led me to discover other masters of creative nonfiction like Tom Wolfe, Annie Dillard, Jo Ann Beard, and James Baldwin. They showed me I didn't have to make up characters or plots to be a writer. The world around me was enough. I could take it for a spin, deconstruct it on the page, and create new meaning from its raw materials.

In the upstairs VIP room, Brooke handed me the mirrored tray and resumed her conversation with the bookend boys. I figured I'd take one bump, just for the sake of appearances. Coke was entertaining at first but I wasn't as enamored with it as everyone else seemed to be. I'd tried it a few times and hated the way it wore off, leaving me with jangly nerves and a blistering headache. And while I liked how it provided me with a steady stream of Big Ideas, I wasn't crazy about hearing everyone else's. But then again, nobody was talking to me about anything tonight. I took a quick hit and passed the tray to Catherine without making eye contact. I would rather sit in awkward silence than make conversation with her. She was dating my college ex-boyfriend, Luis, a brooding, 6′7″ basketball player from the Basque country of Spain who claimed to be a count. We'd been a couple for almost a year in college, and though I didn't love Luis anymore, I didn't want to picture him with Catherine. She took a hit then turned to face me. "Hey, just so you know, I'm not with Luis anymore," she said. She had nobody to talk to either, I could see.

"Oh no?" I feigned indifference at this wonderful news. Not only could I delete the image of Luis and Catherine from my mental photo stream, now I had somebody to talk to. We traded stories, and I learned that Luis had treated Catherine more carelessly than he had me, had broken promises and not returned her calls. This, selfishly, was also wonderful news. My title of Luis's Favorite Girlfriend had been challenged but remained undefeated, and what's more, he had talked about me to her, had not quite gotten over me, it seemed, which gave me an ego boost I desperately wanted but also made me feel genuine sympathy for Catherine, who really was funny and cool, not to mention beautiful, with creamy, black Irish coloring, porcelain skin against ebony hair, a contrast as stark as the keys on the piano in the corner; yes, I saw exactly what Luis had seen in her, for now I saw it too, really I was beginning to love her myself, and I wished we lived closer so we could do this more often, god knows I could use another friend in this town, don't get me started on these people, and sure, I'll have another hit, thanks, and maybe another—are you having one, Catherine? Okay, me too.

I awoke the next morning on my bathroom floor. At some point during the night, I crawled to the toilet to throw up and never made it back to bed. A war waged in my head, a searing pain that obliterated thought. The only sensation I could tolerate was the cool bathroom tiles against my cheek, so that's where I spent the morning, sprawled face-down in front of my toilet like the chalk outline of a murder victim.

My life did not look pretty from this angle. The floor needed cleaning, the tiles were the color of rotten teeth, and the khaki hand towels I'd bought at the mall reminded me of the last phase of a bruise. Everything about the room felt sickly, a palette of bodily rot.

The picture blackened under deeper scrutiny. Formerly disparate puzzle pieces fitted together to form a depressing picture in my brain. My father had long moved on from the Waylon scene, but here I was back in town, working a job I hated, angling to make a name for myself in Nashville and failing spectacularly, soothing my ego with free cocaine on the weekends. Cocaine courtesy of a second-generation member of Waylon's entourage, no less. I was like a bird who returns to her cage once the door has been opened.

Something had to change, I told myself that afternoon as I dragged my body to the sink to scrub the grout marks off my face. First, I'd pass up the tray the next time it came my way. That part would be easy. Second, I'd start plotting my escape route from this town. That part would be harder. But I had a plan. My college roommate Liz had moved to Boston after graduation where she was working as an editorial assistant at a publishing house, spending her days reading manuscripts in an old Back Bay brownstone. Sometimes when you don't know where you're going in life, the best you can manage is to imitate someone who does. In a rare burst of optimism, I applied to journalism graduate schools and was accepted into my second choice, Boston University.

After my acceptance, I flew to visit Liz and discover my new town. It was April 16, 1998, the same day a deadly tornado outbreak struck the mid-South. Three tornadoes ripped through Nashville, damaging over 300 buildings, killing one person and injuring dozens more. The memory seems too odd to be real, but I swear as the plane took off I remember looking down and actually *seeing* one of the black twisters winding in the distance. To this day, I can't say for certain if the event really happened or if it's my own imagination I'm remembering. Our memories are warped and dusty prisms, like antique stained glass. Anyway, it's my memory, true or not, and the meaning I imposed on it was obvious. I was escaping a storm.

PART 3

Earth Mother

CHAPTER 14

A Noble Goal

How will you make it on your own?
This world is awfully big, and girl this time you're all alone
—"LOVE IS ALL AROUND,"
MTM FIRST SEASON INTRO, 1970

The summer after I turned twenty-three, I moved into a prewar walk-up apartment in Boston, a block away from the Mass Avenue turnpike's constant clamor. My street was named Charlesgate East. It was short and L-shaped and lined with cherry trees. For two weeks every spring, I'd walk under a deluge of pink petals that rained down so hard I'd have to pick them out of my hair when I got home. Sometimes I'd stop and stand there like a dumb child, wonderstruck at the cinematography of it all.

When I told Bostonians I lived on Charlesgate East they sometimes said, "You mean West." I'd say no, east, and they'd mutter, "Never heard of it." A few even argued with me about the existence of my own street—Bostonians are like that—and I'd try to rationalize with them: "But if there's a west there has to be an east, right? Otherwise it would just be called Charlesgate." They'd shrug, unconvinced. After enough of these exchanges, I began to imagine the street *did* only exist in my mind. Maybe the real me was still living in the Apartment That Dare Not Speak Its Name, leaving messages for Robert.

CHAPTER 14

My parents had helped me move, and we spent a few days together getting to know the city before we bid another teary curbside goodbye. In the mornings we'd walk through the nearby Fenway Victory Gardens, a colorful jewel in landscape architect Frederick Law Olmsted's Emerald Necklace park system. My dad fell in love with Olmsted's design and bought a biography of him before he left which he quoted frequently over the years. He especially appreciated his lack of ornamentation in favor of organically occurring plants and grasses. "Nothin' wrong with green," he'd say with admiration when confronted with a sweep of lawn. "Nothin' wrong with green."

I didn't have a car, so I walked constantly. The weight I'd gained in Nashville, bloat from Bogle Merlot and cheap pizza deliveries, melted away as I strolled the city, gawking at those townhomes on Charles Street. What a life, to be born into that caste. I thought I was poor but I was only broke, one phone call away from a savior. Still, I couldn't afford good shoes, and every night before bed, I'd peel the dirty band-aids from my heels to clean the baby pink skin beneath my blisters. I was shedding, losing the old me and gaining someone new, someone tender trying to be tough.

In grad school I taught undergrad writing workshops on various genres such as memoir, profiles, and screenplays, genres I was still learning myself. Before each memoir unit, I'd read the opening passage from Eudora Welty's memoir *One Writer's Beginnings*, a brief scene describing a morning ritual Welty's parents shared as they readied themselves for the day. While her father shaved in the upstairs bathroom and her mother fried bacon downstairs, the couple would whistle "The Merry Widow" back and forth to each other. "It was their duet," wrote Welty. No matter how many times I taught it, I always teared up at that line. Rereading it now I still do. The passage is poignant, but why did this slight family ritual affect me so? And why does it still? I must have recognized myself in that scene, that familiar ballad of the only child, always standing on the sidelines peering in.

As soon as I opened my mouth during workshops or courses, every professor and student had the same question: Where are you *from*? On the first day of investigative journalism class, I introduced myself as being from Tennessee and a guy with a buzz cut and chip on his shoulder asked if I used to ride a horse to school. Some classmates snickered, others groaned, and my face betrayed me by turning red. It felt both mortifying and familiar, one more place I didn't belong. But I was also learning something about Bostonians, and by extension the human estate. I'd entered this culture with a presupposition: that everyone in New England was better educated, better connected, more worldly than I was. And while those assumptions sometimes proved true, it was also true that Bostonians could be just as provincial, bigoted, and petty-minded as some Southerners I'd grown up with. Boston culture felt insular, walled by its own set of symbols and myths, ones I could never penetrate.

Before graduation, a professor suggested I apply for a job at *The Bay State Banner*, a news weekly that covered Boston's Black and Latino communities. I took three trains to the *Banner*'s office building, a high-ceilinged, industrial space overlooking a South Boston loading dock. There I met with the publisher and editor-in-chief Melvin Miller, a handsome middle-aged Black man with kind eyes and salt-and-pepper hair, impeccably dressed in a tailored suit and colorful tie. A former US District Attorney who'd graduated from Harvard and Columbia Law, he'd given up a promising law career in the mid-sixties to launch the *Banner*. In his office overlooking the dock, he began the interview by asking where I was from. When I told him Tennessee, he sat up a little straighter. "We are a rare Black family in that we have zero connections to the South," he declared, a glint of defiance in his eye. "None of our ancestors were slaves."

He told me the Millers had immigrated from Jamaica in the 1800s. They'd attended Boston Latin, then pursued law and medicine in the Ivy League. When Melvin was a boy, his father made a point

CHAPTER 14

of introducing him to prominent Black doctors in order to impart models of Black excellence and achievement. Years later I'd read an interview with him where he told how he refused to sing slave songs in an elementary school assembly. The Millers were Boston Brahmins through and through, belonging to no one but themselves. Did I understand?

I did. "Well, I come from poor sharecroppers," I explained by way of apology. "None of my ancestors owned slaves." Melvin chuckled and the moment passed. He asked if I had any questions of my own and I acknowledged the elephant in the room. "Does it matter that, you know . . . I'm white?"

Melvin had a ready answer, maybe a little rehearsed, one I remember to this day. "Miss Curtis, do you know how much of our DNA is composed of race?" I said I did not. He told me the number hovered somewhere under one percent. Race being biologically insignificant, it didn't matter to him that I was white. But unfortunately, he said, it makes up a much larger percentage of our cultural consciousness, our economic and social disparities, our privilege and our power. He glanced down at the bylines I'd sent him from the *Boston Phoenix*, the hipster arts weekly where I interned during grad school, a job that mainly consisted of filing old papers and writing movie reviews to franchise action films nobody else on staff wanted to see. Sure, Melvin said, I could try to land an editorial assistant job at the *Phoenix*, but if I really wanted to understand our country, the *Banner* was a smarter choice for a young reporter. Because as much as people convinced themselves otherwise, America's racial wounds were not the stuff of history books. In the future, our long-simmering hostilities would boil over, the country would have a reckoning with its original sin of slavery, and race would be perhaps the most important issue our country would confront. "Just you wait," he said, holding me in his gaze. "Just you wait." I took the job.

The Millers were as singular a family as any I would ever know. Melvin ran the paper with the help of his wife Sandra and brother John, though John seemed mostly a figurehead, a devout Hindu who spent a large part of each year living on an Indian ashram. John's two sons, whom he'd raised Hindu, helped run the day-to-day operations of the paper. All the Miller men possessed a fine-boned beauty and searing intellect. They held themselves with an arch elegance, aloft from the rest of us—a distance that made them ideal journalists.

I was responsible for writing and photographing four articles a week on issues big and small, from racial bias within the police and fire departments to gentrification to bus delays. In a yellowed paper I saved from October 1999, I wrote a front-page article about the ten-year anniversary of the Charles Stuart case, one of the most horrific blights on Boston's history of race relations. Stuart was a white man who shot and killed his pregnant wife on their way home from a Lamaze class, then blamed the murder on a Black gunman. Not only did the saga exacerbate Boston's deep racial tensions and mistrust, it ignited a national media frenzy, playing on the fears of white suburbanites. The media painted a portrait of the Stuarts as a "Camelot couple" who happened to be on the wrong inner-city corner at the wrong time. Police spent months stopping and frisking Black men in the Roxbury community until they pinned the murder on Willie Bennett, whom Stuart identified in a lineup. When Stuart jumped to his death from a bridge soon after, his brother and accomplice finally came forward with the truth.

The Stuart story alone required much time, research, and reflection, but in addition to that article, I also covered and photographed a piece about a new school assignment plan, another about a forum on racial bias in the justice system, and a fourth about a groundbreaking ceremony for the city's largest low-income housing project. By this point I'd driven my Ford Probe up from Tennessee, and since those were the years before GPS, I spent a good amount of time lost in my car, trying to navigate Boston's baffling web of one-way streets, rumored to be paved-over cow paths.

I reported to Yawu, John's older son. He was slight of build, with delicate features and a deep skepticism about pretty much everything, including me. Eventually we developed a prickly rapport. He made me laugh, especially on Tuesday nights when we stayed late to put the paper to bed, the sunset clouds over the harbor awash in magenta ("Afrocumulus," as he described their shape). Those were my favorite moments at the *Banner*, when the mood relaxed and I was able to see our work coalesce into something I could hold in my hands. Sometimes on those nights Yawu would praise one of my pieces and I'd float back to my apartment on a cloud of my own.

Over time, I overcame my nerves as I grew to know my regular sources, community organizers and politicians who were smart, funny, and generous with their time. I saw activists like the Millers committing their lives to a greater cause in the face of enormous obstacles: separate and unequal resources, environmental blights, and a staggering array of racist politicians. The worst offender I came to know was Boston City Council President Jimmy Kelly.

Jimmy was a former member of the South Boston Irish mob and a close friend and associate of James "Whitey" Bulger, the infamous head of the Winter Hill Gang, who by then had been on the lam for years. Bulger would spend sixteen years as a fugitive until his arrest in 2011, the FBI's second most wanted man after Osama bin Laden. But Jimmy never hid his affection for his old friend, hailing him in the press as a "genius" and a "gentleman." Jimmy was a lifelong opponent of affirmative action and court-ordered school desegregation. During Boston's violent anti-busing riots of the seventies, he headed the South Boston Information Center, basically Bulger's PR team, an operation that disseminated its own racist reality about crime and busing, the fake news of its day. In short, he was a racist wheel-greaser for one of the most nefarious criminals of the twentieth century turned Boston City Council president. And I was supposed to interview this guy about neighborhood school assignments? I had to find a way to be civil to this monster?

I psyched myself up for calling Jimmy as if I were dialing Beelzebub himself. I expected, even hoped, that he would speak to me like the adversary I was. But Jimmy was friendly. "Oh, so you're the new *Banner* reporter? Tell Melvin I said hi!" I steeled myself against his charm and questioned him about the growing racial divisions within the council. A Black councilor named Charles Yancey especially disliked him, and had organized an unsuccessful voting bloc against his reelection as president. Jimmy sounded genuinely hurt that Yancey had "offended" him. "I've always been very good to him," he said, citing appointments he'd given Yancey over the years. Like any good mobster, Jimmy saw the world as a series of quid pro quos, and I knew he was plotting his retaliation against Yancey. But I could also feel an uncomfortable revelation unfurling within myself. Had I met Jimmy without knowing his backstory, I would have liked him. He reminded me of a sweet older uncle who takes care of the family.

I thought I knew racists. I was from rural Tennessee, for God's sake; I could spot a Confederate flag bumper sticker through Gatlinburg fog. But Jimmy Kelly introduced me to a different brand of racist: the beloved uncle, the neighborhood kid from a hardscrabble background made good. If you asked him, I'm guessing he would have said he wasn't a racist, and possibly he believed that was true. Rather, he confronted racial issues from a moral perspective to protect what he saw as his people's self-interests. His politics spoke to a lot of working-class white Bostonians, especially those who bore the scars from those ugly, confused days of early school desegregation. But Jimmy was able to elicit camaraderie from enemies as well (despite their ideological differences, one of his closest allies at the time was Boston's Democratic mayor Thomas Menino). As fellow Boston son John F. Kennedy once said, "The great enemy of truth is often not the lie—deliberate, contrived, and dishonest—but the myth—persistent, persuasive, and unrealistic." Jimmy was a PR man at heart, a first-rate mythmaker.

Melvin Miller had been right—working at the *Banner* was a smart move for a beginning reporter. But the workload was so daunting and the pay so low, the job was a launching ground. It would make or break you, and after a year I started to break. Recently I discovered a journal I kept during my time there, buried in a metal box under my *Banner* bylines, the pages dry and feathery. It reads like a morose love letter to the South. "What's missing for me here is connection," I wrote in November 1999. "Some days I long for everything: old boyfriends, food, memories. I'm so lonely here . . . I constantly feel like an outsider everywhere I go. I'm so scared. I don't know what to do next." About Yawu, I wrote, "He completely ignores me, and in turn my words spill on top of each other when I speak to him."

I'm sad to read how unmoored I was that year. I had lost my accent, but I couldn't seem to shake something deeper in me, a kernel of longing for my native culture. For the nasal vibrato of a honky-tonk song blaring from a juke joint somewhere in the distance. For the easy sisterhood I developed with women there, bonds I thought I'd never find again. For the heavy, cornbread-scented air of a meat-and-three restaurant, its vinegary, sinus-clearing collards going down like fire for the soul. For its unhurried tempo, as moody and slow, as my father said, as cold molasses. For the weight of humidity settling on my skin. For the springtime sunlight, the bright green buds that exploded each March like actors on cue. When I flew home to Tennessee, I teared up each time the view out the airplane window turned from gray to green, my eye trained to the lush carpet of my home state. There was nothing wrong with green.

A new millennium dawned, and each of the few friends I'd managed to make in Boston moved away for jobs or school. Liz moved to North Carolina for a PhD program. My roommate moved home to Dallas to work for her mother. And then there was Neal, a man from Detroit I'd been seeing for a year who'd been accepted into an MBA program in Chicago. Curly-haired and muscular with fair, freckled skin, I thought he looked like the *David* (he was half Italian).

Before I met Neal, I was drawn to the most spectacular screw-ups I could find. I liked the addicts, the tortured artists, the wild cards. Neal was a different breed. He was patient and mild-mannered. He had a steady job, and, unbelievably to me at the time, a gym membership. When my parents visited, I introduced them to Neal over dinner at a Russian tea room. Over plates of schnitzel and potatoes, my dad quizzed Neal about his job in investments and they hit it off right away. In the past, my dad had always felt lukewarm at best about my boyfriends. He'd never given me relationship advice, with the exception of a brief stint when I was living in Nashville dating a banjo player ("Awww honey, not the *banjo*"). But after dinner that night as we were kissing our goodbyes on the curb he said in my ear, "Everyone you've dated so far is a boy. This one's a man." A Texan compliment of the highest order. In turn, I loved that my dad liked Neal, a part of me ever the eager schoolgirl seeking his approval.

Nothing was keeping me in Boston, not even my job. I loved the Millers and was proud to contribute to the legacy they'd created. The paper had changed me on a molecular level, exposed me to systemic inequities, wrecked and reformatted my thinking, and sharpened my skills. The *Banner* gave me far more than I ever gave it, and I'm forever grateful that Melvin Miller took a chance on a naïve white girl from the South. But loneliness and stress were wearing me down, and I couldn't afford to live in Boston on my own. Also, I was tired of beat reporting, of navigating press agents and bureaucracy and dry municipal meetings that dragged late into the night. Nashville was always an option—the streets were familiar, and I knew people there. But despite all my journal longings, the fact was I had changed, expanded. Kurt Vonnegut was right after all: we are what we pretend to be, though what that was, I was still learning. All I knew was that moving back to the South would have felt like pouring a glass of water into a thimble. I would have spilled over.

There was always Chicago. I loved Neal, but not the idea of moving across the country for a man, a path my mom had chosen with mixed results. I knew moving would set in motion a string of events leading to marriage, and I wasn't sure I wanted to marry Neal. Wasn't love supposed to be more turbulent? Arguments between us faded as quickly as they flared. Neal compromised, something I'd never really seen growing up with my parents. My favorite books and films depicted doomed couples, romance as weapon of destruction: Anna Karenina and Vronsky, Bendrix and Sarah in Graham Greene's *The End of the Affair*, even Thelma and Louise. In contrast, the love I felt for Neal was calm as a June day, and what was love without storms? Storms were my native tongue. Either way, Neal followed his own path and moved to Chicago in late spring. I spent a rainy season in my humid apartment all alone, walking back and forth to work under the fleeting pink blossoms.

The shadow of my parents' larger-than-life romance loomed over me, with its star-crossed Hollywood genesis and dramatic airport proposal. It had been my origin story for so long, everything else fell short of its gilded mythology. Some actual stars glittered in my universe, and even the dead ones still emitted light. The workaday routines of a more conventional life felt—can still feel—mundane in comparison. How to find joy in the quotidian is a question every human must grapple with, every doctor and painter and candlestick maker; many a poet has left behind an entire oeuvre devoted to it. Yet it remains one of the central struggles of my life, to find beauty in the commonplace, whether it be a stable, happy relationship, or quiet, fulfilling work.

What I am trying to say is that I moved to Chicago and married Neal.

While I figured out what I wanted to do in my new city, I worked at a tedious temp job in a high-rise office building cruelly located next door to the Tribune Tower, home of the *Chicago Tribune*. That meant that every time I entered or exited the office I was presented with a soaring, neo-Gothic reminder of my failure as a journalist. My cubicle had the better view, a vast panorama overlooking Lake Michigan, layer upon layer of blue. Every day at lunch, I'd eat a limp turkey sandwich and gaze out at the water, the Navy Pier Ferris wheel spinning as slowly as my mind, and feel a mixture of relief and shame.

Relief that I had no state senator to confront, no community meeting to race across town to attend, no deadlines to grind out. And shame because I worried I *should* have those things, that I'd forgotten what I could do. When I quit the *Banner*, Yawu had told me I was a good writer but didn't have fire in my belly, words that pricked my heart, though he was mostly correct. I gravitated toward stories that required research and narrative but I hated confrontations and cold calls. Now I see that simply means I was better at writing than reporting. But I shamed myself for not trying harder.

On one of those boring blue summer days, my desk phone rang. It was my mom, breathlessly telling me an editor from *Rolling Stone* had called their house looking for me. Apparently I'd won first place in a journalism contest.

"It must be a prank, Mom. I never entered a *Rolling Stone* journalism contest." But she was adamant the call was legit. She gave me a man's name and number, a 212 area code I knew meant New York City. After we hung up, I took a deep breath and dialed.

The number did in fact call *Rolling Stone*, and the editor did sound legit. He told me I'd won first place in their annual college journalism contest, essay and criticism division, for an essay I'd written in grad school about Monica Lewinsky and the media's infantilizing of working women. The prize was worth roughly two months of temping work. One of my professors had entered it without telling me.

"Are you currently working in journalism?" the man said before we hung up. For a moment, the world outside my window held its blue breath. The azure waves stopped lapping the sailboats on the horizon, the Ferris wheel paused its incessant funeral pace. My eyes settled on my computer screen's endless spreadsheet, the cursor blinking back at me accusingly. *Shame*. But also, *relief*. After years of writing for school or work, there was a luxury and a liberty in letting go of a hunger, relinquishing a dream. My father had given up songwriting because he craved a similar freedom. I understood that now.

Neal was always encouraging me to start writing again, but I wanted a break from that endless cycle of revision and rejection. I

CHAPTER 14

wanted to clock out at the end of the day, wander the city, observe the world without trying to force it into narrative. I was tired of thinking in terms of ledes and sources, tired of trying to get the bead on every subject. In a famous 1975 commencement address, my hero Joan Didion urged students to do more than endure or suffer the world, but to look out at it and try to see it straight, and to keep those critical eyes open for the rest of one's life. It was a noble goal, and once it had been mine. But it was also exhausting. I don't think people talk about that enough when it comes to writing, or art in general: yes, it saves and heals and redeems and even revolutionizes, but it also warps, changes your brain chemistry. Being a writer is always, on some level, to be a hack, a self-serving magpie mining shiny bits of culture, relationships, and dialogue. I wanted to look out my office window at the bright parachute of blue and see a city on a lake, not a story to be crafted.

No, I told the editor. I was not currently working in journalism.

"Well, that's too bad," he said. "It was a good essay. I mean, obviously. You won."

Like my superstitious Texan ancestors, I constantly searched for signs and patterns in my twenties—in bird migrations, Magic 8 Balls, the numbers on clocks and calendars. For someone who sought to know the order of the universe, you'd think I would have paid more attention to that *Rolling Stone* call, and what direction it might have pointed me in. But I moved on, took a job teaching high school English and journalism, and packed that part of my life away. At the back of my mind, I told myself that one day I'd return to writing. Projects shimmered at the edge of my consciousness like mirages, usually at night when I couldn't sleep. By daylight they'd be gone. But anyway, I could write later, I told myself. Time seemed an infinite resource, both for me and for my parents.

A few years prior my mom found a lump in her breast, mere months after a mammogram revealed nothing. The cancer was fast-moving, already in stage III. So it felt like a miracle that after surgery and six months of chemo, her prognosis was good. Her illness was possibly the best thing to happen to my parents' marriage. They'd begun treating each other with more care, even declaring a ceasefire over politics which they only honored half the time. Still, half was an improvement. They'd finally figured out how to coexist peacefully. It only took them thirty years.

As for my dad, he and the Crickets were enjoying a career resurgence, touring with folk singer Nanci Griffith and releasing a star-studded album in honor of their fiftieth anniversary. They named it *The Crickets and Their Buddies* in honor of their long-lost friend. In 2004, my mom and I flew to Hollywood for the album release concert at the Hard Rock Cafe. Waylon had recently died, but most of the old crew showed up, including Nanci, Bobby Vee, and Phil Everly. Eric Clapton performed, as did, somewhat inexplicably, Vince Neil, who screamed profanities at the crowd ("You motherfuckers ready to *ROCK*?!") before belting out a heavy metal version of "I Fought the Law." Behind him, the Crickets laughed uncomfortably. Sweet-faced Bobby Vee took the stage to restore order to the room. He bounced his signature beach balls into the audience during his hit "Rubber Ball," and for a blissful moment everyone became a 1950s teenager.

In the VIP balcony, my mom introduced me to old friends she hadn't seen since her L.A. flower child days, all of whom startled at the fact I was no longer the pudgy baby in their mind's eye. Over a generation had passed since my parents had left L.A., and yet the Hard Rock Cafe has an unnerving way of compressing time. There was something surreal about the whole scene. The Crickets had aged into performers reenacting a simulacrum of rock 'n' roll, the genre they helped create, in a venue packaged for aging tourists. Rock 'n' roll had morphed into a commodified creature unrecognizable to its makers, a tattooed bully spewing insults at the crowd. The place was crass and commercialized for sure, and yet I felt a potent charge of community. When you stripped away the walls of bedazzled T-shirts and overpriced shot glasses, the music remained, a bonding agent even capitalism couldn't dissolve.

After the show my mom and I escorted my dad outside, where we thrilled to find a small throng of fans awaiting his autograph. It was a starry night on Hollywood Boulevard, a street that loomed large in my dad's mythology. Forty years before, he'd lived in the Sycamore Apartments overlooking this street, the same apartment complex where Bobby Fuller's lifeless body was later found in the parking lot doused in gasoline. Hollywood Boulevard had seen its share of darkness. But that night, it saw a star reborn.

We got time for a nightcap? my dad asked after the fans dispersed.

What a silly question. Time had nothing on us.

CHAPTER 15

Sky Mother

The moon ain't yellow and the moon ain't blue
It ain't made of cheese and it don't have a thing to do with me
and you...

—"HE WAS ONTO SOMETHIN'," 1989

One spring day in the 1930s my great-grandfather Will approached his neighbor, a fellow cotton farmer named Horace, to tell him some news about the sky. He and Horace had some sort of land sharing arrangement worked out, the details of which I don't know except that, according to family lore, it ended badly when Will slept with Horace's wife. But that's a different story for a different day.

On this day, Will and Horace were still friends and neighbors toiling side by side, their backs bent under a mercurial sky. Will had been studying his almanac and told Horace that the moon would pass through Gemini on the following two days, Gemini being the ideal sign for planting cotton. This phenomenon was known as *twin days*. Hey Horace, can you mark the rows you plant on those days? Will asked.

Sure, said Horace, why not? It was their own little science experiment. "Skepticism is a valuable quality," reads an entry in the 1937 *McDonald's Farmer's Almanac*. "But there has been too much skepticism of the power of the moon. Aristotle and the Farmers were nearer right than the skeptics." Despite their hardscrabble values, cotton farmers were, as we might say in modern parlance, a little *woo-woo*.

Over the next two days, Horace tied a ribbon to each fence post marking the rows he planted. And woo-woo or not, the story goes that when the harvest rolled around, Horace and Will could tell to the exact row the cotton Horace planted on the twin days. Their bolls loaded twice as thick as the others.

For years I'd been thinking about the moon as I researched my father's family, trying to imagine the sky through their eyes. I ordered vintage farmer's almanacs off eBay and struggled to decipher the weird, hieroglyphic zodiac calendars. I researched lunar connections to farming, and learned how Indigenous Americans often named the full moon of each month according to animals or crops. These poetic nicknames varied from culture to culture. A tribe with a heavily fish-based diet might call an August moon a Sturgeon Moon, where a more land-locked tribe might call it a Green Corn Moon. January brought Wolf or Spirit Moons, while February moons included Bear, Snow, and Hunger. Summer hunting and gathering seasons saw Buck or Berry Moons. My favorite moon is the first full moon of spring, which some tribes called Pink Moon for the way it illuminated blooming fields of phlox.

And then there is perhaps the most famous moon, the Harvest Moon, the first full moon of fall. The first lullaby I remember my dad singing to me was "Shine On, Harvest Moon." An old Ziegfeld Follies standard, it's not about the harvest at all, but about a horny teenage boy who wants the moon to shine brightly so he can make out with his girlfriend who is afraid of the dark.

The song reminds me of "Moon, Moon, Silvery Moon," the first song my dad ever wrote at age fourteen. Whether or not he was influenced by "Shine On, Harvest Moon," I don't know, but the concept is the same: moon as wing man, co-conspirator.

Moon, moon, silvery moon, light up the heavens tonight
Moon, moon, silvery moon, while I am holding her tight
Maybe tonight she'll give me her love
If you will shine from heaven above . . .

♪

An aunt once told me how my grandma Violet weaned my dad and his five siblings according to the almanac, when the moon was in Sagittarius. Her cardinal rule was never to wean a baby on a full moon. A full moon cannot be a Hunger Moon for a baby, even if it's in February.

My first daughter screamed her way into the world a month early in fetal distress, sick with a never-diagnosed illness. The doctor finally cleared her for discharge one sunny afternoon, and our new family of three stumbled dazed from the fluorescent-lit hallways of Northwestern Hospital onto Michigan Avenue, where pedestrians walked briskly past us, everyone going on with their business as if the world hadn't split in two.

My doctor encouraged me to breastfeed as much as possible in order to give my baby the nutrients to recover. But two weeks of being fed by nurses had acclimated her to the bottle, and she struggled to take the breast. While Neal and my mom set up the nursery, I spent a month of gut-tired days and nights tricking her to my body by guiding her tiny mouth over pointy plastic shields I placed on my nipples, my robe drenched in sweat, milk, spit-up, and tears (hers and mine). Eventually Neal returned to work and my mom to Tennessee, but my life as I'd known it before was gone, my baby and I reborn into a jagged new world. The hum of the city and the jiggle of the stroller against the sidewalk were the only things that soothed her back into the womblike state she longed for. And so we walked.

We'd head east to Lake Michigan, where I'd let her stretch out on the grass as I mouthed words to images: *dog, sailboat, sky*. Then we'd turn south down Clark, past Swedish bakeries and taquerias to an old

German cemetery where I'd wind her stroller past watchful saints to a remote park bench, nursing her to sleep while sing-songing the names on the tombstones: *Enzenbacker, Krebsbach, Schaffrath.* The late spring sunshine felt like medicine after the long, dark winter. Some days, it seemed like our walks were the only thing keeping both of us sane.

Neal worked long hours at his job, now our sole income. When he was home, our marriage sagged under the weight of sleep deprivation, financial stress, and what I now recognize as postpartum depression. I was desperate for five minutes of freedom, to pass our baby off to him when he came home each day, but I was the only star she revolved around, her frayed and tenuous lifeline. To say I didn't know what the hell I was doing doesn't begin to scratch it. I'd hardly been around babies, much less an angry premature infant. I read books and all of them lied. It seemed no expert knew the particular shape of my disaster.

For a few years my bible was *The Baby Book*, Dr. William Sears' guide to attachment parenting, which preached long-term breastfeeding, co-sleeping, and babywearing. Or maybe that was the only book that spoke to me because my baby wouldn't let me put her down. But Sears said I didn't need to put her down, not ever. It was extreme motherhood, an obliteration of bodily autonomy. Yet it made sense in my bleary-eyed state. I didn't see how I could go back to teaching or writing or exercising or hanging out with friends or reading books or any endeavor besides keeping this underweight creature alive. Dr. Sears said staying home with the baby was ideal (he called motherhood "the supreme career"), and so did my mom. I knew that was anti-feminist bullshit, but Women's Studies 101 had nothing against the daily Darwinian battle I was up against.

We lived in a city condo where I could often hear a neighbor woman screaming at her young kids. I might have overlooked these outbursts in the past, but now that I was a mother, my ear was tuned to a hidden language of children's suffering. I did not know that a shadow side lurked within me, that the newborn I cradled nervously would grow into a willful child, then a moody teenager who would test my resolve, and win. That I would say things I could not walk back, that I could snap as easily as a twig. That I would not always be the mother I set out to be. I could only ache for those invisible children next door. My breasts leaked when I imagined their small, frightened faces. I wanted to rescue them, but how? I could barely keep my own child alive.

And yet, I remember those nights with a measure of fondness. The moments of stillness with my daughter as we learned each other's rhythms and delights, the living room awash in pewter moonlight. I felt a connection forming not only with my baby but with all the mothers in my bloodline, like clusters of stars in the same sky, all of us filigreed to each other through the milky heavens. The Milky Way. Old farmer's almanacs like the ones Violet read extolled the virtues of moonlight as a potent force able to stimulate the growth of plants and animals. Farmers would expose their seeds to moonlight before planting in order to encourage their growth. Eventually I removed the nipple shields and my daughter too grew heavier in my arms under a waxing crescent, then gibbous, then full. People say the moon is cold, but that month I felt the moon was nourishing us both like a sky mother. I wanted her to take all the world's children to her breast, but I could only offer mine.

♪

In the spring of 1953, my great-grandfather Will was diagnosed with stomach cancer. By that point, he'd found Jesus and presumably stopped sleeping with other men's wives, but he never abandoned his first bible. He brought his almanac to his doctor's office so he could schedule his surgery according to the sky. But the doctor spread out the contents of Will's file on his desk and shook his head with a grim expression. "I'm sorry, sir," he said. "Your cancer is in its advanced stages. The moon won't help you now."

Will died on August 3, 1953, under a waning crescent. I've wondered about those last days of his life as he lay bedridden in his airless box of a ranch house, the late summer sun baking his bedroom. I imagine him hovering in that hot, blurry limitrophe between life and death, his tumor swelling as the moon shrank in the lawless sky. Did he slip back in time to that horrible day in Arkansas and see his brother's dying face? Did he keep his faith in Christ? Or maybe he reverted to his old pagan self, the Will who bowed at the altar of twin days and early spring rains. The soft cradle of a woman's neck, like a crescent begging to be filled.

♪

One morning a few years ago, my father awoke to a noiseless world. He swears his hearing loss happened that fast, overnight, a possible side effect of the chemo and radiation treatments he'd recently completed. Going deaf is hard on anyone, but for a musician it's especially brutal. Now he can no longer detect if his voice and guitar are in tune. He can no longer hold us to our assigned keys. But he still manages to arrange music on his keyboard, and he can still hear the orchestra in his mind.

When Covid hit and quarantine began, I tried to be more diligent about calling my dad, as much as I dreaded the silences on the line. I worried about him. An octogenarian cancer survivor stood a narrow chance against the disease, yet he didn't seem to share my anxiety. In fact, he sounded cheerful.

"Mom says you've been spending a lot of time in your office," I mentioned one gray April day, referring to his messy sanctuary over the garage scattered with old guitars, dusty music award certificates, and stacks of neatly penciled sheet music.

"Well, yeah, hmmm." He paused. I gazed out the kitchen window at the blooming dogwood, plotting my next conversational move. I hated this space between the notes. "You know what? I haven't even told your mother this," he said. I tuned in. A secret he would reveal to me before my mom? This was a first. "I'm teaching myself to transpose music for the harp."

Oh.

"Do you even *own* a harp, Dad?" I asked.

"No, of course not!" he scoffed. "The last thing I need is a harp! I just think it's a fascinating instrument." For weeks, he said, he'd been sitting at his keyboard, transposing old songs he'd written. "It's been really fun!"

Our conversation reminded me of one of my favorite poems, "Autumn Quince" by Jane Hirshfield. In it, she writes about the discrepancy between the life we imagine versus the life we lead. "And which one is real?" she asks. "The music in the composer's ear or the lapsed piece the orchestra plays?" When I first read that poem years ago, I thought I knew the answer—that reality exists in the space of that lapse, and our happiness depends on our ability to accept that fact. Illnesses wipe clean the slate of our dreams; equality yields to bloodshed and hate; family members fail to say the right words. We spend our days laying the groundwork for a brighter world we may never see come to fruition, transposing notes, like my father, for a song we cannot hear. But watching him age makes me rethink Hirshfield's question. Is the music in the composer's ear not also real? It may be real enough to save us from ourselves.

♪

Slowly, intrepidly, gravity is tugging the moon away from the Earth. The moon distances itself from us at the rate of 1.48 inches per year, roughly the same speed our fingernails grow.

We too are becoming more detached from the moon. Unlike my ancestors, I don't think of the moon when I'm planting tomatoes, or helping that teenager I once struggled to feed apply to college, or tracking my waning period. I read about coming eclipses but forget to go outside to see them. My almanac is an app on my phone. My father can no longer write songs about the moon or anything at all. Life does not unfold in phases like the sky. It waxes as it wanes.

CHAPTER 15

Oh moon, forgive me. Forgive me my skepticism, my maternal failures, my distracted brain. Forgive me for forgetting I am tethered to this Earth. Take me to your breast like a starry-eyed infant, like a moony-eyed poet. *Moon, moon, silvery moon.* Let me never tire of your light.

CHAPTER 16

The Shadow of a Song

You've got the looks and charm
And girl, you know, that's all you need...
—"LOVE IS ALL AROUND," 1970

When the reporter started calling, I was scrubbing potatoes and gazing out my kitchen window at the long slashes of indigo the maples had cast onto the snow. Her first call to the home phone showed up as "unknown number," so I let it go. Thirty seconds later, my cell phone buzzed.

"Hi, this is Kirsten from *Inside Edition*. I'm hoping you can help me—I've called your dad several times, but I haven't been able to get through." I knew that several was an understatement. My mom had told me it was more like twenty. "We just want to do a quick segment on him," she purred. "Maybe you could persuade him to—"

I cut her off. "Kirsten, my dad is an old man who does what he wants. He's tired of giving interviews."

Immediately I regretted my tone. Kirsten was a pest, but I'd been a reporter long enough to know how defeating these calls could be. "Besides, I don't even live near him. You're calling me in Michigan."

"Yes," she said. "I know."

CHAPTER 16

In the January days following Mary Tyler Moore's death, my father seemed to be everywhere: *20/20*, *Page Six*, the *L.A. Times*, and CBS's hour-long prime-time tribute to Moore, *Mary Tyler Moore: Love Is All Around*. He gave so many interviews, he grew wary people might think he was using Moore's death as an opportunity, as he told the reporter for the *L.A. Times*. On the phone to me that week, he seemed flustered. "This has gotten totally out of hand."

At a long red light that afternoon on my way to pick my kids up from school, I lingered on Kirsten's voice. She sounded to be in her mid-twenties, the same age I'd been as a reporter in Boston. *A TV reporter who knows Mary Tyler Moore through YouTube clips, that's rich.* I wondered what the future had in store for Kirsten, if she wanted children, and if so, what she would forsake for them. Would she eventually follow in my well-worn path, feel like a squatter in her own closet each morning as she flipped through button-downs and tweed skirts she had no use for, the vestments of her old identity? No, Kirsten seemed driven, resourceful—how had she gotten my number, after all? I bet she'd balance her ambitions better than I had.

I turned into the icy parking lot at my daughters' school, my dad's lyrics echoing in my head. *You can have the town, why don't you take it?* I'd once carried those words around with me like a charm, but now they felt like a sharp rock in my pocket, one that might nick my palm if I worried it too much. I was used to living with the song, sometimes under its shadow, but at that moment I felt I hadn't lived up to it—fitting, I supposed, for neither had my father.

When my oldest was a toddler, Neal was offered a job at a large foundation in Western Michigan. I reluctantly agreed to visit the town, where I was struck by the storybook nature of the place. Flower beds exploded with rhododendrons and peonies as fat as my toddler's fist. Glass milk bottles sat on door stoops, something I had never seen outside of my childhood Eloise Wilkin books. At the local farmer's market, we learned residents had nicknamed the town "the buckle of the fruit belt." "From the Bible belt to the fruit belt!" we joked. It seemed like an upgrade. We bought a Colonial house on a leafy street, a Norman Rockwell mythology of our own making.

In Michigan, I gave birth to another daughter, and then another. For ten years I was overflowing, drunk on motherhood. I was lonely and never alone, but I found I loved babies. All day long I buried my nose in their round Buddha bellies, their curled seashell toes, the musty creases under their chins where the milk gathered. Even the perfume of their spit-up on my shoulder made me woozy with love.

But had someone asked me back then if I was happy, I'm not sure how I would have answered. I had little room for emotion, for I was but a vessel—first literally to house my daughters' bodies, then metaphorically for their needs. So many things fell through the cracks, as they always do. Career stalled, house destroyed, marriage neglected. The winter I gave birth to my second daughter was the roughest time, a tangle of postpartum depression, sleep deprivation, and loneliness. One day I managed to escape to a therapist's office, where I sat under framed Buddhist etchings anxiously checking the time remaining on my three-hour breastfeeding window.

The therapist asked me what I used to do before I became the hollow vessel before her, using up all her Kleenex. I mentioned that, among other things, I used to write.

"Don't say *used to*," she said. "Say *I am a writer*."

"But that's a lie. I don't write anymore."

She cocked her head. "Well, let's examine that. Why don't you start again?"

"When?" I asked. For years I'd been mired in the vocabulary of early childhood, connecting farm animals to their utterances. It was hard enough making playground conversation with other mothers, much less putting words to a page. I had lost the flow of language.

"Maybe when you're nursing the baby?"

Unbelievable. Did this woman think I was an octopus? I wondered. She had no children of her own, and truthfully, I judged her for it; or rather, I judged her ability to offer me advice because of it. I walked

CHAPTER 16

out that morning in a huff. Writing while breastfeeding! The mere thought made me want to punch a Boppy pillow.

Now that I have the benefit of hindsight, I realize what made me angry that morning was not that the therapist failed to understand the mechanics of juggling a laptop and a squirmy newborn. What made me angry was that she was suggesting I was making a choice by not writing. Hers was a sensible suggestion, even a feminist one. Thanks to role models like Mary Richards, modern-day women have a veritable buffet of choices in front of them. Surely the fact that I was so miserable meant I had made the wrong ones.

While the world was remembering Mary Tyler Moore that week, I was conjuring a different woman, the one I associate with my first lucid memory of "Love Is All Around." It was the late seventies, and my parents and I had driven down to Texas to visit my grandparents at their stucco breadbox of a house. My grandma Violet wore a faded yellow muumuu printed with blue cornflowers—my handful of memories of her all involve a muumuu—as she busied herself in the tiny galley kitchen where she spent the better part of her days. She laid down her dishrag and walked into the living room just as my grandfather turned on the opening credits of *The Mary Tyler Moore Show*, flooding the room with my father's dulcet voice.

"Who's that?" my grandma asked.

"Daddy!"

"Where's his voice coming from?"

I pointed to the TV.

"He's stuck in the TV?" she asked in mock horror.

I laughed along with my grandparents, keen to the joke. My dad had taken me to the recording studio, its endless rows of candy-colored buttons irresistible to my curious fingers. Even at three, hearing his voice replayed on TV no longer held the power of surprise for me.

But what ran through my grandma's mind as she listened to her son usher in a show about a single career woman? She'd quit school at seventeen to marry my grandfather on a Thursday morning and, as my father tells it, was back in the field pulling bolls by midafternoon. It was October 1926, the year the dirt really started to kick up, a year as dry as the heart of a haystack. A month later as they celebrated their first Thanksgiving as a married couple, a black duster blotted out the sun so opaquely the chickens went to roost in the middle of the afternoon, mistaking day for night. My grandparents feared it was a bad omen, and they were right. It was the start of the Dust Bowl.

What could the second wave of feminism have meant to my grandma Violet, this mother of six who by the age of thirty survived at the fickle mercy of disaster? I'd like to believe she saw the show as a good omen, a whirling spoke in the wheel of progress. But my hunch is that she saw it as an amusement, a frivolity. She probably viewed Mary as she might have viewed me if she were still alive: a woman born with the dubious fortune to choose her own fate.

Around the time my youngest started full-time preschool, I saw an internet meme of a cartoon military man named Captain Obvious above the words: "When life shuts a door, open it again. That's how doors work." It was stupid, yet reading it opened a door in my own head. Life shut the door on writing when I became a mother. Could I really just . . . *open it again*?

It's absurd to say that a Captain Obvious meme changed my life, but it did make me realize how much I'd accepted society's definition of myself as a stay-at-home mom without questioning the cultural myth behind it, its bitter stew of sexism and ageism. Full-time mothering is after all a stage of life; barring extenuating circumstances, nobody is a stay-at-home mom forever. The intensity of the early years fades, children grow and fly away, new opportunities present themselves.

I began writing again in the small hours of the morning, or for an hour after dropping off the kids at school. The blog *Scary Mommy* accepted two of my parenting blog posts and I bought myself a bottle of champagne as if it were the *Paris Review*.

Chapter 16

Motherhood enriched my understanding of humanity and made writing feel urgent, necessary. At the root of my desire to write was preservation, to make some kind of mark in the world to pass down to my daughters. But just as desire begets sex which begets desire, the urge to write begets the act of writing, which begets a deeper urge to write. And therein lies the problem as it relates to my life as a mother. It's still jarring each time I have to leave my writing behind to pick up the kids from school. Hours spent spinning life into language leave me feeling hollowed out, often with a headache. Some days, I'm distant from my daughters, my brain still stuck on the page. Or I feel resentful that I can't make a simple phone call to say that I'm working late, resentful that I have no support system like the one I provide for Neal, or the one my mom provided for my dad.

The image of an artist modeled for me since birth was a solitary figure, alone with his thoughts and musical scores. Somewhere in the periphery, a pan banged against the stove, a child cried out in frustration, but these distractions barely pierced the bubble of the artist's thoughts. On hearing children playing happily outside his window in Prague, Franz Kafka wrote, "It drives me . . . out of the house in despair, with throbbing temples through field and forest, devoid of all hope like a night owl." The artist must not be disturbed!

This age-old mythology of the seclusive male artist didn't work for me. In order to make my own art, I'd have to kill it.

I was too young to watch *The Mary Tyler Moore Show* during its initial run, but in the early nineties Nick at Nite syndicated "Marythons," which gave me a chance to watch it with my dad. He was biased, but he loved everything about the show (especially Lou Grant's cranky character). I was a sullen teenager by then and found the show dated, my image of a modern career woman having been carved indelibly by Candice Bergen's Murphy Brown, who strode big-shouldered into the office each day prepared to take zero flak from her male coworkers. Compared to Brown, Mary Richards came across as loopy, toothless, safe.

Later, I'd learn that Richards paved the way for Brown and others of her kind, in part because she was the first notable female TV character to choose work over family life (the series memorably ended with her giving a stirring speech declaring her coworkers her family), as well as the first female character openly on birth control. The show suggested Richards' success was made possible by her decision not to have children, making her career trajectory inversely proportional to my own.

And so "Love Is All Around" stirs in me strong emotions and ideals regarding women and success. In this way, I'm not alone. Gloria Steinem once told my father how much the song meant to her, as did Moore, who gave him a framed copy of the song's sheet music cover that hangs in his office. She titled her 1996 autobiography *After All*, a reference to the song's hook, "You're gonna make it after all." As I watched a teary-eyed Oprah on the CBS special invoke my dad's lyrics to explain how the show instilled in her the belief that "I own my own life. I'm in control. I'm going to make it after all," I considered how unlikely it would be to see, say, Bill Gates or Elon Musk give an equally emotive interview about believing in himself. To put a point on it, women relate to "Love Is All Around" because it's a song about success for those who have been told they can't succeed. The song doesn't say, "You're going to make it, baby," but "You're going to make it *after all*," the implication being "*after all you've overcome.*" This was a pep talk women yearned for in the seventies, when offices were rife with blatant sexism.

When I explain to my daughters that their grandfather wrote a song inspiring women to believe they could succeed at work, I'm greeted with blank stares. The idea that women would need encouragement entering the workforce is a concept as foreign and irrelevant to them as Mary Richards' manual typewriter would be to Kirsten. And how different their work will be from the work of Violet, whose hands clawed the crust off the West Texas earth and sowed the cotton, dug the milkweeds from between the stalks, and plucked the soft clouds from the razor-edged bolls until her cuticles bloomed and bled. Did she have hopes and dreams beyond the fields, or is dreaming itself a frivolity if you're born with such limited choices? Then again, choices can be their own kind of burden, and who am I to place a value judgement on Violet's life? It's not the life I would choose, but that doesn't mean she wasn't happy or fulfilled. In my memories of her, she's always laughing.

♪

The April after Mary died, I sat in a vast auditorium at Lubbock's Texas Tech University watching my dad perform a songwriters-in-round show. Midway through the concert, he began strumming the six cascading notes that begin "Love Is All Around." The song requires no introduction. People clapped and whistled even before he opened his mouth to sing—especially women, or so it sounded to my ears.

Even without its feminist cachet, it really is a lovely song. I've always been proud my father wrote it, though it's far from perfect. Like my own history with it, the song has a darkness, a shadow side: the second verse. "You are most likely to succeed," it begins before flying completely off the rails with "You have the looks and charm, and girl, you know that's all you need/All the men around adore you/That sexy look will do wonders for you."

When I became old enough for my mother's tawdry gossip, I gradually learned a startling piece of information. Nearly every successful female country music star in Nashville slept her way to the top. My mother had a story about them all. Though she never repeated them in front of my dad, they came from him, or from his friends, or from his friends' wives (Loretta Lynn was notably exempt, probably because she married at age fifteen—a tough way to extricate yourself from the rumor mill). As I became an adult I began to see these stories for what they were: propagandized narratives spun by the good old boy network on Music Row, tales told over burgers and beers at Brown's Diner. They served a purpose in the Nashville music scene, to diminish women's power and maintain the status quo of men as music business gatekeepers and women as sexual objects of desire and scorn. And certainly they served a purpose for my mother and her women friends for the same reason tabloids sell, to level the playing field. *Well I may not be a big star, but at least I'm not a whore.* Today my mom and I both recognize the misogyny behind these stories. The culture has changed, and so have we. But I cringe when I think of the initial effect it had on me as a teenager, how it perverted female power and warped my expectations for success. Some of the stars were women I admired, and even with my new perspective, I could never see them the same way.

When I hear the second verse of "Love Is All Around," I'm reminded of those stories. After Moore died, I asked my father about the verse over the phone. I told him I thought it was sexist. "I don't think I'm a sexist," he said.

I said I didn't think he was either, but that's not the whole truth. My dad is a gentleman in the vintage sense of the word, the kind of man who will perform an impromptu quick-step to open a door for a woman, or praise her appearance when she gets "dolled up," cordial relics of days gone by. He raised me to be strong and confident, to never apologize for raising my hand in class. He also wrote a verse suggesting women need nothing more than raw sex appeal to succeed in life. There exists in him a nugget of chauvinism that is undeniable, generational, and, while understandable, not wholly excusable.

So I gave him an out, and asked if he'd write the same verse again today. "Yeah, I think I would," he replied airily. "I still think it's clever." I let out a long sigh, but I didn't push the issue as I would have a decade or two ago. Time with my father increases in value with each passing year. I certainly don't want to spend it arguing about a fifty-year-old theme song.

But as I sat in that Lubbock auditorium a few months after our conversation, something strange happened. I watched my father do what I'd never seen him do before, not in the countless times I've seen him perform "Love Is All Around." He played the two different versions of the first verse that appeared on the show. He skipped the second.

CHAPTER 16

Growing up in the shadow of a famous song is a curious thing. It's a part of me when it suits me, but a part I don't pay much attention to, like a knuckle, when it doesn't. It suited me when I was young, but after I had children, I began holding it at arm's length. "The child goes through the full-time mother like a dye through water," wrote Rachel Cusk. "There is no part of her that remains uncolored." For me, motherhood tinted everything, even this seemingly benign theme song that helped put me through college. If I hear it on the wrong day, it invokes all that could have been, had I just believed with each glance and every little movement that I could make it after all, had I invested less energy in my mothering life and more in my career. Or the song reminds me that even if my father drops the second verse, he did indeed write—and defend—a line that undermines values I hold dear, both as a feminist and a mother raising three daughters of my own.

But if I hear the song on the right day, it lifts me out of my domestic minutiae and makes me applaud my father's willingness to revise. Good art can do that, help us reconcile our messy, "imperfectly mingled spirit," as Thoreau put it. The man with sexist tendencies who raised a feminist daughter. The feminist who quit her job and became a full-time mother. We're not dualistic creatures defined by our instincts; after all, Mary Richards was just a character on TV. The real Mary Tyler Moore was a divorcée, a flawed mother, a recovering alcoholic, and a raging Hollywood success.

A few years ago, a friend sent me a link to a print she'd found online, a folk artist's rendering of a hand tossing a beret in the air below the caption, "You're going to make it after all." It was a crude picture, one my child could have scrawled, but to me it looked like a scruffy patch of earth on which to stake my flag. So what if the hand was cartoonish, the fingers all the same length? My oldest daughter once said, "Sometimes mistakes make the best art."

I ordered one for my father, who was coming off a grueling year of chemo and radiation. Then I thought of Mary Richards and bought one for myself. Later, I hung it over my desk in the room I'd recently converted from a nursery into an office. It is the space where this book was born, and the writer in me was reborn there too under that clumsy print, making mistakes on the road to art. Adrienne Rich was right: domestic chores *are* often in direct conflict with the subversive function of the imagination. I want a family, and I want the writing life. I want the love that's all around but I don't want to be crushed by it. I want creativity in the face of reactivity. My father had the former, my mother the latter. My lowly, holy purpose in life is to find a way to have both.

Since I returned to writing, my daughters have grown. The creases on their thighs have filled in, the dimples on their knuckles, the hours in their days. They grant me my own space now, often more than I'd like. Now I am the one asking them to come out of their rooms and hang out with me. I couldn't imagine that shift twelve years ago in the therapist's office, but if I could go back in time and sit in her chair, this is what I would tell the empty vessel before me: one day the fog will lift from your brain and the bonds will loosen. In the meantime, try to write some things down. It doesn't have to be pretty or fine. Do it as a gift to the future you, for the bright morning on which you'll awaken to find a door has opened in your mind and you're finally free to enter.

After all, that's how doors work.

CHAPTER 17

The Winter Dance Party

And you know the levy ain't dry
And the music didn't die
'cause Buddy Holly lives every time we play rock and roll
—"REAL BUDDY HOLLY STORY," WRITTEN IN 1978

A few years ago, a bar in my town hosted a concert memorializing the sixtieth anniversary of Buddy Holly's final performance in Iowa, his last stop on the doomed Winter Dance Tour. I decided to check out the scene—or more accurately, Neal shamed me into going. "You're writing a book involving Buddy Holly. It's pretty lazy if you don't show up for an hour." I hate it when he's right.

That Saturday night, we hired a sitter and headed into the bitter February wind. The show was held at the Old Dog Tavern, located in a gutted paper factory with bruised oak floorboards and exposed piping. The place has a sort of rustic Michigan charm I've grown to recognize and love, the walls mounted with moose heads and blue marlins and the ceiling lined with ancient canoes. If you squint hard enough, you can envision Hemingway in the corner, drinking a whiskey and soda and scribbling the first draft of "Big Two-Hearted River" (actually written about Michigan's Fox River, such a beloved mythology in my town that our hometown brewery Bell's named their famous IPA after it).

CHAPTER 17

We arrived to find the Old Dog's parking lot full, as was the tavern, every table taken. Even the back room was crammed body-to-body, Buddy Holly still turning them out. Not only was there no place to sit, there was little room to stand. The prospect of squeezing next to strangers all night to hear songs I'd already heard enough to last three lifetimes made me grouchy, and I wanted a drink.

The crowd was mostly white with the average age above sixty—which made sense, for Buddy is an eternal teenager. I told Neal I thought we were the youngest ones there, and he pointed out a couple in their twenties practicing the jitterbug. The man was dressed like a greaser with a glossy black pompadour and a Harley-Davidson T-shirt. Everything about him appeared slick, as if he were a figure in a wax museum. His dance partner was a pretty redhead in beatnik attire: black turtleneck, black capris, and ballet flats. They knew the steps but they looked like reenactment performers.

A few days before the show, I'd reached out to the lead singer of the headlining rockabilly band on Facebook, a woman named (or stage named) Delilah DeWylde. I told her a bit about my connection to Buddy, and we'd arranged to meet at the bar. I spotted Delilah immediately—a Bettie Page look-alike with dark rimmed eyes and vampy red lipstick. She made her way toward us wearing a black fifties swing dress with a sweetheart neckline, a red carnation tucked behind her ear. After I introduced myself, I asked what drew her to Buddy's music.

Delilah told me her parents had been too young to appreciate the singer in his heyday, so she'd discovered him on her own during the rockabilly resurgence of the 1990s. When she told me she did the singing in the band, I asked if she attempted Buddy's signature hiccup, his famous vocal trick. She looked caught, like I'd presented her with a pop quiz. "I try, but I can't really get it," she said. I told her my dad had never quite pulled it off either and she seemed relieved.

Delilah turned to see a man with a gray-haired ponytail paying his admission near the entrance. "Oh no, that guy's kind of a stalker," she said, ducking low beside Neal. I said she must get a lot of older men who projected their 1950s fantasies onto her.

"Oh my God, you have no idea. They'll cite some obscure song and tell me I have to cover it. Then I'll go home and Google it and it will be so stupid, not even from the right era."

"Maybe they got their first boner to it." Delilah shrieked with laughter, and in that moment it felt like we became friends.

Just then a knee-walking drunk man stumbled up to tell us it was his birthday. He had a cherubic face and eyes that were sloshing around in their sockets like fish in a bowl. I could tell by the way the bartender greeted him that he was a regular. "I died the same day Buddy was born!" he announced. "Wait . . . that's not . . ." I told him I knew what he meant. Then, because I felt a little sorry for him, I mentioned that Prince had died on my birthday a few years before.

Fish Eyes stopped swimming. "Now all we can do is celebrate them," he said, clinking his glass against mine. It was a surprisingly lucid statement, if one I didn't buy. I loved Prince, but I wasn't going to spend my next birthday at a Prince tribute concert. I would treat myself to a nice bottle of wine, dinner with family or friends. I would celebrate my own cherished life. Because life, as a widowed friend of mine sometimes says to cheer herself up, is for the living.

Delilah excused herself to perform. Fish Eyes unceremoniously weaved into the crowd. Neal squeezed his way to the bar for another round, leaving me alone with my empty drink and addled thoughts. My legs were tired from running after my daughters all day and I longed to sit down. I waited for the lights to dim and thought about the good old days of the Crickets, when there was always a front-row seat reserved for me. The best period was when my dad rejoined the band in the nineties—Paul McCartney had bought much of Buddy's catalogue (the Beatles admired Buddy and the Crickets so much, they famously chose an insect name to emulate them), and for years he hosted an annual concert gala honoring him in London or New York, with the Crickets as the headliners. I attended a few, my favorite in London when I was twenty. I was living in Oxford on a study abroad program at the time, and two of my girlfriends and I took the train to see the show.

CHAPTER 17

After the concert (enjoyable if typical Crickets fare; the set list never diverged much) my mom escorted us backstage, where Paul and Linda were holding court. The McCartneys occupied a mythical space in my brain. I learned Beatles melodies before I could form words, and I knew the couple's romantic backstory by heart: their passionate love affair, their animal rights activism, how they'd only spent that one night apart when Paul was arrested for marijuana possession. In my mind they were immortal as gods, and here they were in the flesh acting like normal people, especially Linda, who was dressed as if to pull weeds in faded jeans and a baggy sweatshirt without a lick of makeup on. My mom introduced me to her and she threw an arm around my shoulder and led me to her table, where she seated me next to her teenage son James. I locked eyes with my mom across the room, and she winked and gave me a thumbs-up. James was too young for me, but how she loved to tease me for years that if only I'd played my cards right, I could have been a McCartney. I remember that night so well, how the giddiness lasted into the next morning when my mom barged into our swanky hotel suite and made a show of checking under our beds. "Oh Jaaaaames!" she trilled. "Come out, come out, wherever you are!" My friends and I lay in our 600 thread count splendor, howling with laughter, all of us so young—especially my mother, the beautiful clown. That night, the best night of all.

It was all downhill from there. My mom and I grew jaded at Crickets concerts, rolling our eyes at each other when my dad told his worn-out stage jokes ("Folks, this song's the reason I'm able to drive a Buick"). In the band's last decade leading up to their retirement in 2015, they performed less and less and when they did, I rarely bothered to go.

How I wish I could see them once more, I thought. *I'd do it right this time, take my daughters, appreciate every lame joke, every sentimental song.*

Back in the Old Dog Tavern, a tall man with salt-and-pepper hair and a chiseled face tapped me on the shoulder, crashing my VIP pity party for one. "Excuse me," he said. "It's okay if you stand here, but do you mind staying between these two points?" He stretched out his arms to demonstrate the narrow coordinates of the space he wanted my body to occupy. "You see, when you move too far right, you block my view of the stage." I'm barely 5′4″ and slight of build but apparently I wasn't small enough for this asshole, who wished me damn near invisible.

Oh, gentle reader. Words cannot fully express the fire that lit within me at that moment. It was a standing-room-only fire, a woman-alone-in-a-bar fire, a woman-who's-paid-her-Buddy-Holly-dues fire. It was the fire of my father and all the Dust Bowl farmers before him, the fire of a polite young man who chartered a plane because he wanted to arrive at the next gig a day early to wash his underwear and catch up on sleep, but ended up dead in a snowy cornfield, a field as flat as the ones in West Texas he'd managed to transcend. It was all those fires and more. All the petty grievances and inequities in my life leading up to that moment I placed squarely on this handsome man's shoulders as I turned to him slowly, sparks spitting from my flaming eyeballs.

"Hey man, back off. My dad played with *Buddy Holly*."

As soon as the words escaped my lips, I envisioned my dad's embarrassed face, his furrowed brow. Humble Sonny. He would not approve of my name-dropping.

"Um, that's cool?" the man said, backing away slowly.

Finally, mercifully, the lights dimmed and Delilah sashayed into the spotlight. She had an effervescent stage presence, transitioning nimbly from one song to the next, her voice equal parts honey and spice. Her curves were mirrored in her massive upright bass, which she slapped into submission. It was easy to see why men fell in love with her; hell, I was falling in love with her. She evoked a bygone feminine mythology, a good time gal, a gal before the days of #metoo, back when you could tell women where to stand in bars.

The beatnik and the greaser had some competition on the dance floor, a young couple who seemed out of place, both because of their age and because they didn't fit a discernible mold. They weren't older Baby Boomers. They weren't dressed like rockabilly fans. They weren't pervs. They just seemed like average college kids who liked Buddy Holly. I couldn't stop watching them. The boy was tall and preppy in a golf shirt and khakis and, surprisingly, he could dance. At one point, he threw his arms in the air and did a little shimmy, making his date laugh.

Maybe it was the bourbon in my blood, but they gave me hope. I felt like the universe had presented them to me as a reminder that Buddy Holly's music really *is* special and enduring. I'd been feeling jaded and bitter when what I should have been feeling was lucky—lucky to claim even a distant connection to this rare talent gone far too soon. I wanted to remember this glorious young couple, so I snapped several pictures of them on my phone, but they turned out to be blurs of motion, one more fleeting moment in my life I couldn't pin down. Though I did manage to capture the shimmy.

The next afternoon I called my dad. It helps when we have something to talk about, and I figured my attending a Buddy Holly tribute concert would give us plenty of material. But he seemed unimpressed.

"Sounds like a good time," he said flatly. The line fell silent.

"I remember you used to dread playing the Winter Dance Party," I said, referring to the annual tribute held at the Surf Ballroom in Clear Lake, Iowa, Buddy's last stop. The four-day event includes a sock hop, meet and greets with oldies performers, and a big concert finale. For years before the Crickets retired in 2015, they were the headliners.

"Oh yeah," he sighed. "It was exhausting. People were always in my face." I could picture them. *What was Buddy Holly really like?* Pervs. "We'd close out the show the final night. It didn't end until one or two in the morning, and then we'd only get a few hours' sleep before we'd have to catch a plane to fly home. J. I. always wanted to get out of there early."

I said I remembered that he usually came down with a cold or flu after he returned. "Always. Those shows just about killed me," he said, no trace of irony in his voice.

I could tell this line of conversation was weighing on him, so I changed the subject and asked what he'd been up to. He said that he and my mom had met J. I. and Joanie for breakfast at Cracker Barrel that morning. I asked if they'd talked about the fact that it was the sixtieth anniversary of Buddy's death. He paused. "No," he finally said in a low whisper. "We would never bring that up to J. I. It would just make him feel blue."

After we hung up, I looked out the window at the ash-gray February light, the bare tree branches scratching the sky. What a depressing month to revisit a death. I considered what the Winter Dance Party must represent to my father, what a mind warp his life must be when it comes to Buddy Holly, always having to answer the wrong question, decade after decade. In my research on his interviews, I found only one instance where a reporter, Raoul Hernandez for the *Austin Chronicle*, asked the right one: "Do you find it strange that forty-five years after Buddy's death, audiences . . . are essentially celebrating a moment frozen in time? A twenty-two-year-old frozen in time?"

"I've definitely always tried to be my own person," my dad said. "I've never tried to imitate Buddy. When we do a performance, we're obligated to do 'That'll Be the Day' the way folks remember hearing it. I don't overplay the hiccup, but I put that in there, because it fits, it belongs."

You might note that my father did not answer Hernandez's question, so I'll answer it for him. Yes, it's strange that audiences still gather once a year to jitterbug their way through one of the saddest events in rock 'n' roll history. Yes, it's strange that people—and I am one of them—still ask my dad what Buddy Holly was really like, as if it's an accurate gauge for the kind of man he would have become had he lived past twenty-two. Yes, it's strange how we hold onto our heroes, how we require them to recreate themselves for our amusement (as I write these words, a theater in Allentown, Pennsylvania, is running a musical featuring a Buddy Holly hologram. A Hollygram?). As if the world will finally freeze on our command, and for one brief moment we will become young again, or brave again, or relevant again, or just a little less broken.

CHAPTER 17

Did you talk about the sixtieth anniversary of Buddy's death? What a silly question. In that moment I saw I had become like the greaser and the beatnik, resurrecting Buddy on the page while forgetting that his death affected—still affects—actual living people. He's not just a hologram or a ghost on the radio. He was a real man gone too soon, far too soon.

CHAPTER 18

The Meanders of the Creek

As I look back down that winding road of life, here's what I see
The dreams of all my yesterdays, the total sum of me
From childhood trails and swimming holes to what I've
   grown to be
I owe the biggest part of me to Tennessee
          —"TENNESSEE, I LOVE YOU," 1976

🔥 HOT NEW HOME ON MARKET! FABULOUS CALIFORNIA CONCEPT HOME! Originally Built as a Custom Home for a Rock & Roll Legend (One of the "BUDDY HOLLY & THE CRICKETS" Band Members) Long time personal home *Nestled on 5.01 Picturesque Acres *SUPER COOL VIBE *SOARING 2 STORY GREAT ROOM & Incredible Windows* Huge Detached Shop/Garage/Barn* Awesome Country Setting yet Easy Access to I-40/ I-840 *SUPER HOT LOCATION for Nashville/Franklin COMMUTERS *If these Walls Could Talk . . . You Feel the History of this Home!

A high school friend sends me the listing on Facebook. I click through the photos of the glass house feeling alternately sad, possessive, and confused, but mostly confused. The rooms are so different.

The longtime owner has made a lot of upgrades (no more shower greenhouse, wisely) and I can't find my bearings. Am I looking at my father's office, or our guest room? What floor am I even on? I finally recognize my old bedroom by the off-kilter angle of the windows. Like the rest of the house, it's been staged by a realtor and wiped clean of history, as if each room has taken a bath and donned a cheap interview suit.

I fly down a month later for my annual fall visit. Fall is my favorite Tennessee season, when the humidity lifts and the air turns musky, the trees shedding their ruby leaves dramatically, like country singers flinging off their sequined jackets.

"Isn't this nice, just the three of us?" my father says over dinner the first night.

My mother chimes in. "Well, of course, we *love* Neal and the girls, of course we do! But still. Isn't it nice?" This is our routine, to say these words whenever it's just the three of us. And it is nice. It's a relief reverting to our old familial language. Nobody outside our triangle will fully understand our history, our jokes, the off-kilter angle of our myths. I suppose that's one definition of family.

The next morning my mom and I drive to the glass house while my dad stays back with his crossword. I don't think he enjoys going out there much. He's driven me past the farm a few times over the years, and it always bothers him the way the owner let the pastures go. Under his regime, the fields stayed bushhogged within an inch of their lives, the land neatly studded by hay bales each spring, the trail to the Piney River cleared of brush. Once when the farm was particularly overgrown, he fought back tears. He has the soul of a poet but the heart of a farmer. Show him a swath of grass and he'll look for a plow.

We arrive before the realtor and wander around the yard just as the sun is starting to burn off the last wisps of morning fog. The angles, the palette, everything is the same and not the same. The lawn still rises to a wild pasture, the pole barn still sags in the distance, the place still smells of decaying leaves and grass. But much has changed. So many people who bore witness to this land are gone: our farmhands Phillip and Clyde, and nearly all those jolly songwriters who used to toss horseshoes in the spot where I'm now standing. Yet my narrow, two-story wooden playhouse, built by my dad and J. I., remains.

"Look, someone scratched out your name!" My mom points to the arch at the top and sure enough, I can make out the word *Sarah* carved into the wood. Another child tried to scribble it out in black magic marker, but did not leave their own name. Only mine, a child's existential announcement. *I am alive.*

The realtor, Missy, arrives in a big black SUV. She wears stylish workout gear and a baseball cap pulled low over her wavy brown ponytail. Immediately she apologizes for dressing down, a Southern lady habit I know too well. We head up the outside stairs to the second floor, where we enter through the kitchen just like we used to. Immediately I'm hit with the familiar, herbaceous scent of cedar. Oh the kitchen. This was the room where we gathered every night to laugh or argue, where my mom peeled enough potatoes to feed Ireland, where she sauteed so much okra that to this day when I taste it, I'm transported to the grassy scent of a Tennessee pasture and the sweet vanilla of dogwoods in bloom. My mom always regretted not building a dining room, which I never understood as a child. The kitchen felt perfectly sized to me, room enough only for the three of us and the characters we created.

"You couldn't build this house today," Missy says. "No contractor would touch it. Just the wood alone would cost maybe a million." Looking around, I feel a phantom pain from all my childhood splinters.

I look out over the wraparound balcony to see a rope fence lining the driveway, a knife-edge separation between the house and the woods. Missy tells us that's because the owner is selling the house with only five acres attached, and those five acres do not include the surrounding trees. *Do not include the trees?* This takes a minute to sink in. Given Nashville's massive housing sprawl—Missy tells us she's negotiating thirty closings this week alone—it's likely a developer will come in, clear the trees, and build who knows how many homes. Doesn't the owner understand that the glass house and the woods are a package deal, the woods necessary to cloak the home's nakedness? From a merely aesthetic view, the home would lose its treehouse vibe. People who live in glass houses shouldn't throw stones, and they also shouldn't build subdivisions in their backyard.

As I'm mentally arguing with the owner, he drops by in the flesh to say hello. It's hard to dislike him. A chatty, flannel-clad man in his sixties with kind, tired eyes, he tells us he's retired from the music business and currently living in the small white house, which he's renovated. We sit on the couch and he pulls up photos of it on his phone. My mom and I sit in disbelief as he scrolls through one bougie scene after another. It looks like one of those tiny houses you see on HGTV, all sliding barn doors and sleek gray cabinetry, a perfect blend of modern and farmhouse. It's come a long way from raccoons in the attic and a porch bathroom.

He tells us he's selling the glass house because his children are grown and he doesn't need so much land anymore, but it was a great place to raise kids. Yes, we all agree, the glass house is something special alright (*with the woods attached*, I think). Before we leave, I ask if it's okay if we come back and stroll around the farm the next day by ourselves. Yes, of course, he says, though he warns us the pastures are wild. "And it's copperhead hatching season!" my mom says.

The owner cocks his head. "You know what? In all my years living here, I never saw a poisonous snake."

While my mom regales him with snake stories of her own I quietly slip away, up the stairs to my old bedroom. It's now an office with pastel paint and a geometric rug. How many selves were molded in this small, crooked room? I picture my old bed, cream-colored and girly with an etched mirror on the headboard, how I would lie there for hours looking at my face, at the bump on the bridge of my nose and pimples spreading across my forehead, at my eyes blue like my mother's and cheeks fat like my father's. The bed where I flung myself and cried one Friday afternoon in sixth grade because Brandi Wilson didn't invite me to her roller-skating party, though I didn't know how to skate because nobody had taught me. The bed where I spent weeks at age fourteen with a bad case of mono, wearing a red flannel nightgown and watching reruns of *Batman* until my mother forced me to turn off Eartha Kitt and bathe. The bed where I read *Love Story* as a teenager, and envisioned living in a place as far away and sophisticated as New England, and eventually I did, though I learned it was just a place like any other, flawed and complicated. The bed where I suffered my first periods, my first heartbreaks, my first hangovers, my first secrets I could not tell adults. Where I tried to learn how to be a girl in America. Where I wanted most to stay, and most to leave.

Walking through the glass house, I feel as if a part of me has never left. And if you count the thousands of dreams and nightmares I've had about the house over the years, that's true. Maybe those are some of the truest things in life, the ones we try to leave but can't, like my father's twelve-by-fourteen shack. All the rooms that claim us in the end.

The following day my parents and I drive back to the farm under a bright bluebell sky. My dad pulls down the gravel driveway and continues past the house, past the pole barn, into the first pasture, which is indeed wild. My mom grunts in disgust. "Look at this mess! It looked so much better when we lived here!"

Yep, my dad agrees. I'm clearly not a farmer at heart because I'm not sure why the sight of tall grass offends them so. My dad wants to turn back, but I beg him to drive us to the old log cabin and he reluctantly agrees. We pull up to find it's collapsed into a pile of rubble. Only the brick chimney remains standing. Circling the ruins feels morbid, so I announce I'm going to walk to the Piney.

"*The Piney?*" My mom balks. Don't I remember when a Piney water moccasin once swam dangerously close to one of my cousins? she asks. "They're very aggressive! They'll even jump into boats!" I tell her

CHAPTER 18

I don't plan on entering the Piney by foot or by boat; I only want to see it. My dad sighs and shakes his head. Our beautiful farm, still a treasury of peril.

Water moccasin microaggressions be damned, I leave my anxious parents at their Jeep and begin my slow descent into the third pasture. The grass has swallowed the path and I keep my head down, my old routine, scoping the ground for those elusive hatching copperheads. But then the owner's words echo in my head: *In all my years living here, I never saw a poisonous snake.* Huh. Come to think of it, I never saw one either, at least not a live one. Garters were common, and Phillip showed me several dead copperheads when I was young so I knew what to look out for. ("How can you tell it's a copperhead?" my dad once asked him. "It's a copperhead until it's dead," was his sage reply.) But I'm tired of walking head down. And anyway, I'm wearing a flannel jacket, jeans, and hiking shoes. If a baby copperhead is that hungry for human flesh, it will have to make it through a layer of denim first.

Soon the grass clears into a spongy field of river weeds. I make my way to stand at the bank. The Piney looks exactly as I remember: clear water, pebble stone bed, wooded cliff, downed tree. *Downed tree?* My eye catches on the tree. Why does it look so familiar? I feel like I could paint it by memory, but I haven't been here in over twenty years. Then I realize that this log, this stream—it's the exact scene I conjured when I wrote about Will and the Arkansas gunfight, the same rotting tree that hid him from the gunmen, the same cold waters that clotted his blood and kept him alive. I was writing about Arkansas, but I was picturing the Piney.

If Will had died in that river, I would not be here. Pearl and the children—my grandfather Arthur being one—would have remained in Arkansas. They would never have migrated to West Texas. My grandfather would never have met my grandmother, my father would never have been born, my DNA never expressed. I consider this as I peer down the Piney to where it disappears at the bend. *Does this river connect to that one?* I wonder.

The noonday sun beats down like a drum and I grow hot under my heavy flannel. I say my final goodbyes to the Piney before turning back. In response it says nothing, just continues its unhurried flow, unaware of its confluence in my life and all my writerly associations. As I approach the gate leading to the third pasture I see my worried father standing at the base of the hill, shading his eyes to look for me. When he spots me he jumps up and down and waves his arms above his head, as if I've returned from a dangerous mission. "Oh Dad," I cry out. "I didn't mean for you to walk this far!"

As we make our way up the hill to the Jeep, I ask him where the property ends to the east. I never thought much about the actual borders of the farm as a child; it seemed like a boundless kingdom of green. "It follows the meanders of the creek," he says with a shrug.

"Aw, that's poetic, Dad."

"No. It's in the deed. 'The farm is bordered by the meanders of the creek.' That's what the deed says."

"Oh. Well, it's a poetic deed, then."

"I reckon so."

We climb the rest of the hill in silence, my dad leading the way. I examine him from behind, his thin shock of white hair, the black hearing aids cupping his ears, his careful but agile gait. His shoulders slump from age and cancer surgery, but he manages the incline with ease. I'm gripped with a moment of gratitude for my 84-year-old father, still game for my misadventures.

Maybe what matters isn't so much the geography of the land as the geography of the mind, the myths I have spun. My memory too follows the meanders of the creek; it rolls and rushes over stones, overflows its banks and dries back down, catches on small twigs and ripples, drains down dead-end tributaries. It decomposes, breaks apart, regenerates in new forms. The downed tree might have been here since my childhood, though probably not. Even giant trees decompose quickly in a river. The Piney might connect to the river that saved Will, though probably not. But as I am the one telling the story, the rivers are forever merged. It is the image I saved and served, whether I knew it at the time or not. That is the power of the memory keeper, the mythmaker, the songwriter. The storyteller.

I fly back to Michigan the next day. As usual, my dad spends all morning lecturing me about interstate traffic. As usual, we spend ten minutes negotiating a departure time. As usual, he gets me to the airport two hours early. I hug my parents goodbye on the curb and my dad presses a folded bill into my palm. It's hard to tell behind his dark sunglasses, but I think he's tuning up.

When I arrive in Michigan, nobody greets me at the airport. Neal's at work, and my daughters are at school. The sun is shining but delivers no heat. As I bundle into my puffer coat and crank the heater in my car, I long for the blue skies and warmth of my home state.

My family and I live in an old farmhouse on a property its former owners named Pine Song Farm, though the farm is long gone. The family sold it to a developer who built an Arts and Crafts subdivision behind our house, inhabited by amiable, retired doctors who walk their designer dogs more than I feel necessary. But trees remain from the old property, the tallest being two massive Norway spruces that shade our driveway like benevolent overlords out of Tolkien.

Inside my house, I'm greeted by my crazed poodle and a pile of mail on the kitchen counter. In a few minutes I'll leave to pick up my daughters from school, and then this home will be filled with the cacophony of rowdy girls competing to tell me about their weekend: the meals, the errands, the injustices. There will be lunch bags to clean and homework to finish, laughter and arguments and chaos. It is the life I've created, so different from my own solitary childhood in the glass house. Often it feels like too much for me, and often it is. But in the silence of that moment, I miss my family's song. *This is it*, I think, *our happiest time*. My parents still alive, my father still adored, my daughters still at home. One day all of that will change, I know. It will change and change and change again until we become like the family who lived in the log cabin on our Tennessee farm, leaving ruins behind for others to sift through. But not exactly. My father's songs will live on, and maybe so will my words.

As I'm backing out of the garage to pick up my girls from school, I notice that Neal has cleared out our vegetable garden for the winter while I've been gone. A few summers ago, he built four cedar beds surrounded by steel mesh walls to keep out the deer. It's a lovely space, one deserving of better gardeners. Every spring our hopes are high as we fill the beds with heirloom seeds. But by July, half our crops are struggling. Slugs and earwigs devour our kale and collards. No matter how early we start the tomatoes from seed, the Michigan summer never lasts long enough for them, and all but the cherry varieties end up mealy. Our pole beans are stringy and our berries lack flavor, which seems to be the number one problem with our crops. They're serviceable but not luscious like the offerings at our local farmer's market: plump tomatoes bursting with summer juices, candy-sweet strawberries, snap peas tender enough to be eaten straight from the basket.

After a particularly disappointing crop last summer, Neal threw up his arms and suggested we give up the garden entirely. "What's the point of going to all this trouble when we can just go the farmer's market?" he said. "Those people know what they're doing. Unlike us."

I promised him we'd get better at it, that I'd spend more time working out there—promises I knew, even as I made them, I wouldn't keep. The truth is, I suspect we'll always be middling gardeners, outsmarted by slugs. It's not so much the product but the process I've grown attached to: the feeling of my hands in the loamy Michigan soil. I buy myself new gardening gloves every summer but never wear them. I like digging in the dirt. It's nice to think that sensation connects me to my Texan ancestors, but I am living miles away, toiling under a forgotten moon. Rather, my garden connects me to something inside myself I cannot name, a wind-blown scrap of DNA, the shadow of a man who named himself, a thin yet stalwart root anchoring me to a world beneath the ground.

CHAPTER 19

The Ghosts of Lubbock

*Often I am permitted to return to a meadow
as if it were a given property of the mind
that certain bounds hold against chaos,
that is a place of first permission,
everlasting omen of what is.*

—ROBERT DUNCAN

*When the wind gets up you can hear that old panhandle groan
Kickin' up dust with a gust and a Texas moan
But that's my home
That's my home...*

—"WHEN AMARILLO BLOWS," 1982

My parents and I enter the auditorium through a side door, where an intern awaits to guide my father backstage. He fiddles with his hearing aids and trails after her into the shadows, his guitar case slung over his shoulder. "Knock 'em dead, Dad," I say, but he cannot hear me.

This show, part of an annual Lubbock music festival, is his first since he's begun to lose his hearing. In the past, I probably would have skipped this concert. He's played hundreds of these songwriter-in-the-round type gigs over the decades. But during his cancer battle, I realized how much I missed seeing him perform. And so I've left my husband and three daughters behind in Michigan for this chance at redemption.

My mom and I sit in the center of the empty auditorium, a large Texas Tech lecture hall that smells of brass instruments and pencil dust. Soon the doors open and the audience floods in, wizened older Texans who know more than the words to the songs they are about to hear. They know the route to the 640 acres outside Lubbock where my great-grandfather planted cotton and sorghum, and to the joints where my dad and Buddy used to pick. The land is out of cultivation and the joints are long gone. But in the weathered faces surrounding me, I think I see the flicker of those ghosts.

The room dims, the ceiling explodes with pinpricks of light, and my father walks onstage as easily as if he's strolling into his living room. He is just starting to get his strength back from the cancer, and he looks elegant in a navy sport coat and dark jeans. The room erupts in applause for him and the night's other two performers, fellow Lubbock sons Joe Ely and Lloyd Maines. A hush falls over the crowd as the three men take their seats.

"To my immediate right, Mr. Sonny Curtis," says the silver-haired announcer. He delivers a fawning introduction, calling my father "a terrific songwriter, a terrific vocalist, a terrific guitarist, and a terrific human being." He doesn't mention the name Buddy Holly because he doesn't have to. Their connection is well known in this room. Anyway, that was over sixty years ago, and tonight is about what remains.

After the introductions, the announcer asks my dad to go first, to sing a song and tell a story about the song, standard procedure for a songwriter-in-the-round event. Yet my dad seems confused. "What's that?" he asks, cupping his ear and leaning in, though the announcer is sitting right next to him. The man repeats himself. A nearby audience member laughs and my heart seizes. But when my father starts talking, I exhale.

"First I'd like to say what a pleasure it is to be back in Lubbock. I always feel real warm when I look out the window while the plane's about to light, and I see my old home." He draws out the words *real warm* and narrows his eyes for effect, slowly sweeping his hand in front of him as if he's surveying the land from just below the cloud line, how Lubbock sprawls like a quilt of brown and orange squares. It's a striking view, all that expanse made so tidy. *This place has owners, a system*, the land says.

He kicks off the show with "I'm No Stranger to the Rain." His voice is weakened by surgery to remove a tumor close to his vocal cords, and it wobbles between the notes. Yet his guitar playing remains nimble, his chord changes exact. After a few turns at the mic, his voice warms up and he appears to relax. A casual observer watching him would assume he's enjoying himself. It's clear the audience loves him, and the feeling is mutual. But I am his daughter. I see his forced smile, his rushed introductions. He stares into the middle distance after each song—once Lloyd has to tap him on the shoulder to alert him it's his turn. My father wants off this stage.

For the finale, the three men close out the show with "That'll Be the Day," a song I've heard enough to last two lifetimes. And yet my eyes burn with tears as I watch my dad show off on lead guitar, the audience singing along as if the song represents hope now instead of tragedy. What I don't know as I sit in this auditorium is that soon my father's hearing will deteriorate so rapidly, it will be the last time I'll see him perform.

The next morning my parents and I decide to pay a visit to my uncle Pete, a retired farmer who still lives in my dad's hometown of Meadow. But first we stop for breakfast at the Pancake House, a Lubbock diner that caters to Texas Tech students and burly farmers in Carhartt coveralls. The place is filled with antique tchotchkes and signs about Jesus and cotton, like *All I Need Is Coffee and Jesus* and *Cotton: It's What You Wear to Dinner*. A middle-aged waitress appears with a wink and a refill. Her shirt reads *Today's Special: Jesus*.

CHAPTER 19

"Can you tell I just had Botox?" my mother asks me, touching her cheek. I lie and say no. Possibly due to her deepening anxiety about my father's health, she suffers from a hemifacial spasm, a twitch that overtakes half her face. Invisible to the naked eye, it is maddening to the sufferer. Her doctor calms it with Botox, which immobilizes the area around her eyes, altering the planes of her cheekbones. As the Botox wears off, her face appears more natural but the twitch returns. I can tell she's recently been injected by the way her blue eyes freeze when she smiles. My parents' aging has become a series of bargains straight out of a Grimms' fairy tale. My mother's beauty for her sanity. My father's hearing for his life.

We talk about the shrieking wind the night before, a West Texas night sound I remember from childhood visits to my grandparents. It's been a long time since I've heard that sound, a long time since I've been in Lubbock—not since my grandfather's funeral twenty years ago.

"I always hated that sound," my father says, stabbing his eggs. "Lonesome."

Outside the Pancake House the wind has settled into a mild April day, the air weightless on my skin. My father gestures to a strip of gravel lots in the distance. "A few blocks that way was the 16th and J Club, a joint I used to pick with Buddy," he says. "Man, you talk about some orchestrated fistfights. *Woo-eee.*"

We climb into the Jeep, with me in the passenger seat so my dad can hear my questions. Downtown Lubbock appears completely empty except for a group of weatherworn men in front of the bus station on Crickets Avenue. They sit on piles of beat-up suitcases, smoking cigarettes and squinting into the sun. Across from the station, a mural of Buddy Holly is painted across a beige brick building, sandwiched between a shuttered laundromat and a bail bond company.

The mural is made up of three scenes. Painted on the left is the titular Peggy Sue, J. I.'s first wife whom he forever immortalized in song. She died a few months after our trip, but on the mural she is forever young, blonde and angelic in a strapless prom dress, practically levitating amidst a haze of blue light. In the center, Buddy and the two main Crickets, J. I. and Joe B., lean in to form a triangle, with Buddy at the top. On their right is a rendering of Buddy's famous close-up, his earnest gaze penetrating his black horn-rimmed glasses.

My father pulls our rental Jeep to the curb so I can get a better look at it. I try to place where I've seen another pair of bespectacled eyes overlooking a bleak, urban landscape. Then I remember: the billboard bearing the eyes of Dr. T. J. Eckleburg that haunts the Valley of Ashes in *The Great Gatsby*. The metaphor writes itself. This vista, this street—Crickets Avenue no less—is Lubbock's own Valley of Ashes. Yet Buddy Holly continues to breathe much life into this town. As I write this, the city has recently completed construction on the Buddy Holly Hall of Performing Arts and Sciences, a $154 million project that features two state-of-the-art theaters, a ballet school, a symphony orchestra, a bistro, and multiple community spaces. The campus spans 220,000 square feet and is expected to revitalize downtown Lubbock.

After more than fifty years together, the Crickets officially retired following Joe B. Mauldin's death in 2015. Even my mom had to admit the band came a long way from that disorganized Swedish tour in the mid-nineties, the one that nearly broke up my parents. In 2012, the band was inducted into the Rock & Roll Hall of Fame as part of a special initiative to include previously overlooked backup bands. Buddy Holly was inducted alone into the hall's inaugural class in 1986, and J. I. and Joe B. were deeply hurt by the oversight. J. I. and Buddy had formed the Crickets together; the band was half his creation. The late induction was a nice gesture but one that came too late, and after hemming and hawing for a few months, the band decided that instead of attending the ceremony in Cleveland, they'd throw their own party in J. I.'s barn. That night, my dad, J. I., and Joe B. sat on overturned buckets drinking cans of beer surrounded by J. I.'s tractor equipment and rusty tools. My mom took a photo of the three of them laughing, probably at something J. I. said. Later I captioned the photo, "The Real Rock 'n' Roll Hall of Fame," and gave a framed copy to each of them. Fame, finally on their own terms.

CHAPTER 19

I lean out my window to take a picture of the mural on my phone. Beside me, my dad waits patiently for his nosy daughter to make meaning of a ghost. "You ready to move on?" he asks. I say I am.

I've learned the problem with ghosts isn't that they're not real. It's that they lure you from what is.

Outside the city center, my father makes a sudden right-hand turn down 36th, a residential street of neglected ranch homes on parched lawns. He stops the Jeep in front of the first one on the right, a tan house with peeling siding.

"Right there's where my high school girlfriend Jeanie Kate lived."

"Oh yeah? How long did you date her for?" I ask.

"Uh, I don't know. Three or so years."

That's a long time for high school, I say. I ask if she's still alive. "No, she died fairly recently. Cancer, I think. She was a good ol' girl." He examines the house from behind his black shield sunglasses.

"And a beautiful girl!" chirps my mother. "I've seen pictures of her."

I roll down my window to get a better view of the house. It looks abandoned, as do all the homes on this street. I start to wonder how long we're going to sit here and stare at it. My father breaks the silence. "I'll tell you a story about this house," he says with a smirk. I reach into my purse for my notepad and flip to a clean page.

Before my father turned seventeen, Jeanie Kate planned to throw him a birthday party at this house, he tells us. The night before the party, he was booked to play a show five hours south with Buddy and Bob Montgomery. He gave Jeanie Kate his word that he'd be back in time for the party, but after the show, a high school principal offered the band a gig at a jamboree the following evening. Buddy and Bob felt they could not pass it up.

"But I'm supposed to be back at Jeanie Kate's house tomorrow night for my birthday party!" my father claims to have protested, though I'm betting he didn't put up much of a fight. Back in those days, gigs trumped everything for my father. In some ways, they always did.

He leans in to deliver his punch line, making a gun with his thumb and index finger. "So at that house right there, Jeanie Kate threw me a seventeenth birthday party." *Click, boom,* he pulls the trigger. "Sans moi." He laughs lightly and eases on the gas.

I laugh too, but as usual, I have questions. "Was she mad?" I ask.

"Aw, no, I don't think so."

"*Really?*"

"Well, yeah, maybe a little," he admits.

We drive for a minute in silence. My father scans the landscape, tapping out a beat on the wheel. I wonder if he is remembering Jeanie Kate, the cheeky way she nibbled her pencil, how she stood in the front row of his shows and winked up at him between songs. In my mind, she's the stock 1950s girl next door, the spurned, bobby-socked heroine whose loyalty is never enough. More Betty than Veronica, more Debbie Reynolds than Liz Taylor. But surely she was more than that, and maybe my father's not thinking of her right now anyway. Maybe he's thinking about the boy on that stage, what kind of life he would have led had he married Jeanie Kate and not my mom. Would he have managed the music store he worked at through high school, selling guitar strings and giving lessons to teenagers who wanted to pick like Scotty Moore? Or would he have become a farmer like so many who came before him, relegated to writing songs from the seat of his own tractor?

On the outskirts of Lubbock, strip malls give way to farmland, green and brown stripes of cotton and soybeans, the West Texas of my memories. The horizon is so flat it appears sliced by a paper cutter, the view all heaven, no earth. The seam between land and sky trained my father's eye from an early age. You're not crazy or stupid in West Texas; you're half a bubble off plumb. Anything other than level is viewed with suspicion.

Every landmark cues a synapse in my father's brain. The place where he first spotted his friend Glen D. Hardin riding a bike barefoot while playing a ukulele (Glen D. would grow up to play piano for Elvis, John Denver, Emmylou Harris, and many other luminaries. What was in the drinking water in West Texas?). The exact elm tree under which, in third grade, he first kissed a girl. His voice is as rich as warm molasses, and it lulls me back to a place deeper than memory, to our green Tennessee farm. It smells of cut hay and vanilla with a base note of cow manure. It sounds like the lonely call of a bobwhite, my mother yelling up the stairs, *Sarah, dinnertime!* It feels like the smooth edge of the oak dining table where I sit night after night listening to my father tell old rock 'n' roll stories, or to my parents argue. My dad talks us all the way to Meadow. At some point, I lay down my pen and close my eyes behind my sunglasses. I lose the thread.

Once again, I'm left to find the story hiding in the details. He'll tell you about Jeanie Kate's birthday party sans him, but he won't tell you how desperate he was back then for a break, or how impossible it felt to leave Texas. He'll show you the joints he played with Buddy, but he won't tell you what it felt like to bury his friend at twenty-two or live out the remainder of his life wrestling with the shadow of a ghost. It's a magician's trick. First comes a sudden sparkle in the periphery, an old pickpocket move, though he uses it to protect his own pockets. *Over there*, he'll point, and in a wink you'll laugh, and look away.

Parallel to the highway a freight train blows by, the words *Texas Star* emblazoned on its steel belly. My father squints at it. "Wonder why that's passing so late in the morning?" he mutters. I'm not sure how he knows the Lubbock train schedule, but his memory is a bit of a mystery. He still knows who owns every square inch of land on this farm-to-market highway, and this knowledge seems to cheer him. "See that metal shed? That's the Jenkinses' quarter. And look, Louise, there's the old Burleson place!" He points in the direction of a tumbleweed.

Finally we reach a sign announcing we're in Meadow (pronounced "MED-ah" by its residents), population 593. He turns right over the railroad tracks into his hometown, passing a dingy white brick building on the corner. "There used to be a restaurant right there! And that's where I had my first bite of hamburger with mustard."

All those mom-and-pop businesses are gone, squeezed out by cheaper competitors in nearby Brownfield or Lubbock. But when my father was a teenager in the 1950s, the town was bustling for its size, a place where kids rode their bikes from dawn to dusk, where mothers baked each other pecan pies and fanned themselves on porch stoops. The town had a grocery store, a variety store, a blacksmith shop, three cotton gins, several diners, two Mexican cafes, and a feed store that served as a hangout spot for farmers, a place to share almanac predictions about rainfall.

Today Meadow is a motionless suburb, mostly populated by retired farmers and Mexican immigrants seeking cheaper housing outside Lubbock. Even the post office is shuttered. All that remains of Meadow's heyday is the Meadow Music Hall, a local bluegrass venue with the false front of an Old West general store. Bisecting the town north to south is Sonny Curtis Street, formerly First Street, renamed in the late nineties. I make my father pull over so my mother can photograph the two of us standing under the sign. As we're walking back to the Jeep, he waves toward a vacant patch of dirt. "I own both those lots," he says.

"You *do*?" I ask. This is news to me. I know he owns a share of his family's farm, but I had no idea he still owned land here in town—if Meadow can be called a town anymore. "Yeah, this was where we lived, where the yellow house was," he explains. "Before he died, I said, 'Daddy, I sure do like those lots in town,' so he left 'em to me." The house was torn down years ago.

"Could use a little landscaping," my mother says. I look at the dirt lots and try to imagine the ghost of a yellow house filled with two parents and six children, one of the only houses in town with no indoor plumbing. My dad couldn't wait to leave this house behind when he was a teenager. Now he's an old man nostalgic for the ground on which it stood.

Back in the Jeep, he turns down Renfro Street, a series of larger brick homes with neatly kept lawns ("Silk Stocking Row," a Texas cousin once joked). One of them belongs to my uncle Pete. We park in the driveway and walk up the single cement stair leading to the porch. The door creaks open and Pete appears behind the screen wearing a white Barstow shirt and a gray Stetson cowboy hat. At eighty-eight he is growing frail, though he still cuts an imposing figure. Pete is taller and more classically handsome than my father, with chiseled cheekbones and a square jaw. When my father first brought my mother to Texas to meet his family in 1970, she told me she swooned over Pete and their late brother Dean. *Man oh man, were they somethin'. Real live cowboys.*

Pete gives me a one-armed hug, his other hand gripping his cane. I pull back and see tears in his eyes. "This place is a mess," he mumbles, "what with Glena away . . ." Glena, his wife of over sixty years, is in a rehab center in Lubbock recovering from knee surgery. My dad rests his hand on Pete's shoulder as if to say, *Don't worry, brother.*

We enter through the living room, where Pete's wooden rocking chair has been replaced by a leather recliner he gingerly lowers himself into. The walls are cluttered with portraits of weddings and grandbabies in cowboy boots. Photos only get added here, never subtracted. On the wall behind Pete, I glimpse my floozy-haired high school portrait. Beside it, a copy of the Ten Commandments hangs directly above a yellowed print of a gunfight scene, a rogue cowboy on a horse shooting at a stagecoach. Imposed over the scene is a revolver and the caption, "Cold Wells Fargo, .31 caliber." It's quintessential Texas: Thou shalt not kill, but in case you need to, here's the gun for the job.

My parents and I sink into the pink sofa across from Pete and listen to his slow, hypnotic Texan drawl. "Sonny, do you remember them ranchers rippin' out Daddy's fence?" We all know that story.

"Well, I can't quite remember it, Pete, so go ahead and tell it," my father says. This is their ritual, their dance. Their love, their history, their values, their connection to the land—all they hold dear expressed within the arcs of timeworn stories they repeat like hymns, like prayers.

The 640-acre farm remains in our family, passed down and divided among the branches, but whole. One day my parents' eighty-acre share of it will be mine. It's land I can never sell, as my father has instructed me over the years: "Not because it's worth much, Sarah, but because of the mineral rights, *the oil*." Perhaps he is preternaturally attached to the land for what it represents: an upward social tick for his family, his grandfather Will's journey from sharecropper to landowner. The realized dream of the West.

I've asked Pete and my parents to show me the homeplace this morning, the section of the farm where Will and Pearl built a house in 1925. This will be my second trip there. My parents took me to the house once when I was a girl to visit my father's uncle Argust, Will and Pearl's son who lived there after the couple died. Argust was tall and awkward, the kind of man Texans describe as having "a funny look out of his eye." I remember how he and my father made strained chitchat in the living room, and how, when I started to fidget, my mother whispered in my ear, "Follow me."

She took my hand, explaining to the men that she was off to fetch me a glass of water in the kitchen. But once we turned the corner she continued straight, past the kitchen to a closed door at the end of the hallway. I stood behind her as she turned the knob slowly to lessen the whine from the rusty hinges. A stagnant odor wafted over us, like what I'd smelled when I'd buried my nose in the pages of old library books. Inside I saw a standard oak bedroom set, some framed needlepoints on the wall. On the bedspread, a yellow bathrobe had been staged intentionally, as a teenage girl might display a prom dress. A pair of worn slippers lay on the floor beside the bed. My mother had described this scene on the long drive down to Texas, so I knew right away the bedroom had belonged to Pearl, who died twenty years before. Argust was so close with his mother that after she died, he refused to touch her bedroom. Back in the doorway, my mother turned to me with wide eyes. "*Spooky*," she whispered.

What is the lifespan of a ghost? The lifespan of Buddy, the lifespan of Pearl? Her son Argust was an oddity to my mother, but he stands as an apt symbol of my father's family, held tight in the grip of the past. I spent years building a fence of my own to separate myself from them, but maybe I'm as strange as Argust. I wouldn't keep my father's bathrobe on a bed for twenty years, but I do obsess over details of his life, turn them over in my brain and press them into words on a page. Preservation takes many forms.

Distant relatives I barely know live on the family farm now. The land has been out of cultivation since the late eighties, when Pete turned it over to Texas's soil conservation program. Now its cotton rows are but a memory, the fields overtaken by desert flora: vermillion shoots of Indian paintbrush, bright blankets of red-and-yellow firewheel, blackfoot daisies, barbed mesquites and cholla cacti, and through it all, feathery lovegrass. Pete likes the lovegrass best; he tells us it replenishes the soil. As we drive to the homeplace, he nods out the window at it, pleased to see it thrive. Rumi said there are hundreds of ways to kiss the ground. The Dust Bowl taught West Texans a few.

After a ten-minute drive through cotton fields, we reach our farm, wilder than its neighbors. My father turns left down a long, gravel driveway that cuts through a grassy prairie. Pete asks him to stop the Jeep.

"See here . . . this is the southwest corner of the homeplace, and this is the old Speckman section," Pete says, gesturing to an overgrown field on our right. His hand trembles with neuropathy, a result of severe frostbite he suffered while stationed at Heartbreak Ridge during the Korean War.

That's right, my father nods.

"See here, this was pasture . . . all this was pasture," he continues haltingly. "And the lake where they shot the cows was over by where that mound of dirt is."

The lake where they shot the cows. The story is fresh in my mind. Pete had told me about it during a phone call I made to him before my visit. It happened in 1935, a year deep in the bowels of that devastating trio: Dust Bowl, Depression, and drought. The drought was so severe that year, President Franklin D. Roosevelt established the Drought Relief

Service, a delicate title for a brutal act. Under the DRS, government men traveled throughout the Great Plains and Texas paying farmers anywhere from four to ten dollars a head to take their cattle off their hands. Some of the cattle were drought-starved, or at least that's how the government framed it. But many were healthy—the program was designed to relieve the farmers, not the cows.

My grandfather Arthur was a young father in his twenties at the time. The morning the men came to Meadow, he brought along five-year-old Pete. While the little boy watched from the sidelines, Arthur and the other farmers corralled their cows into the bone-dry crater of a lake. They sorted them according to age and condition, herding mothers with their young calves. Then half a dozen government men made their way to the center of the corral, where they loaded their .22 rifles and began to shoot.

I imagine Pete, his childish excitement turning to horror as the wild-eyed cows crumpled on their sides, legs twitching, as the calves cried out in terror watching their bawling mothers go down. In little more than fifteen minutes, 250 head of cattle lay dead.

"You must have been so scared that day," I say. Pete looks straight ahead from the shotgun seat, a muscle rippling in his jaw. I think maybe he does not hear me, so I say it louder. He still does not answer.

My father takes his cue and continues down the dusty driveway. I stare out at the haunted field, thinking of my young uncle, almost the same age as my youngest daughter, and wondering why my grandfather brought him to the slaughter that day. Maybe he knew Pete would one day inherit the responsibilities of this land, a life that left no room for childish attachment to animals.

We park in front of a redbrick ranch house, where a man and woman I've never seen come outside to greet us. I'd place the woman in her late seventies, maybe younger; it's hard to tell. The sun has had its way with her. She has close-cropped blonde hair and is missing a few molars. Pete introduces her as my father's step-cousin Linda. Her son Lanny is a stocky, middle-aged man wearing a baseball hat and glasses. He seems excited for visitors and immediately begins showing us his self-rigged farm equipment. His crown jewel is a shooting circle he's devised out of a remote-control clay pigeon thrower and an old Lawn-Boy mower. To designate the area, he's hooked the Lawn-Boy up to a pole, then set it loose to mow a perfect sixty-foot circle. "It's pretty neat watchin' that thing go," he says.

"Well, all right, Lanny," my father responds with a wry smile. It's hard to entertain the entertainer.

My mom spots a cluster of star-shaped flowers blooming by the side of the house and plants her face in it. "*Mmmmmmmm, jasmine,*" she coos. "Reminds me of California."

Linda asks if we're ready to see the homeplace. The site is only a few hundred yards away, but the field is completely uncultivated, impossible to reach on foot. Lanny and Pete lead the way in a golf cart while the rest of us ride behind them in the Jeep. When we reach the site, I open the car door and step into a tangle of knee-high grass. "Watch out for rattlesnakes!" shouts Linda. My father had also warned me of snakes before the trip, so I've dressed in jeans and an old pair of Frye cowboy boots. I glance down at my father's feet. He's wearing European sneakers.

The homeplace is no longer home to anything but varmints and a collection of rusted relics planted deep in the windblown soil: a house in shambles; the skeletons of a Studebaker and station wagon; my grandfather's tractor; the top half of a windmill fanning out of the grass. Genealogical tourism has become a booming business. My mother and her sister spent two weeks sailing around majestic Norwegian fjords, stopping occasionally to stroll through graveyards in search of their father's surname. My father-in-law is planning a trip to a hilltop village in Italy's Campania region, where he will explore his family's history among the ruins of the Roman empire. I am trudging through a metal graveyard, watching out for rattlesnakes.

I weave down what passes for a hill in West Texas to the stucco house where Will and Pearl and, later, Argust lived. After he died, the house was left to rot. Earlier my father had told me it wasn't

My grandfather's tractor. (From author's collection.)

safe to enter. *Come on*, I'd thought. *How bad could it be?* I nudge the screen door open a few inches before I get my answer: a noxious smell of rotting animal flesh and feces. It stops me cold. Through the screen I see a living room destroyed, the floor buried under smashed glass and upended furniture, its stuffing ripped out by looters and raccoons.

My father's getting nervous. He yells down for a second time that the place is a snake pit, and I turn back reluctantly. I'm not sure why I'd been so eager to enter; it's not like I have fond memories of this particular snake pit. Maybe a part of me wanted to prove I've got the guts of a Texan like my relatives, though my relatives are standing by their vehicles looking uneasy. Linda and Lanny never come out here. The only reason we're all standing in this ghostly field is because of me and my curiosity. I don't have the guts of a Texan. I have the guts of a tourist.

I walk back to my father's side. He takes my arm and points to a faraway spot on the prairie to show me where the dugout used to be, the underground shelter where he was born. I'd hoped to see the dugout up close, but the terrain is too wild; even if I could reach it, the lovegrass has claimed it. Now the dugout exists only in memory. A faded scar of a home, an absence of an absence. I cannot reach across this fallow field to the dugout any more than I can reach into my father's mind and know what he is seeing as we look at the same landscape. I could ask him, but his silence has trained me over the years to know the answer wouldn't fill the void.

We wind our way around the wreckage of the house to where my grandfather's tractor remains half-buried in the earth. The green paint has rusted off, but you can still make out the brand, which my father says aloud as if recalling the name of an old lover. *Allis-Chalmers.* He affectionately runs his palm over the grass spiking from its metal carcass.

I wonder if he's remembering the tedious fall day when he was fourteen, perched on the seat and running a stalk cutter behind, staring down a sea of cotton. *Moon, moon, silvery moon, light up the heavens tonight.*

It was an afternoon like so many others, row upon row of work before dusk. What made it different was the notes, notes only my father could hear above the dissonant growl of the engine. He listened for them while keeping an ear to the ground that had borne him, spewed him from a Dust Bowl dugout onto this hard, flat plain.

Moon, moon, silvery moon. It was a hymn to the heavens, a game to fill the space between the turn rows. It was his way out.

Long after I say my goodbyes to Pete, Linda, and Lanny, the homeplace will stay with me. Perhaps it was always a part of me, though I struggle to see what part. A DNA spit test once told me my father's side is mostly English and Irish, though his family has no records dating back to Great Britain. If you ask my father where his family came from, he says Texas. If you ask him where before that, he says Arkansas.

My research suggests they were likely tenant farmers from Great Britain who came over in the late 1700s, part of a mass migration to the New World. Most of the emigrants were Scotch-Irish border residents fleeing poverty, sectarian conflict, or, in the case of the Northern Irish, famine. One journalist reporting from an Irish port in 1774 called them "the scum of two nations." But though they were poor, they were fiercely proud, which the Quakers and Puritans of New England found crass and perplexing. The colonists pushed them westward, using them as a physical buffer against the Native Americans. It was a role the new immigrants were born to play. The men were warriors and the women laborers, raised on bloodshed and expecting little more from life than raw survival, with maybe some music along the way.

In the past few years, scientists have made surprising discoveries in the field of epigenetics, the study of the myriad ways genes express themselves, which biological chords get plucked and why. It seems we may carry more than our ancestors' DNA. Some research suggests we carry their traumas, their memories, and their experiences, possibly for up to fourteen generations.

What does my father carry? A fear of rattlesnakes, an ear tuned by Revolutionary War melodies? A sullen pride, a made-up mind, a black hole low enough to keep him humble for the rest of his life, no matter how high he ascends?

And what about me? Do I carry Pete's drive to nurture? Argust's nostalgia? My mother's vanity? The grief of early morning news of a plane crash in Iowa? My father's daydreams and quick temper, his wandering heart? Pluck the wandering string and it clangs against my breastbone, the string that longs for home. The chord is atonal as the West Texas wind crying in the night. *Lonesome.*

CHAPTER 19

Before we head out for dinner in Lubbock that evening, my parents and I meet for a drink in the hotel lobby. A young man working the reception desk, clean-shaven with dark hair and black horn-rimmed glasses, stops my father on our way to the table. "Excuse me, sir," he says with a shy smile. "Is it true you played with Buddy Holly?"

An *aw, shucks* grin spreads across my dad's face. My mom and I stand smiling behind him while he scribbles his autograph on a hotel notepad. "How's it feel to be so famous in Lubbock, Texas?" my mom asks him with a wink as we settle around the table with our drinks. He shrugs and says he reckons it feels pretty good.

I tell him I didn't know he owned so much land around Lubbock. Then, after a few sips of liquid courage, I ask him what he plans to do with it all when, you know, the time comes. He explains matter-of-factly that he'll leave me the two lots he owns in Meadow, along with his eighty-acre share of the farm. I know I'll keep the farmland, but I immediately start thinking how to unload those dirt lots. Yet before my mind can wander too far, he tells me he's set to inherit an additional ninety-six acres of the farm from his brother-in-law which he's willed to my three school-aged daughters. Thirty-two acres apiece of wild pasture outside Meadow, Texas—a place my daughters have never been. He has several Texan nieces he could leave the land to, relatives who would treasure the acreage. What will my three Yankee daughters do with it? As much as I believe in epigenetics, I find it unlikely they'll be drawn to this remote brown square of earth.

"Why leave it to them, Dad?"

He takes a sip of his scotch and looks out the window at the dying sun, sinking over the parking lot in this city where people still know his name. From dust he came, and to dust he will return. But he's not a ghost yet. "Well, you never know," he says. "If things ever get rough in life, it's good to have a little land to fall back on."

For a brief moment, the bubble wobbles and the universe rights itself plumb. After all these years, he's given me a perfect answer.

ACKNOWLEDGMENTS

Thank you to my agent Katie Kotchman, fellow farm girl and country music lover, for helping me hone this project for years, and for believing in it when belief was a rare commodity. Thanks to my editor Travis Snyder, and to the talented team at Texas Tech University Press. Travis, your passion and skill breathed life into this book when I could no longer see past the words on the page. You were a joy to work with, a true muso in the best sense of the word.

This book was birthed at Vermont College of Fine Arts' MFA program, and I'm indebted to its rich community of writers. Thanks to my mentors Bret Lott, Douglas Glover, Harrison Candelaria Fletcher, Sue William Silverman, and Barbara Hurd. To Jeniah Johnson, Bailey Gaylin Moore, and Natalia Perch, thanks for keeping me sane on my memoir journey. John Browning, thanks for reading my unedited prose about Buddy Holly and finding it interesting. God bless musos.

Thanks to early readers Marc Sheehan, Patricia McNair, and Marty Levine. Thank you to Bill Janovitz for keeping the music alive. Huge thank you to Mo Rocca for your wonderful segment on my father for *CBS Sunday Morning*.

Thanks to the editors who published excerpts from this book, especially Joe Mackey at *River Teeth*, Jill Talbot at *The American Literary Review*, Hattie Fletcher at *Creative Nonfiction*, Wendy Lesser at *The Threepenny Review*, and Stephanie G'Schwind at *Colorado Review*.

Thanks to Allison K. Williams and Dinty Moore for their wonderful Rebirth Your Book retreat, and for gently nudging me across the finish line.

Thanks to Amy Wilson for being a light in the darkness.

Thank you to my dear friends who kept my spirits up during this seemingly endless project: to Shelley Roberts McLay for making me laugh through thirty-plus years of friendship, and for saving me when I needed saving. To Liz Markovits, whose deep intelligence and strength continue to inspire and challenge me. To Shannon Bevins, for being my North Star and wingwoman for life. To Meg McCroskey Blum, for your excellent marketing perspective, and for being my biggest cheerleader and most wickedly funny friend in my pocket.

I wrote this book partly to preserve a bygone era, and since its completion, Pete Curtis and J. I. Allison have both passed away. They were legends on this earth, and I hope this book serves in some small way to honor their memories. Thank you to all the Curtis family, especially Karen Curtis Rodgers, for sharing your weird and wonderful DNA with me. I am proud to be cut from your cloth.

Thanks to my Crickets nuclear family: Joanie Allison, Jennifer Mauldin, and in loving memory of Joe B. and Jane Mauldin. Joanie and Jennifer, I love you both so much. We sure had some fun, didn't we?

Thanks to Gene and Jo Graziano for your enduring love and support.

Thanks to Martha and Richard Davis for giving me details about L.A., and for being the coolest aunt and uncle a kid can have.

Thank you to my dad Sonny for giving me the hook, and my mom Louise for filling in the notes. It's not easy to have a memoirist for a daughter, but you both encouraged me to tell my truth, and you were generous with yours. Whoa whoa, yay yay, I love you both more than I can say.

This book would not be possible without my family, especially Neal. Thank you, Neal, for supporting me through this project, and for always steering the boat away from the rocks. I love you. And to Estella, Mira, and Sylvie, you are my everything: my sun, my moon, my stars. Whenever I'm with you is my happiest time.

INDEX

Note: Page numbers in italics refer to images.

Acuff-Rose Music, 62
Adair Music, 56
Allison, J. I.: coins term *pervs*, 46; and Crickets' induction into Rock & Roll Hall of Fame, 264; and death of Buddy Holly, 67, 247; and death of Eddie Cochran, 87; as drummer for Crickets, 62; early days with Buddy and Sonny, 52, 75–77; with Everly Brothers, *93*; and heating of farmhouse, 130–31; leaves Waylon Jennings' tour, 156; marriage of, 102; moves to Tennessee, 115, 122; at seventies party, *152*; and Sonny's military discharge, 94; Sonny's relationship with, 164; and "Walk Right Back," 89
Allison, Joanie Sveum, 98, 102, 115, 122, *152*
Allison, Peggy Sue Garron, 76, 262
Armstrong, Jennifer Keishin, 104–5
astronomy, 132–33
Atkins, Chet, 55, 140–41
"Autumn Quince" (Hirshfield), 227

Babcock, Jack, 91
back-to-the-land movement, 114–15
Barthes, Roland, 36, 194
Battelle, Phyllis, 56
Baxter, Charles, 63
Bay State Banner, The, 209–15

Beatles, the, 243–44
Bellis, Mark, 176
Bennett, Willie, 211
Black, Bill, 55
blood harmony, 84
bluegrass, 49
BMI, 195–96, 199
Bobby Fuller Four, 74
Boston, 204, 207–15
Boston Phoenix, 210
Bowen, Jimmy, 173
Bowman, Don, 142
Bradley, Owen, 57–59, 140–41
Bragg, Rick, 79, 80
Brooks, James L., 104–5
Brown, Charles, 56
Buddy Holly Hall of Performing Arts and Sciences, 263
Buddy Holly Story, The (1978), 58–59
Bulger, James "Whitey," 212
Burns, Allan, 104, 105

Cadillacs, 89
Campbell, Glen, 103
car trips, 168–70
Chicago, 215–17
Church of Christ, 78–79
Clark, Carlie McCummings, 101–2, 110–11
Clark, Gene, 110
Clash, The, 74
Clinton, Bill, 191, 192

279

Cobble, Clara, *70*
Coburn, Henry, 25, 28–29, 34–36
Coburn, Ida, 24, 25–28, 29, 34
cocaine, 142–43, 148–49, 198, 202–3
Cochran, Eddie, 86–87
Colter, Jessi, 146, 147, 148, 151
Cotton Club, 56–57
cotton farming, 20, 25, 30–32, 78, 221–22
cows, killed by Drought Relief Service, 271–72
Crickets: career resurgence of, 219–20; fame of, 62, 63–64, 67; following Buddy's death, 75–78; inducted into Rock & Roll Hall of Fame, 264; as influence on the Beatles, 243–44; leave Waylon Jennings's tour, 156–57; retirement of, 264; Sonny leaves, 164; Sonny rejoins, 68, 192–93, 243; springtime tour of England, 83–87; tour with Waylon Jennings, 127–29, 140, 149–53. *See also* Holly, Buddy; Two Tones
Crickets and Their Buddies, The, 219–20
Curtis, Alene, 11
Curtis, Argust, 269–70
Curtis, Arthur: builds family home, 11–12; and cows killed by Drought Relief Service, 271–72; early years of, 25, 26; as father, 19–20; and fight with L7 ranchers, 32–33; occupation of, 10; and Sonny's birth, 7–8; and Sonny's musical career, 60
Curtis, Dean, 11, 49, *70*, 129–30
Curtis, Dick, 26–27, 28, 34–36
Curtis, Etta, 25–26, 28, 29, 34–35
Curtis, Freeman, 25, 26, 48–49

Curtis, Jean, 12
Curtis, Karen, 25–26, 38–40
Curtis, Lorena, 48–49
Curtis, Louise: attends *Mary Tyler Moore Show* premiere party, 105; and birth of Sarah, 109–10; cancer diagnosis and treatment of, 218–19; and Carlie McCummings, 110–11; difficulties between Sonny and, 105–6, 129–30, 192, 193–94, 200; family and background of, 96–101; as farm wife, 124–26; fertility problems of, 109–10, 130; friendship with Judy, 158–59; health issues of, 262; on Joe Osborn, 136–37; life in Los Angeles, 101–2, *107*; marriage of, 106–8, 185–86; and meeting with McCartneys, 244; moves to Tennessee, 115–17, 121–23; and music parties, 143, 146, *152*; on Pearl Curtis's preserved bedroom, 270; personality of, 160–61; reports sexual harassment by football coach, 178–79; Sonny meets, 95–96, 102–3; on Sonny's insensitivity, 130–31; on Sonny's rejoining Crickets, 192–93; on Sonny's touring with Waylon Jennings, 150–51; visits Dickson farm, 252, 253–54
Curtis, Pearl, 28, 30–31, 270
Curtis, Pete, 7, 12, 20, 40, 49, *69*, 268–72
Curtis, Sarah: birth of, 109–10; college years of, 186–95; employment at *The Bay State Banner*, 209–15; and motherhood, 223–25, 233–34; moves to Chicago, 215–17; moves

INDEX

to Michigan, 230–31; postgraduate education of, 204, 208–9; relationship with Sonny, 167, 168–69, 173–75, 190–91; returns to writing, 231–32, 233–34, 239; at seventies party, *152*; with Sonny, *138*, *169*; worldview taught to, 183–86

Curtis, Sonny: ancestry of, 274–75; on Arkansas justice system, 29; birth of, 7–8; and Buddy Holly, 46–48, 50–54, 59–60, 67–68, *70*; cancer diagnosis and illness of, 9, 13–14, 16–17; career of, 8–9, 219–20; and Curtis Brothers, 49; and Curtis family shack, 12–13; with daughter, *138*, *169*; daughter's relationship with, 41, 167, 168–69, 173–75, 190–91; description of, 69–71; difficulties between Louise and, 105–6, 129–30, 192, 193–94, 200; early years of, 10–12, 15–16, 19–21, *69*, 78–79, 161; on Elvis Presley, 54–55; with Everly Brothers, *93*; on fame, 148; first performance of, 49–50; goes to Nashville, 61–62; as gun owner, 36–37, 41–42; hearing loss of, 226, 259, 262; on high school girlfriend, 264–65; on "I Fought the Law," 73–75; imitations done by, 165–66; insensitivity of, 130–31; insomnia of, 166; interest in Olmsted, 208; J. I. Allison's relationship with, 164; jingles and theme songs written by, 103–5; leaves Crickets, 164; leaves Waylon Jennings's tour, 156–57; lectures of, 81–82; marriage of, 106–8, 185–86; meets Louise, 95–96, 102–3; meets Neal, 214–15; on memorialization of Buddy Holly, 247; military service of, 87–94; on missing out on Crickets, 63; moves to Tennessee, 115–17, 121–22; musical education of, 48–49; name of, 8, 11, 66; as pioneer, 54; plays Lubbock music festival, 259–62; political shift of, 191–92; poster commemorating, 23; quits songwriting, 176–77; rejoins Crickets, 68, 192–93, 243; sleepy era of, 131–33; tours with Waylon Jennings, 127–29, 140, 149–53, *152*; and Two Tones, 46–47, 57–61; visits Dickson farm, 253–54, 255; visits Lubbock and Meadow, 261–69, 271–74, 276; way of speaking, 190–91; on Winter Dance Party, 246

Curtis, Sonny, songs written by: "Blue Days, Black Nights," 59; "Cowboy Singer," 139; "Destiny's Child," 141; "Eager for the Edge," 155; "Girl of the North," 94; "He Was Onto Somethin'," 221; "I Fought the Law," 23–24, 73–75, 78, 80, 111; "I'm No Stranger to the Rain," 175, 176, 197, 261; "It's Not Easy Being Fifteen," 127, 183; "The Last Song I'm Ever Going to Sing," 171; "Laughing Stock," 66; "Love Is All Around," 104–5, 229, 232, 235, 236, 237–39; "Moon, Moon, Silvery Moon," 80, 222–23; "The Real Buddy Holly Story," 45, 241; "Rock Around

with Ollie Vee," 58; "Soul Fever,"
109; "The Straight Life," 103, 121;
"Tennessee, I Love You," 117, 249;
"That'll Be the Day," 261; "Walk
Right Back," 83, 88–90, 92–93;
"When Amarillo Blows," 259;
"Wrong Again," 66
Curtis, Violet: and Curtis family
shack, 12; gives birth to Sonny,
7–8; married life of, 232–33; as
mother, 19–20, 223; occupation
of, 10–11, 15; and Sonny's first
performance, 49–50; and Sonny's
military service, 87–88; work of,
235–36
Curtis, Will, 24–34, *42*, 221–22,
225–26, 254
Curtis Brothers, 49
Cusk, Rachel, 238

Daum, Meghan, 201–2
Davis, Edward Everett, 20
Dead Kennedys, 74
Decca (Records), 57–59, 60, 70
DeWylde, Delilah, 242–43, 245
Dickinson, Charles, 168–69
Dickson, Tennessee, farm: Curtis
family moves to, 121–23; Curtis
family visits, 249–56; description
of, 123–25; glass farmhouse on,
133–38, 249–50; operation of,
125–26; purchase of, 115–17;
songwriting in, 126–27
Dickson Country Club, 159–60
Didion, Joan, 201, 218
domestic violence, 37–39
Drought Relief Service, 271–72
drug abuse, 110–13, 141–43, 146–47,
148–50, 198, 202–3

dugout, 7, 11, 274
Duncan, Robert, 259
Dust Bowl, 8, 10, 15, 19, 32, 78, 233,
271
Dylan, Bob, 114

Ebarb, Cheryl, 165
Elektra Records, 172–73
Ely, Joe, 260
England: Sonny's love for, 85; spring-
time tour in, 83–87. *See also* Great
Britain
epigenetics, 275
Everly, Don, 84, *93*, *152*. *See also*
Everly Brothers
Everly, Karen, *152*
Everly, Phil, 13, 84, *93*. *See also* Everly
Brothers
Everly Brothers, 83–86, 89–90, 92–93

Faber (Women's Studies teacher),
188–89
fairies, 124–25
fame, 66–67, 174–76
feminism, 103–4, 189, 232, 233,
236–37, 238. *See also* sexism
fence posts, taken by L7 ranchers,
32–33, 268
Fender Stratocaster, 57, 59
First Presbyterian, 163–64
Foley, Neil, 53
Fort Ord, 88–90
frog gigging, 179–80
Fuller, Bobby, 111

Garrett, Simon, 27–28, 34, 35
Garron, Peggy Sue, 76, 262
Gladstone, Steve, 167, 173
"good road, the," 151

Gordon, Jim, 112–13
Gordon, Osa Marie, 113
Gore, Tipper, 192
Gornick, Vivian, 68
Great Britain, 173. *See also* England
Grech, Ric, 111
Green Day, 74
Green River Boys / Mayfield Brothers, 49, 50
Griffith, Nanci, 219
Guess, Don, 55, *70*
guns, 24, 31, 33–40, 41–42, 88–89

Haber, Jim, 165
Hansen, Patti, 147
Hard Rock Cafe, album release party at, 219–20
Hardin, Glen D., 265
harmony, 170
harp, 226–27
Hatch Show Print Shop, 23
hearing loss, Sonny's, 226, 259, 261
Hellard, Ron, 175
Hells Angels, 140, 143
Hernandez, Raoul, 247
Hirshfield, Jane, 227
Holly, Buddy, *70*; concert memorializing, 241–43; death of, 67–69, 75–78, 128; impact on Lubbock, 263–64; inducted into Rock & Roll Hall of Fame, 263; and María Elena Santiago, 65; memorialization of, 244–48; reaction to Elvis Presley, 55; significance to Curtis family, 45–48; Sonny's early experiences with, 50–54, 57–61; Sonny's last interactions with, 66–67. *See also* Crickets
Holly, Ella, 60

Holly, Larry, 59
Houriet, Robert, 114
Howard, Harlan, 164

Inside Edition, 229–30
insomnia, 166
Ives, Burl, 191

Jackson, Andrew, 168–69
Jeanie Kate (high school girlfriend), 264–65
Jeanne d'Arc army base, 90–92
Jennings, Waylon, 61, 62, 65, 127–29, 139–41, 142–43, 144–47, 148–53
jingles, 103, 122
Johnson, Lyndon, 97–98, 99
Judy (Louise's friend), 158–59

Kafka, Franz, 234
Kelly, Jimmy, 212–13
Kennedy, John F., 213
King, Thelma, *70*
KLLL, 65, 66
Kooken, Richard, 91–92

L7 Ranch, 31, 32–33, 269
Lambton, Lady Lucy, 85–86
lectures, 81–82
Lisa (author's second cousin), 37–40
Lottie (Louise's mother), 96, 98–99
Loveless, Brother, 79
Lubbock, Texas, 30–31, 53, 262–67, 276
Lubbock music festival, 259–62

Maines, Lloyd, 260, 261
Marshall (Women's Studies teacher), 188–89, 195
Martha (Louise's sister), 96, 97,

100–101, 122
martinis, 91–92, 102
Mary (Louise's sister), 96, 97, 100
Mary Tyler Moore Show, The, 103–5, 232, 234–35
Mauldin, Joe B., 13, 62, 77, *93*, 147, *152*, 263
Mauldin, Father, 161–62
Mayfield, Edd, 49
Mayfield, Herb, 49
Mayfield, Smokey, 49
Mayfield Brothers / Green River Boys, 49, 50
McCartney, James, 244
McCartney, Linda, 244
McCartney, Paul, 243–44
McCummings Clark, Carlie, 101–2, 110–11
McGuire, Echo, 52
McKinley, William, 168
Meadow, Texas, 20, 31, 266–74, 276
melons, 46
Memphis, Tennessee, 199–200
Merron, Jeff, 58
Michigan, 230–31
military service, Sonny's, 87–94
Miller, John, 210–11
Miller, Melvin, 209–10, 213, 215
Miller, Roger, 191
Miller, Sandra, 210
Miller, Yawu, 211–12, 214, 217
misogyny, 236–37. *See also* feminism; sexism
Monroe, Bill, 49
Montgomery, Bob, 50–51
moon, 221–23, 225, 227–28
Moore, Mary Tyler, 230, 235, 238. See also *Mary Tyler Moore Show, The*
Moore, Scotty, 55

motherhood, 223–25, 233–34
myths, 36, 194–95

Nashville, Tennessee, 61–62, 197–200, 203–4
Nashville Skyline (Dylan), 114
Nashville Sound, 140–41
National Coalition on Domestic Violence (NCADV), 39
Neal (author's husband), 214–16, 223, 224, 241, 242, 257
Neil, Vince, 219
Norman Petty Trio, 59

O'Brien, Tim, 21
Ol' Bob Place, 24–25
Olmsted, Frederick Law, 208
Olympia Beer, 103
Osborn, Gwen, 136–37
Osborn, Joe, 115, 136

Parsons, Gram, 111–12
parties, 142–46, *152*
Peer-Southern Music, 65, 66
Pee-wee Herman, 165–66
Perkins, Carl, 54
pervs, 46
Petty, Norman, 59, 64, 76–77
Phillip (farmhand), 125–26, 135, 179, 251
Piestrup, Don, 103
Piney River, 40, 253–55
politicians, 167, 168
politics, 191–92
pond, 171–72
poster, commemorative, 23
Preacher Bill, 163–64
presidents, 168–69
Presley, Elvis, 54–55

INDEX

Quanah, Texas, 30

racism, 212–13
Radle, Carl, 113
rape, 188
"Real Buddy Holly Story, The," 45
religion, 78–80, 161–64
rhythm and blues, 53–57
Rich, Adrienne, 189–90, 239
Richards, Keith, 147
Richardson, J. P., 77, 128
Rock & Roll Hall of Fame, 264
rock 'n' roll, 56
Rolling Stone, 217–18
Rose, Wesley, 62

Santiago, María Elena, 65–66, 76, 77
Sears, William, 224
segregation, 53
sexism, 145, 185, 236–37. *See also* feminism
sexual assault, 188
shack (Curtis family), 11–13, 14–17, 18–19, 20–21
Sheeley, Sharon, 86
Shihab, Naomi, 177
Silent Generation, 168
snakes, 40, 41, 252, 253–54
Snapp, Landon, 142
Snyder, Rachel Louise, 40
Sowell, Thomas, 192
Stan's Record Rack, 53
Steinem, Gloria, 235
Stener (Louise's father), 96–97, 99
St. James Episcopal, 161–63
Stone, Dave, 52
Stuart, Charles, 211
substance abuse, 110–13, 141–43, 146–47, 148–50, 198, 202–3

Sullivan, Niki, 64
Sveum Allison, Joanie, 98, 102, 115, 122, *152*

Taylor, Peter, 200
Texas, ideology of, 53. *See also* Lubbock, Texas; Meadow, Texas; Quanah, Texas
Thoreau, Henry David, 238
toolshed, 12–13, 14–16
Toul, France, 90–92
Tree Publishing, 164, 173
Two Tones, 46–47, 55, 57–61. *See also* Crickets

Vee, Bobby, 13, 219
Vee, Ollie, 58
Vee, Willie, 58
Vietnam War, 97–98, 99–100
Vincent, Gene, 86
Vonnegut, Kurt, 177

Walker, Wayne, 61–62
Washington, George, 168
Welty, Eudora, 208
White Scourge, The (Davis), 20
Whitley, Keith, 175, 176
Whitman, Slim, 61
wine, 91
Winter Dance Party, 246
Winter Dance Tour, 77, 241
Women's Studies 101, 188–90
Wood, Father, 162–63

Yancey, Charles, 213

ABOUT THE AUTHOR

Sarah Curtis's essays have appeared in *Creative Nonfiction*, *Salon*, *The Threepenny Review*, the *Los Angeles Review of Books*, the anthology *River Teeth: Twenty Years of Creative Nonfiction*, and elsewhere. She lives with her family in Michigan. More of her writing can be found at sarahcurtiswriter.com.

AUTHOR PHOTO BY LORI GOTTSCHLING

www.ingramcontent.com/pod-product-compliance
Lightning Source LLC
Chambersburg PA
CBHW031430160426
43195CB00010BB/677